I NEVER SAY GOODBYE

A Personal Story

of

Undying Love

by

Kira S. Redeen

"I have written books without any copyright--no rights reserved--because it is a gift of God, given by God, as much as sunlight. Other gifts of God are also free."

       from a talk by Kirpal Singh with the author of a book, after speaking to students of religion at Santa Clara University, San Jose, California, on November 16, 1972.

First edition--1985 (40 copies)
Second edition--1987 (800 copies)
Third edition--1991 (1000 copies)
ISBN 0-9615501-1-2.

DEDICATED TO

PARAM SANT SATGURU

KIRPAL SINGH JI MAHARAJ

THROUGH WHOM

ALMIGHTY GOD

WAS WORKING

A Murshid-i-Kamil* is not content with
imparting mere theoretical knowledge. He gives
a practical demonstration of what He says, and
therein lies His greatness. One who cannot
grant on the soul-level some actual experience
of What he asserts at the level of the intellect
is not a Master-soul in the true sense of the
meaning of the word Master, and his words cannot
carry weight and conviction.

--Kirpal Singh

____

*Murshid-i-Kamil. A Perfect Master.

MASTER KIRPAL SINGH

PREFACE

The preface to this third edition of "I Never Say Goodbye" has been written by some of its earlier readers.

"It is a wonderful book and very beautifully captures the feel of Sawam Ashram in 1969." -- Russell Perkins.

"I liked it immensely and appreciate deeply the help rendered to the Sangat by writing it. Couched in healthy and hilarious idiom, it provides extremely useful insight into the teachings of the Great Master and His life and lofty mission. In sum, it is excellent on all counts and makes very interesting reading, and to crown all means profound remembrance of the Master Soul we had the good fortune to come in contact with." -- A.S. Oberoi, India.

"Margaret and I have devoured the book; it will be a lovely addition to our library. Others are now waiting their turn to read it." -- George Arnsby Jones.

"There are no words to describe how much this book has meant to me." -- Lucille Gunn.

"Your book is a great blessing in a darkened world." -- John MacIntosh, Victoria, Canada.

"Its reading touches the heart and soul and reminds one of the Inexhaustible

PREFACE

Love, Compassion and Uplift that one
received from the Holy One, Dear Master
Kirpal, while in His Physical Body, and
fails not to bring copious moisture in
one's eyes." -- Gyani Ji, India.

"As page after page is slowly read,
tears of gratitude trickle down my
cheeks.... Not only your lines are
pleasurable reading, your topic is divine and your Hero is God himself in the
form of the Godman." -- James Nicholson.

"From the depth of my being, I thank our
beloved Master for laying it on your
heart to write it.... I have, and am,
enjoying this precious book so very
much." -- Betty Posey.

"I savored it word for word, line by
line, being all the while reminded of my
own very special trip to India in Feb.
1974 during the Unity of Man Confer-
ence." -- Eva Ide.

"Your reminiscences of those wonderfully
'soul-stirring' days when Master actually walked among us can't but elicit the
profoundest nostalgia." -- Veera and
Desmond Montague, Canada

"Thank you for 'I Never Say Goodbye'
which has made a permanent impression
and become an important part of my edu-
cation." -- Paul Nieman, London.

"I am delighted to acknowledge the receipt of the book 'I Never Say Good-bye' for the circulating library of the North Carolina Initiates of Master Kirpal Singh. I am glad to think that they will enjoy it as much as I have."
-- Charles Fulcher.

"Thanks for sending me the loving, devoted Spirit expressed in your gift book containing wonderful experiences with Master Kirpal.... Oh Master, you truly are still with us." -- Norah Lee.

"You remember I asked you a few months ago to send a copy of 'I Never Say Good-bye' to the initiates in South Africa. They have just written to say they have received it and how they are enjoying it. They feel they cannot put it down and the friends who came to visit them happened to pick it up and they also felt they must go on reading it."
-- Kathleen B. Melvin, Malta.

"Such a work of love. Words cannot tell how much we appreciate it and enjoy it, Mother, Bjorn and myself.... The one you sent to (the late) Etta and Phil (Perrin) came in record time... They, too, were overjoyed as it brought back so many memories." -- Benthe Secher.

"It is so wonderful to have all these thoughts, to share these loving events

PREFACE

with Master_oh God! To feel with Kira,
Bob and Khuku, to be in India, to be
with Him again. It makes me so happy."
-- Erhard Donig, Germany.

"Your beautiful book ... has been
received and read with great pleasure;
thank you very much for this so interesting and lovely story." -- Jean-Pierre
Frey, Geneva, Switzerland.

"How can we thank you for such a beautiful gift ... it is thrilling to experience Master at the Ashram so intimately
as I never had the privilege of going
myself." -- Consuelo Taylor.

"The book you gave me is bringing the
sweet remembrance of the Great Master,
and also the other Satsangis in Italy
are enjoying it." -- Pier Franco Mar-
cenaro, Italy.

"The book came to me at a very important
time when it was so necessary for me to
read something like this. It brought so
many memories of my time with our Master
in India." -- Isabel Blanco.

"The stories in it are wonderful. The
beginning of your book brought tears to
my eyes as I reminisced my first arrival
in India in 1984 and my own drive to
Sawan Ashram across the sewer canal." --
Chris Adamski.

PREFACE

"It is beautiful and one always receives a 'lift' and joy reading about another's experiences with our Beloved.... My husband--a non-initiate--enjoyed the book as well as I and I shall pass it on for my beloved son to read."
-- Arlene Weintraub.

"Every disciple of Sawan Kirpal should read this book carefully because the discourses explained in the book stretch us all to our Beloved Satguru.... I want to read the book again one time; thereafter I'll offer it to other Satsangis to read." -- Joginder Painter, Vadodra, India.

CONTENTS

FOREWORD

The "Redeens have enjoyed their short stay over here when they were privileged to tour with the Master for some days.

They shall be bringing with them some precious rich stories of their divine pilgrimage."

- - - LETTER FROM MASTER KIRPAL SINGH IN OCTOBER 1969 TO WILLIAM CAIRNS.

After a sixteen year delay the stories have finally been written down to share with any others who may have interest in reading them.

The subjects we talked about remain, but the actual words uttered have been replaced in many instances with exact quotations from the Master to avoid any errors. That, in turn, compelled a slight change in some people's names but not in their characters or personalities.

Since the Great Master delivered His talks either in Punjabi or Hindi we learned of their contents only through translators. To avoid possible error their words have been replaced with exact quotations on the subjects as found in Kirpal Singh's English-language books and talks.

Kira says she has been influenced by the leisurely style of the 19th century Russian novelist Goncharov.

But certainly more influential than Goncharov was the love that was developed for the Guru Himself. One hears and reads throughout life of those who have achieved perfection in character and action but despairs of actually meeting such a personage. Thinking back on the thousands of people we have known--we are both in our sixties--only one could be described as "perfect." We both agree that His name was Kirpal Singh.

Robert Redeen

A good friend of ours, who has mastered the art of dying while living, once said:

"THE TRUTH IS MORE FANTASTIC
THAN FICTION!"

His name is Al Oshinsky, and he lives in Florida.
Let us keep his words in mind as we read the following pages.

CHAPTER ONE

INTRODUCTION

There is only one Truth—God Absolute. When this Power came into vibratory action, It emitted light and sound. This flaming sound was called Word, Naam or the Conscious Audible Life Stream.

Whosoever by the Will of the Almighty God becomes one with It is the Beloved of God or His Elect and is called Param Sant or a Saint of the Highest Order. Did not Christ say, "I and my Father are one?"

This manuscript deals with the glorious game of eternal love where the Beloved is One while the wedded brides are many, just as many as there are living souls under this blue sky of ours.

He, the Beloved, is the one and only King of Kings and is God personified at Whose Holy Feet bow emperors, kings and consorts, at Whose Saintly Feet the tears of love flow in blessed silence as the heart becomes lost in adoration and the Light of God begins shining within, at Whose Blessed Feet forever are sacrificed all attachments to the world and worldly relations, at Whose Feet name and fame become as naught and kneel in reverential supplication, and the ever-oscillating mind stands still in awe.

By His one glance of Grace, eternal salvation is granted, and the wheel of life and death stops rotating as in the luminous company of the Beloved one crosses worlds beyond worlds, one more splendid than the other, until man, the prodigal son of God, returns to his True Home from whence he was exiled and thrust into creation since times out of mind.

Yet until that glorious fate befalls one, he remains an integral part of humanity that is groping and is doomed to grope endlessly in an impenetrable dark illusion remaining constantly subject to different degrees of subjectivity or untruth, as it is properly called.

The density or degree of this subjectivity is in reverse proportion to the brightness of the Light of God within oneself.

"See that the Light within you is not darkness" was no empty phrase uttered by the Sage of Galilee.

The realization of the complete oneness with that sonorous, effulgent Light of God is not attained, however, until the ego is crucified and abolished through holy baptism in the Lake of Immortality in the inner sphere of Par Brahm*. Only then Truth dawns on the soul of man who now has become an immortal. Further up, the soul proceeds by degrees until it merges into the Absolute Word or Truth.

None unaided can achieve this stupendous goal. Only a Son of God—God Personified, a Godman, a Saint—Who has Himself attained the unattainable, He alone can aid the aspiring soul on this wondrous Path of Love.

---

*The Lake of Immortality, Amritsar, lies in the fourth plane of creation called Par Brahm.

And in this lies the Saint's inestimable greatness. In wonderment on the banks of Amritsar, the Lake of Immortality, the soul exclaims in awe and adoration: "All the glory is yours, oh Master. Wahi Guru!"

The deep meaning hidden in the prayer of the Christians: "Lead us from darkness to light, from untruth to Truth, and from death lead us to immortality" thus stands revealed.

So says the Master.

To the agnostic and materialist what follows will be just another tale of Scheherezade, to others a romance, a novel. To those who are mystically inclined its contents may touch on the Ultimate Truth as God's unerring will gives every human being the power to spin out his own opinions and come to his own conclusions.

Let us remember always that each of us lives quite alone in his own self-created world, neither understanding himself nor others, although in self-assumed righteousness he may think otherwise.

For two of us this game of never-ending Love began on a trip to India in 1969 where by the will of Almighty God my husband and I met His physical embodiment, the Great Saint Sat Guru Kirpal Singh, the Godman.

The reader is asked, however, to keep in mind that the author and the editor have not so far crossed the egg of Brahmand*, and no matter

---

*Brahmand (egg) 3 planes of Creation: material, astral and mental.

how they tried to adhere to the exact happenings and words uttered, the report will have to remain in the multifarious domain of subjectivity in its evaluations and reactions.*

Only a Godman, the Word or Naam** made flesh, knows what this mighty play of God's Light and Sound called Cosmos is all about.

We can only pray in all humility that He may shed His holy blessings on us all, on each particle in His vast Creation, and then surrender completely to His unerring Will.

---

*Subjectivity is an unavoidable law of nature. Our Master once told us in a parable: "If 4 men go to Kashmir and on return give their separate reports, one would be prone to believe that they had visited 4 different countries."

**Word or Naam, the audible life stream or the flaming creative Sound.

IT'S A LONG WAY TO TIPPERARY.

IT'S A LONG WAY TO GO.

  _old song.

CHAPTER TWO

FLIGHT TO INDIA

After years of intense search for the goal and purpose of life which we conducted first separately and then, after our marriage, together with double zeal, we were at last initiated into the Mysteries of the Beyond. This occurred on August 4, 1968 through Master Kirpal Singh's representative in Washington, D.C., T.S. Khanna.

Kirpal Singh, Param Sant*, Sat Guru**, a living master of the Surat Shabd Yoga***, the royal yoga**** of the Audible Life Stream, the Word or Naam, lived in Sawan Ashram located at Shakti Nagar, Gur Mandi, Delhi 7, India.

So we decided to finish with talking, thinking, theorizing and travel to the Saint's home in Delhi and meet the living, perfect Master face-to-face, eyes-to-eyes and sit at His Holy Feet.

---

*Param Sant--A Saint of the highest order, a perfect Saint.

**Sat Guru--The Teacher of Truth.

***Surat Shabd Yoga--Yoga of union of the Soul with Naam or Word.

****Yoga--Teaching which links the Soul to its source.

FLIGHT TO INDIA

In September 1969 we found ourselves at New York's Kennedy Airport ready to board a plane—destination: Delhi. In our mind's eye we could see ourselves closing in on the glorious peak of a spiritual Mount Everest—a little more effort, a little more time and we would surely find that we had ascended to the very pinnacle of spirituality.

Although we had read much about a Living Master, had hoped for much and imagined much, the Truth later surpassed all our wildest expectations.

The years spent in reading, listening to a galaxy of lectures, trudging all sorts of so-called paths to the Ultimate Goal, crawling on radiant roads to reality—from all that effort the only benefits we got were bloated egos and bewildered, stuffed minds.

Nevertheless, the confusion did not stop us from regarding ourselves as great pundits, researchers, missionaries and the creators of our own destinies. In this state of hypnosis we pulled out our air flight tickets and presented them to the uniformed Lufthansa clerk.

We didn't know, of course, that the next three weeks were to find us exposed as spiritual neophytes, void of any correct understanding and filled with self-created delusions. The sign on the wall behind the clerk's head offered Lufthansa patrons trips to "London, Frankfurt and around the world."

"Around the world!" With a thrill I thought, "This means us!" And there we were, Bob in an immaculate suit with matching tie, tall, blond, fair-skinned, age 52, and I, age 48, standing next to him in a fashionable knee-length dress, bare feet clad in patent leather shoes, a touch of lipstick and a bit of makeup. We watched as the clerk busily processed our tickets.

The travel sign made me think of another 'round the world trip taken 130 years earlier by the Russian novelist Ivan Goncharov. The famous writer was a secretary aboard the frigate "Pallada" as, sails subject to the whims of the wind, she departed from St. Petersburg, the capital city of the Lord's anointed Tsar of Russia, headed for Japan, the country of the Son of the Sky, the Mikado.

It took Goncharov three years to complete his dangerous trip. But today just 130 years later we would cross the land and ocean by jetliner in a mere 19 hours for our trip to India and return in a similar amount of time. What a spectacular change, I mused, through technological progress.

However, the spiritual achievements of the Western World, in my view, have been few and far between. With the advent of the pseudo-teachings of Karl Marx and the crushing influx of materialistic thought, not only has humanity not made much growth in spiritual stature, but has rather suffered an enormous setback landing somewhere in the morass of the Baskerville Swamps*.

---

*The Hound of the Baskervilles by Conan-Doyle.

My thoughts returned to the present as I heard Bob ask, "What movie will be shown aboard our Lufthansa flight today?"

"None," the clerk answered without raising his head. "We cancelled movies permanently long ago."

"How come? Maybe I want to choose my plane according to the movie," said Bob.

The clerk, pausing in his paperwork, round eyes fixed on his odd American passenger, stared in complete disbelief as silence reigned supreme. "So was! Unglaublich!*" he exclaimed, lapsing into his native German. Nevertheless regaining his composure, with commendable personal discipline, the clerk finished his paperwork.

Until then, I had not flown on a Boeing 707 turbojet, and it would not serve the interests of truth to say my heart was filled with courage. On the contrary just looking at the five story-long, three story-high metal structure caused my body to break out in cold perspiration.

Keeping my fears under control, however, I joined my husband in taking a last look at the airport and the familiar Manhattan skyline: the city of glass and steel skyscrapers, friends and relatives, our familiar haunts. We were leaving our beloved country and going to a strange foreign land. Who could know what would happen there? Would we ever come back, I wondered.

---

*My goodness! Unbelievable!

Now, though, there was no time to waver, no time to lose. Our plane's passengers were moving ahead energetically, and, swept by the crowd, we climbed the steps to the jet's doorway weighed down as we were with handbags, photo and movie cameras, a brave, but phony expression fixed on my face. In the plane every one was settling down, putting hand luggage in compartments above the seats. Parents were quieting their children. All was filled with fuss and bustle, yet it seemed unreal; somehow it did not fit the danger of the situation. Conversation about an evening meal on the plane was surely premature since we might not live long enough to begin it!

Our seats were in the last row, and the seat backs were set against the restroom wall. Ahead of us through the entrance people were still pouring in.

Tall and bulky, Bob sank heavily into the middle of a trio of seats fussing with a few belongings while the last passenger, a blind, stocky man, was led in and told to take his place next to Bob.

The entrance door was slammed shut, the door-bolt securely fastened, and our neighbor introduced himself. "My name is Herr Burgmüller," he began. "I am blind. Lost my sight long ago. Kindly please tell me, did I board the right plane? Is it Lufthansa to Frankfurt am Main?

"Yes, yes, it is indeed, sir," Bob answered reassuringly and immediately launched into his favorite subject. "Did you know, Herr

Burgmüller, that vitamin A can help the eyesight?"

While both my male traveling companions engaged in a neighborly conversation about the value of vitamins, I looked apprehensively out the small window, as a calm voice sounded on the plane's intercom system. "This is Captain Schultz speaking. We are ready for takeoff."

The huge Boeing 707 slowly moved to the runway and stopped, taking its position in a long line-up of planes.

When our turn came, we lifted off smoothly and imperceptibly, flying up and up into the wild, blue yonder. The planet beneath had the appearance of a topographical map. Above it drifted soft, white clouds.

A stewardess rudely interrupted the conversation on vitamins by tossing steaming, odoriferous green cloths at each of us with the aid of a pair of tongs.

"Nein, nein, sehr schön, sehr schön*," yelled Bob, exhausting his German vocabulary in the process. But it was too late. The cloth had already arrived in the palms of his hands, burning his fingers. Instinctively, he threw it back to the blond stewardess who stood still for a moment, then remarked with an impersonal, professional smile on her face, "What a nervous passenger."

"For goodness' sake," Bob continued loudly, shaking his scorched fingers in the air,

------

*No, no, very nice, very nice.

"I can't breathe with the wall right in back. There's no circulation here. This pollution is utterly suffocating."

"Murder," proclaimed Herr Burgmüller simultaneously as he vigorously poked a long finger through the stench in protest.

In a few minutes the objectionable odor had disappeared, and quiet was restored to the back of the plane.

Newspapers and magazines were now distributed, and Herr Burgmüller informed us, "I am most surely not as blind as you may think. I can read if I want to, but I hate newspapers, and I stopped reading them a long time ago. All this news is junk and annoyance, and I get a headache from it."

"What did he say?" Bob asked, as Burgmüller had spoken in German.

In spite of Burgmüller's opinion, Bob, a life-long newsman and correspondent, looked at the newspaper out of professional interest. But seeing it was printed in German he swiftly handed it back to the stewardess saying, "Nein, nein, nein!"

As he listened, Herr Burgmüller grinned in complete approval. "Didn't I tell you so?" he chuckled. "Now you've realized for yourself that news is indeed nothing but annoying garbage."

The clear voice of Captain Schultz crackled over the plane's intercom system as he informed us that our destination was Frankfurt am Main. He then reported with exactitude the speed and height of our plane, when precisely we would land and the kind of weather to expect.

The sunlight outside the window slowly faded as we ate our vegetarian meals, the sky turning a velvety black while dazzling stars appeared, inviting us to another, somehow better world.

The Captain's matter-of-fact voice awoke us from slumber announcing that we would reach our destination in 23-1/2 minutes exactly since we had encountered no delays, no unusual incidents and all had come about as planned earlier in the timetable. In 23-1/2 minutes as predicted, we landed in Frankfurt am Main, West Germany.

"Please unfasten your seat belts, put the blankets and pillows back in the appropriate places," Captain Schultz requested. "Bitte schön, leave the plane in order and quietly. Danke schön."

The stewardess helped Herr Burgmüller to the door, and as we followed him through the exit we found ourselves at an airport bustling with efficiency. Crowds of people, young and old, streamed around us in brisk, businesslike fashion, while a disembodied voice informed the multitude of the latest plane arrivals and departures over a public address system which at times was not very intelligible.

"Good lord, where did they all come from? Where are they going and why?" Bob wondered.

Burdened with luggage, carry-alls and cameras, everyone seemed preoccupied with his own immediate problems. Parents transported children in bags, on their backs, carried them in cradles and baskets, wheeled them in perambulators and small carriages and dragged them along by the hand. The children in turn yelled, shouted, cried inconsolably and giggled with amusement. Some parents relieved their frustrations by spanking misbehaving youngsters with admirable vigor.

"Noone understands children," I sighed, "'except old maids, hunchbacks and shepherd dogs.' That gloomy old American author, O. Henry, was right."

As the agitated multitude swarmed around us, I wondered what would happen if this tendency is permitted to continue. Will the people of this planet stand shoulder-to-shoulder with no room left for pastures and fields?

Bob's eyes were shining with excitement as he, carrying two handbags, a cassette tape recorder and a camera, urged me to hurry. "We don't dare to be late!" he said. Hastily scrambling aboard a British airliner we sighed with relief, settled comfortably in our seats and relaxed for the next hour as the plane did the same. "We're falling behind schedule," Bob worried.

"This is Captain MacMillan speaking. Rome is not letting us in," a voice on the intercom explained the delay. "Traffic is very heavy there. We'll have to wait."

Accepting the mandate of Rome, we spent our waiting time observing our fellow passengers in this plane as they were quite different from those on the previous flight. Many dark-skinned, unusual-looking faces were in evidence with brown, quiet eyes, moist and deep, and hair as black as the wings of a raven.

Here and there we noticed a bright turban, a multicolored saree embroidered with gold. The colorful East had almost entirely replaced the pale and anemic West. We felt, with a thrill, that very soon we would be entering a new and wondrous world. As in legends of old, a secret door then would suddenly open, and on its threshold a perfect man, a Godman, the greatest wonder of this world, like blinding sunlight would appear.

The plane's takeoff with Rome's approval interrupted our reverie. Piercing through thick clouds, we quickly left them far below. Like a fluffy, white Afghan rug, they covered the space beneath.

Bright light poured through the windows and, sucking caramels presented by the stewardess, we read from books which had been brought along. My reading in turn produced a variety of thoughts and I began writing some of them to my daughter, Raisa.

"Who is normal? A person should be considered normal who has finished his inner evolution and lived up to his full inner potential, a potential made available to all by their Creator, no exception to the rule.

What is this potential? It is complete freedom from the illusion of mind and matter through the knowledge of self, the knowledge of the Ultimate Truth or God.

Such people who have achieved this knowledge are extremely rare. They are called

Godmen. Fortunate indeed and blessed is one who in his lifetime is allowed to encounter such an exalted Being.

One who meets such a Godman sees what perfection truly is. He realizes that a Godman controls life and death, that He holds the forces of nature in His hand as a mechanic manipulates a machine, and as Julian Johnson puts it in 'The Path of the Masters,' "Life to the Masters holds no unsolved problems. Death to them has no terrors. To them the future is an open book and there are no limits of time and space to their sway."

Such is a pale pen-picture of a man who has completed His inner evolution and has lived up to His God-given birthright, to His divine potential. Such, and only such, a man could be called a true 'homo sapiens,' a normal man. Everyone else, truly speaking, is not up to the mark. Humanity in its entirety cannot be called normal if observed from this lofty angle of vision.

We all differ only in the degree of our imperfection or abnormality. Man is only in the make, in the process of becoming. He is, as Dr. Johnson writes, 'Only a suggestion, a promise of what is to come.'" (1)

Quo vadis! Oh soul of man, in which direction are you strolling?

The British stewardess, a red-headed girl with a splendid complexion, created a diversion by placing trays with meat loaf and scraps of fish in front of us.

"How come meat?" exclaimed Bob in dismay. "Our order was for a vegetarian dinner. We don't eat fish, meat or eggs."

"Meat, fish and eggs," the stewardess instructed us calmly, "are common everyday foods and everyone eats them so why can't you?"

"Because," Bob said firmly, "humanity became carnivorous strictly out of ignorance of spiritual and health laws. Meat-eating creates binding karma*, flares up animal passions in man and in doing so becomes detrimental to a person's inner evolutionary progress. In this sense it is a sin.

On top of all that, meat-eating, contrary to human beliefs, destroys one's physical health slowly and imperceptibly and is the cause of all sorts of diseases." After this brief verbal exchange the meat was removed and we were told to sit and wait.

Bob turned to me, eyes bubbling with laughter. "You see how delightfully wonderful it is here? They know nothing, mix and confuse everything. There is no system and no timetable. I feel comfortably at home on this British liner. The Germans within the 7 hours of our flight with them bored me to distraction with their exactitude, accuracy and precision. If I ever moved to Germany," Bob declared, "I'd die there from a headache."

---

*Karma. The law of causation: as you sow, so shall you also reap or an eye for an eye, a tooth for a tooth.

Sitting this time in the first row of seats, we were just behind a rumpled, unsightly curtain which divided the first class passengers from tourist.

A clumsy, heavy-set man making his way back to his tourist seat accidentally entangled one foot in the curtain and down it came.

From that moment we enjoyed the privilege of viewing the first class passengers without hindrance and, of course, absolutely free of charge.

"You see," Bob beamed triumphantly, "nothing like that could have happened on the Lufthansa plane. I'll bet the curtain will remain on the floor till we arrive in India."

He was right. It remained where it had fallen.

Eventually, our cold vegetarian meal was served after the empty trays of the meat-eating passengers had been picked up.

"Thank you!" We smiled at the stewardess, while thinking, "Better late than never!" and peered at the new meal with some caution. It consisted of small, slimy mushrooms with a marked resemblance to undeveloped death-caps*. Next to them on the plates lay a spoonful of wrinkled, stale, green peas.

"Excellent, excellent," Bob enthused. "You should note that the death-caps are moldy and smell musty. Well, the mold is penicillin,

---

*Death caps. Poisonous mushrooms found in Russia.

a very valuable medicine and here we find the British are generously distributing it free of charge. This is grand indeed!" And Bob began eating his death-caps with gusto.

Verily, hunger is the best cook!

Captain MacMillan, however, effectively destroyed his appetite. "The final decision of Rome," he announced, "is negative. We have not been granted permission to land. Another city has now been assigned to us. All passengers will have to go to Rome on their own. And please," he admonished, "don't forget your luggage."

"Imagine," I exclaimed in dismay, "going to Rome without knowing the Italian language and hauling our heavy luggage as well! This is grand indeed!" Uneasy, I gazed out the window for a while at the moving clouds below, then thought, "Still, it's a well-known saying that all roads lead to Rome, but..." At this point, sleep took over.

When Bob woke me up, the plane was on the ground. "Despite any previous announcements," he said, "we have arrived in Rome. Just look out the window."

"Roma," the sign distinctly read. The personnel at the luggage platform were obviously Italian, as the agitated movements of their bodies, hands and legs clearly betrayed them. Although their animated conversation was utterly inaudible, it presented no problem whatsoever in understanding its topic. They were all swearing like troopers.

FLIGHT TO INDIA

What a picturesque scene in the style of Leonardo da Vinci!

So this was truly Rome! Once a great and powerful city and now not so any more. Once, legendary wealth and unlimited powers belonged to her emperors, victorious Roman armies mercilessly swept the continents, gladiators entertained audiences while dying in the arenas, Christians were fed to the lions.

We decided to forego a brief visit to Rome, so as to avoid the nuisance of a search at the entrance gate.

A new and different crew took over at the Eternal City.

"This is Captain Cafarelli speaking," our new pilot said in a pleasant baritone. "This plane will fly to Karachi, not New Delhi," and he turned off his microphone.

"Mama mia," a woman groaned in a seat behind us.

"Not to New Delhi!" Bob cried out in frustration, "What do we need Karachi for? Stewardess, stewardess, our tickets say 'New Delhi.' Stewardess, do you hear me?"

The stewardess played deaf as she noisily operated at the plane's door. The metal bolt of the lock clicked into place, and the door was shut fast.

Bob held his breath, listening to that click, then suddenly realized the irrevocable nature of what had happened and gasped. At that moment Captain Cafarelli's pleasant baritone filled the plane. "Gee," he said, "pardon me. A mistake crept in somehow. We are not flying to Karachi but New Delhi, India. I beg your pardon, please."

Stunned, Bob slumped back on his seat but kept silent as a true philosopher should.

The plane was also silent as we were grounded once again and the sign "Roma" that was decorating the terminal building, glared brightly into our eyes.

The blue sky above was empty. No planes were in sight, just a few little clouds which like soap bubbles swam placidly towards the East. No planes were taking off.

"Strange traffic," Bob mused. "Maybe it's traffic Italian style. It's well-known, of course, that everyone interprets the same event in quite a different manner."

Now, we were informed by Captain Cafarelli that because of heavy traffic our flight would be delayed for at least another half hour.

Bob reclined once again and sighed, hoping to catch up on his sleep. He was completely devitalized from the endless exasperations and perturbations. As his head fell on his breast, he drifted off into the world of dreams.

Finally, Captain Cafarelli's jet took off like a roaring lion. Within seconds the sight of Rome was replaced with a vast ocean.

"Arrividerci, Roma!"

We continued flying towards our unknown fate, towards the land of a Satguru*, ever closer and closer and closer. As the evening

____

*Satguru. Teacher of Truth.

fell, our stewardess announced that we would arrive in New Delhi at 7 p.m., New York time.

"Did you hear that?" Barely keeping his eyes open, Bob mumbled weakly, "What that means is that noone will be at the airport to meet us as we'll be landing two hours ahead of schedule. We'll be lost there like babes in the wood."

"Well," I remarked rather smugly, "Lufthansa from the beginning to the end; Lufthansa all the way through; that's what we should have flown. We would not have been so shattered and done in by now, you know!"

Bob's head rested against the back of the seat, a weary look on his face. But he was to get no more sleep.

Someone in a uniform, like a whirlwind dashed through the plane with a can of disinfectant solution in each hand instantly and vigorously spraying everyone and everything.

Again an unbearable stench spread heavily in the air as passengers coughed and choked. Bob, now fully awake, wiped the smelly liquid from the top of his balding head.

"I beg your pardon," said Captain Cafarelli with a notable lack of concern. "This is done at the orders of the Indian Government."

A Japanese neighbor across the aisle politely passed us a scrap of paper. We read the following: "A mistake crept in somehow. We will arrive in Delhi, India, 2 hours later, not earlier. I beg your pardon, please." It was signed by Captain Cafarelli. We handed this remarkable document to another passenger, a man who was snoring loudly.

I switched on the overhead light, as it was already dark, and began reading Master Kirpal Singh's book, "Naam or Word."

He wrote: "Life originates only from life. A living Master and noone else can transmit a life-impulse to others. The sages and seers have always emphasized that Naam or Word should be made manifest within by whoever may be able to do it; and then the experience obtained from the competent Master-soul must be developed."

Then He quoted the founder of the Sikh religion, Guru Nanak: 'Go wherever thou wilt to get contact with the Divine Link, (Naam) and then with the grace of the Guru develop this experience.'

Kirpal Singh continued: "A Muslim divine says the same thing: 'Should you like to go on a Haj' (pilgrimage to Mecca), take with you a Haji (one who has been to Mecca) for a guide, no matter if he be a Hindu, a Turk or an Arab.'

For an experience of the Divine Link (Naam), it is necessary to contact a Sant Satguru, for he alone can explain the theory and grant a practical demonstration of the Reality within each one of us.

The charged words of the Master, his magnetic influence and the life-giving rays emanating from him, quickly help in withdrawal of the sensory currents from the body; for unless the spirit, surging downwards and rushing headlong into the world through the outgoing faculties, is concentrated at its own seat behind the two eyebrows, it cannot reflect upon itself. It is a practical experience of self-analysis or separating the inner man (Soul or the Higher Self) from the outer man (lower self consisting of mind and material body).

By force of age-old habits we are unfortunately clinging to the outer man and are reveling all the time in the outer world with which we have identified ourselves.

There is a regular process of inversion or receding, 'tapping inside' as Emerson puts it, or 'conversion into a little child' as Christ called it; and none but an adept on the spiritual path can help in cutting the Gordian Knot and separating the spirit for awhile from the mind and outgoing faculties.

It is, in other words, a supra-mental experience of the spirit on a super-sensual plane and can successfully be imparted by a Master soul.

This experiment cannot be practically performed by reading scriptures and holy books, for they can neither speak nor explain their true import; nor can they be a guide to the spirit as it transcends the physical plane and traverses higher regions, most of which are fraught with subtle dangers and difficulties from which the Master in His luminous form* can protect and lead the spirit safely from plane to plane. Those who take up the Way without a competent Master are likely to be deceived by the Negative Power and misled.

----

*Guru Dev. The light form of the Master.

FLIGHT TO INDIA

In Surat Shabd Yoga, the importance of the Master cannot be over-emphasized. He is in fact the central figure from the beginning to the end, in life and after life, helping visibly and invisibly beyond the ends of the earth, right up to the Judgment Seat of God and even beyond.

Spirituality can neither be bought nor taught but may be caught like any infection from a spiritually infected person, a Satguru, a Sadh or a Saint.

An adept in Spirituality may in compassion and grace grant a spiritual experience of Naam, now lying buried within each one of us. We have, of course, to develop a receptive attitude and then the grace flows in automatically.

The riches of Naam or Word come to a Gurmukh* and not to a manmukh**, who constantly grovels on the sensual plane.

'Search within, for everything is within.
Only a devotee of the Guru can unearth
Naam,
And remain in touch with It all the time.
Inexhaustible as is the treasure of Naam,
It comes to one so ordained.'

                              --Guru Amar Das.

It is through the grace of God alone that one is initiated." (2)

----

*A devoted disciple of the Master.

**A man who follows the dictates of his mind.

FLIGHT TO INDIA

As I closed the Master's book, I thought what a strange fate! By the grace of Almighty God we were initiated into the Mysteries of the Beyond, and now we shall meet the Godman, the embodiment of Naam, the Word made flesh, the very chosen of God, who has full knowledge of all that is visible and invisible. (3)

We shall see with our own eyes and hear with our own ears and witness that which the whole world does not even suspect exists!

The closer to India, the more inner tension and strain. The expectations and trepidations mounted as my heart began beating faster.

Sleep did not come. Thoughts like endless clouds pursued by the wind crowded the mind, restlessly and persistently.

Over the horizon, a pale yellow light began to kindle, turning primrose, growing brighter and brighter, while the stars slowly dimmed and died out.

The sky began to flame and sparkle with southern intensity in golden, purple and red colors until everything turned into a veritable festival of gleaming lights, and then, like a shining swan, slowly and majestically the sun made its appearance in all its blinding glory.

The plane was landing. The stewardess opened the door and the new unknown world, a world of different culture and ways of life, the ancient land of India, welcomed us with the aroma of cow dung and a hot, humid caress.

This odor and the stifling heat pursued us from that moment on, day and night, like a living visitant who never left.

"How can one move here? How can one breathe here? Good Lord! How does one live here?"

"Never mind, Kira. We shall have to get accustomed. Let us move on," Bob answered as he bravely fought his way through the liquid heat.

Perspiration rolled down his face in large, glistening drops. I silently trailed behind him, pondering whether we would be able to survive in India.

Entering the glass terminal building we looked around.

The Indian personnel at the airport, the exotic Eastern attire, the structures—all was strangely beautiful, picturesque and deeply mysterious.

Following the other passengers, we passed through the customs inspection and walked apprehensively into the waiting room.

Standing amidst the milling crowd, we sought some clue as to what would happen to us next.

THE ONLY IDEAL FOR MAN
IS TO BE PERFECT AND COMPLETE.
THIS WOULD DISTINGUISH HIM
FROM THE IMPERFECT AND MUTILATED MAN,
COMPLETELY IGNORANT OF THE GODHEAD
IN HIMSELF, TORN AS HE IS BY PETTY
JEALOUSIES, AVARICE, GREED, DECEIT,
ENMITY, RECRIMINATIONS AND ALL
TYPES OF VICES, A TRUE ABODE FOR
SATAN AS AT PRESENT. (7)

BE YE PERFECT AS THY FATHER IN
HEAVEN IS PERFECT.
        ___CHRIST
        (ST. JOHN 1:1-3)

CHAPTER THREE

IN THE ASHRAM

Two girls in their thirties approached us. Both were clad in white Indian-style outfits resembling our Western pajamas: a loose shirt with a cut on both sides, and wide comfortable-looking trousers held tight at the ankles with a rubber band. Their heads were covered with light, white shawls from under which a long pigtail fell down the back.

One was Indian; the other looked British; and both were positively beautiful, each one in her own way. Large, dark eyes, resembling doe's eyes, gave a natural mystery to the Indian girl's lovely and animated face, while her British companion displayed breeding and delicacy in her features that were most attractive.

"Are you the disciples of Master Kirpal Singh Ji?" asked the British girl, giving us a searching look.

Overjoyed, and grinning widely, we both exclaimed at the same time, "Yes, yes, yes, that's us. That's us!" and like a drowning man to a straw, we clung to them from there on.

"The jeep is waiting for you outside; please come with us," said the British girl, visibly enjoying our sincere enthusiasm. "My name is Elaine."

"And I am Mira," her companion introduced herself with both Indian accent and laughter in her voice.

IN THE ASHRAM

We loaded our luggage into the old, battered jeep and sat down on a bare, iron-back seat. Mira was the driver. Elaine sat next to her.

"Master is at His home in Rajpur," Mira informed us without taking her eyes from the road. "He will be back in a week."

"That's all right," said Elaine soothingly, "you will have a week's rest."

"True," sighed Bob, and as we had no other choice but to wait anyhow, he added, "It will be very good to rest as we had a rough flight over here, you know."

India!

The country of Gautama Buddha and legendary maharajas, the land of the ancient Vedas, of Rama and Sita, darvishes, wizards and magicians, the fatherland of Guru Nanak and Kabir Sahib, the ground in which the roots of all religions rest! Finally India was before us!

The jeep rumbled along sometimes wide, sometimes narrow streets. We passed by dirty, shabby houses with flat roofs, some of them with no windows, paint peeling from the walls.

These structures were surrounded by solid white fences. Mud huts about 3 feet tall clung to them like birds' nests.

A black hole in the middle of the huts served as a door in front of which was a chalked-out square which denoted the territory that the owner claimed for his use.

On one of these squares we noticed an empty plate, while next to it a baby wept, its mother crouching by its side fanning off the flies with a banana leaf.

As we rode along, delightful and rich-looking three-story high dwellings appeared, the architecture reminiscent of Mohammedan mosques. These villas were figuratively drowned in lush, exotic foliage, and the gardens brimmed with bright, fragrant flowers.

We crossed a bridge, and on its railing right above a precipice a fakir sat cross-legged, lost in deep meditation.

We passed modern glass buildings, banks, hotels, offices. Stores and shops were there in abundance.

Some stores looked utterly appalling, reminiscent of the mud huts we had passed a moment before with similar black holes as entrances. Around them all was filth and untidiness. It seemed that to enter places like that would surely require unimaginable bravery.

Merchandise lay both outside and piled up inside these shops. One could buy here a variety of items ranging from old, torn-up automobile tires to imitation Aladdin lamps.

On Connaught Circle, everything looked different. Here were rows of magnificent stores located on a wide circle which surrounded a park. Here one could acquire almost anything one could afford: gold, diamonds, beautiful light silks, bronze statues, hand-carved folding screens, the hides of tigers and leopards, shoes, to mention a few.

On a side street Tibetan refugees had their own rows of dilapidated shops.

'It seemed that to enter places like that would
surely require unimaginable bravery.'
(Page 25)

The sidewalks were crowded with people in a hurry, clad in white, rumpled outfits, filthy rags or in some cases only a loincloth. Everywhere one could see men wearing turbans and Nehru caps, but most heads were uncovered.

Against this overall background of white, the multi-colored ladies' sarees stood out like living flowers, lending a beautiful touch of cheerfulness to the whole picture.

The streets were jammed with bicycles. There were so many of them that one assumed they were the principal means of transportation in India. Not just 1 but 2 and 3 persons were sometimes carried on one bicycle which often had a cart fastened to it loaded with either people or things.

Motorcycles roared threateningly, cars honked, dirty buses with deafening noise thundered along the cobblestones, while military jeeps from World War Two rumbled mercilessly.

Wagons to which men had harnessed themselves inched along squeaking pitifully on rusty axles. Oxcarts straight from Biblical times creaked and moved slowly on two huge, wooden wheels, wheels so big that one could not see the man sitting between them on a bundle of straw.

Add a herd of cows and goats, a flock of chickens and geese to all this swarming madness and only then one would have a pale pen-picture of street traffic in this Indian city.

The only creatures maintaining an unruffled calm amidst all this turmoil were the fabled Indian white cows that stood peacefully or lay unconcerned on the cobblestones.

A white hump rose in the middle of their backs. Their brows were adorned with curved horns which looked like ancient lyres, presenting quite a stately sight.

With utmost care, the mind-boggling traffic skirted around them thus avoiding any disturbance to their royal repose.

Mira was an excellent driver, and with admirable skill she maneuvered the old, battered jeep in the midst of all this chaos.

Occasionally, she stopped the car, half-opened the door, leaned out of it and loudly reprimanded in Hindi some miserable offender of the traffic regulations, reenforcing her words with strong gestures of the hand.

The offender would invariably talk back no less loudly, and his hands would fly around no less energetically.

This excitement would last for a few moments, and then everyone would start moving ahead once again.

And all this in such heat! No wonder that heat strokes do not surprise anyone over here.

Settling down behind the wheel again, Mira would laugh heartily and explain to us what went wrong.

Roasting and sweltering on our hot iron-back seats, we slowly regained our composure after this brief encounter with the city of Delhi, and Bob started a political conversation, believing it would be quite appropriate for this particular moment. He wanted to know what the foreign policy was of the current Indian Government towards the United States.

Drily, Elaine replied: "In the ashram we do not talk about such insignificant and unimportant subjects as politics."

"No?" Bob could hardly believe his ears. "Then what do you talk about?"

"The Satguru," she said.

Silence fell, deep and long, as we had nothing at all to say about the Satguru.

And this little episode was just our first blunder as we slowly entered the unfamiliar world of spiritual life.

I attempted another conversational approach, having heard a rumor at Satsang* in New York that the Maharaja of Jind owned a spectacular palace containing rooms without number, filled with solid gold statues, Persian rugs, objects of art and other priceless treasures; that numerous servants worked in the palace and gardens, tasters were checking the meals before they were served; that the Maharaja, being a passionate hunter, kept 3 thousand dogs for his pleasure in separate quarters and there were servants to wait on the dogs.

He had a beautiful daughter, a princess who renounced the world, left the palace and became the disciple of Hazur Kirpal Singh Ji, the Master, and lived somewhere in the ashram.

---

*Satsang. Spiritual gathering.

I began by saying, "Mira, we were told that a real princess lives in the ashram. It would certainly be a thrill to have a glimpse of a real princess at least once in one's lifetime. Do you think you could point her out to us from a distance, of course, so as not to disturb her Serene Highness in any way?"

"Why from a distance?" smiled Elaine quietly. "You can see her from close up. This princess is Mira."

Stunned, I flinched away with an expression that must have resembled that of the first Pilgrim as he fell off Plymouth Rock.

"The miracles of India have already begun," Bob muttered in disbelief. "The princess, the daughter of the Maharaja of Jind is our chauffeur!"

Elaine looked amused. "You see," she explained, "our angle of vision is spiritual, not worldly. Princesses, caste, riches, fame, name, worldly achievements, politics, cultures, religions, nationalities—all that and much more have no value for a spiritual person. Why? Because they do not guide and lead mankind to the goal of human life on earth which is God-Realization through Self-Realization.

This goal sets all other goals to shame, for beside it there are no goals at all, but empty baubles and toys, at best half-way houses.

When this light of Self-Knowledge dawns, all doubts and all differences vanish (4) because 'a person possessed of this Knowledge then actually sees nothing but God in His creation and creation as established in God; the two as identical and not separate from each other.' (5)

It is all oneness. It is all the manifestation of the Absolute God in action called Naam or Word, and besides this oneness there is nothing at all in the whole creation. So says our Master."

"That is akin to the pantheistic view of religion," (6) mused Bob from his back seat.

Elaine continued, "So, in reality none is high; none is low. There are no princesses, no castes, no maharajas. These are all man-made badges and meaningless dreams conjured up by the unillumined and dark human mind."

Elaine fell silent for a few moments as Mira honked at two cows with gilded horns who began moving slowly towards a long, dirty wall. Then Elaine added,

"Our Master says, 'There is only one nobility, the nobility of the soul. There is only one caste, the caste of humanity. There is only one religion, the religion of love. And there is only one life, and this life is Naam, the flaming sound.'"

From a narrow street we crossed a small bridge over a deep, smelly canal. "This is a sewer canal," explained Elaine, "and on the other side of the bridge is the entrance to our ashram."

We drove in to the ashram through a shabby gate, noting on the fence the painted words, "Be good, do good, be one," as a passing train rattled and whistled loudly somewhere close by.

IN THE ASHRAM

The jeep stopped on a large, wide central area where, as Elaine told us, thousands of people from all over India came once a month to listen to Master's discourse.

The courtyard was covered with sand. To the left, behind a black, floral cast-iron gate, stretched a beautiful roomy house, Indian-style, with a flat roof surrounded by a balustrade. A few lush trees and bright flowers grew in front.

"This is Master's house," Mira told us, "and in front of you are the quarters for the Western disciples. In the back to the right, you see rows of empty rooms for the Indian satsangis* visiting overnight."

The gates to the lovely Western quarters were opened. We entered and walked along beside a green, square lawn, surrounded on three sides with white buildings. An Indian, bending over, mowed the grass with a hand sickle.

We were assigned a small room where we found two hard metal beds, each with a mattress, sheets and a flat pillow, a narrow table under the open window, and two chairs squeezed in on the side. A tiny rug decorated the wooden floor.

There was barely room to turn around here. The back door led in to a large bathroom with noisy old-fashioned equipment. Another opened on to a screened porch where a lonely straw chair stood at a bare wall.

---

*Satsangis: disciples of the Master.

The gates to the lovely Western quarters
were open.
(Page 32)

Clinging with its sharp claws to the ceiling, a pink lizard observed us peacefully with his black, beady eyes. On the floor a small animal resembling a mouse lurked in a corner chewing busily. Above it in the breeze of an overhead fan, caught in a delicate spider's web, the dead body of a scorpion, void of its contents, was placidly swaying.

Everything here was simple, modest and unassuming. It was a real monk's cell, and we loved it.

Stretching out on the hard, hard beds in utter exhaustion, we instantly sank into blissful oblivion.

Ramji, the ashram's servant, woke us up with a loud invitation to come to the breakfast being served in the dining room. Smiling, he bowed, hands folded. Sleepily, walking behind him, we entered the eating hall.

The room was not very large. A long table, surrounded on all sides with plain wooden chairs, stood towards one wall, leaving just enough space to walk past.

Further up, a door led into a kitchen where we noticed an old refrigerator proudly displaying a slightly rusty chromium door handle.

Screened windows and 2 doors formed the wall facing the ashram lawn, a wall through which oppressive heat and humidity entered in profusion.

Two Westerners sat at the table eating rice with lentils. Thus we met Kim Knutsen, a 20 year old lad from Hawaii, who barely said 3 words during his whole stay with the Master, and Gerald Stern from Fort Lauderdale, Florida.

Gerald, dressed in a white Indian outfit, was a tall, well-built man in his late twenties with wide, strong shoulders. His brown hair fell softly on his forehead. Behind dark-rimmed spectacles his hazel eyes smiled at us in a warm, outgoing and very attractive manner.

A small, beautiful child—perhaps a year old—sat on his lap, letting saliva bubbles out of her mouth.

"The baby's name is Sushila-Mira," Gerald grinned in welcome. "My wife Jodi is washing her diapers in the bathroom, and I am busy taking hundreds of pictures of Master. Actually, I'd like to snap a thousand since I'm a portrait artist and have my own studio in Fort Lauderdale.

When I moved to New York from Africa where I was born in a family of African Jews, Cy Winters and I made a living by dancing on the stage. Are you acquainted with Cy?"

"Oh, yes," we answered. "Cy is an exceptionally advanced disciple. He sees the Radiant Form of the Master within and without and talks to Him."

"What a terrific guy," Gerald exclaimed happily. "I am so delighted to hear that he's made so much inner progress." Pushing up his slipping spectacles, he inquired, "And what is he doing now?"

Mira and Elaine entered the eating hall just then. With a smile Elaine repeated again that in the ashram one should talk only about the Satguru, the path and inner illumination, the rest being a mere dissipation of mind disturbing to one's meditation.

"You see," said Mira, "between God and soul stands the oscillating mind. In agitated waters the sun does not reflect. Still the mind, and you will see God."

She looked at us warmly and then added, "It is all so simple. Do not agitate the mind, and pay no attention to the outside world. Otherwise, your meditation will suffer."

"Mira," asked Bob, "is there anything that could help us to still the mind?"

"Sure," she replied. "One should simplify his life. Our Master says to take our irons out of the fire one by one. The more you are involved in outer things, the less peace you will have inside. Stay away from and do not think about the worldly people as whomsoever you think about, his very radiation will be absorbed by you.

It is an old well-known truth that the worldly people are given up to lust, anger, greed, attachment and vanity—all the 5 deadly sins. Your mind will be infected by them and lose its stillness.

As long as you do not see the Radiant Form of the Master within, you will have acquired no conviction, so avoid wavering individuals. They will instill doubt in your mind which will prove to be detrimental to your inner progress.

Also, 'forgive and forget' is another helping factor. Hatred, revenge, an eye-for-an-eye, and a tooth-for-a-tooth will create unending, harmful agitation within you.

Truthfulness, too, is very necessary. What we think, we should say, and what we say, we should do. We are scheming, fibbing all the time. A person will have to tell so many other lies just to cover up the first one, and then more lies to cover the second one. There cannot be any peace within such a person, and where there is no inner peace, there will be no good meditation.

Do one thing at a time and with full attention, wholly and solely, so that your thoughts do not start wandering. Such a way of life will make your mind single-pointed and whole.

Sink from the circumference of your being to the center and stand there soul-centered, poised and still. Only then will your meditations be successful."

A voice called to Mira from outside and both girls left, wishing us a good appetite.

The delightful Indian tea spread its delicate aroma to all of us at the table. Mixing yogurt into his rice and lentils, Gerald carefully swallowed a spoonful, and then continued his biography with great deliberation:

"After our daughter was born, we wrote a letter to Master asking him to name her, and He obliged by calling our little girl Sushila. However, when we arrived here, Taiji, master's housekeeper, recalled that in Indian history

Sushila was a bad woman. So Taiji suggested that Master should give the baby a different name. After a little thought, He changed her name to Mira. Mira was a princess, and the whole of India still sings her heart-warming songs. The only problem is that Sushila does not respond to her new name at all!"

After breakfast we went back to our room and resumed our slumber. By evening, having somewhat regained our strength, we stood silently on the portico admiring the charming grounds. The green lawn, smooth as velvet, was bordered with an array of bright, colorful flowers that glowed like precious stones in the oblique, last rays of the sun.

The white, clean structures of the ashram were as pure as Italian marble. The blue, silken tent of the Eastern sky stretched placidly above.

Surrounded by all this beauty in the middle of the lawn, our new acquaintances from the West and a few local disciples sat in a circle, motionless, cross-legged, Indian-style, resembling white, chiseled statues.

Nothing was stirring, not the leaves, not the men, not their thoughts. Nature itself seemed lost in meditation enticed by the voice of a faintly twittering, invisible bird exhorting her to, "Do it, do it, do it!"

Peace and bliss saturated the atmosphere of this quiet estate, its grounds, buildings, life, and permeated our thoughts, hearts and souls through and through.

I basked in this reverential glory and could not have enough of it. "Verily a Garden of Eden," I thought.

Bob had vanished like a phantom somewhere amidst this silent splendour. On returning, with fascination he repeated a story that Mira had just related.

"When she was younger," Bob began, "a palmist predicted that the number 26 would prove fatal in her life.

Mira's husband was a pilot in the Indian Air Force, and in a vision she saw him crash into the side of a mountain, the plane going down in flames, his dead body sprawled on the ground.

Fearfully, she pleaded with him never to fly on the 26th day of any month. But the vision came true in spite of it.

Descriptions of the fatal accident given by eye-witnesses coincided to the minutest detail with her vision, but the date was not the 26th.

She then went to another palmist who said, 'Oh, I see that at the age of 26 you lost your husband in a fatal accident.'

Deciding to leave the world, she became Master's disciple.

Once, when in her ashram quarters, another vision was granted to her. She beheld her husband in the lowlands of the astral world in ominous and gloomy hospital-like surroundings, his face distorted with horror and fear.

Frightened she rushed immediately to the Master. 'Is it true?' she asked with apprehension.

'Yes,' the Satguru answered, 'it is so.'

Sobbing, Mira begged Master to help her suffering husband.

'All right,' He answered.

One day as she was alone in her room, her husband, radiant, shining and happy, suddenly appeared before her. His beauty was such that, entranced, Mira could not take her eyes from that glorious being.

Folding his hands, he smiled and bowed humbly. 'Thank you,' he said. 'Thank you so much!' and vanished forever from her sight."

Bob fell silent as I exclaimed in utter wonder, "Oh, truly then, it is so. A Godman controls life and death and there are no limits of time and space to his sway!"

Next morning the golden rays of the sun lay on the floor of our room in liquid patches. In ornamental patterns they adorned the empty walls. Hot air poured in from the doorway to the porch while somewhere in a distant backyard a rooster crowed.

Standing on the porch we peeked through the screen door into the adjoining large room. On top of a colorful Indian rug stood a small table with a lamp. To the right we saw 2 beds; to the left an open window under which a soft couch and 2 club chairs were placed creating a cozy corner. Next to them were shelves built into the wall.

Two fans were idling on the ceiling. In the back of the room was an entrance into our bathroom.

"You like it?" someone asked with a laugh.

We turned around in surprise to see Mira standing behind us, her lovely face all smiles.

Flushed with embarrassment, I muttered, "Yes...a large room."

"That is good," she said. "Why don't you both move in there as your small cell will be used by a new disciple who just arrived today."

We noticed then that a tall, blond, handsome young man with a wide grin on his face stood behind her.

"Swen," he introduced himself. "Swen Olson from Canada. Our group of Satsangis in Vancouver owns a health food restaurant. Whenever we save enough money, by turns we travel to India to stay with the Master, and this time it was finally my turn!"

His large blue eyes gleamed with happiness.

"Excellent, dear neighbor," I exclaimed. "We'll leave right away."

As Swen settled in our little room, everything became quiet and calm once again as Swen happened to be just like Kim. He was silent and kept meditating all the time.

"A Dane?"

After weighing all pros and cons, Bob said with an extra ounce of warmth in his voice, "A Swede!"

Verily, I thought, our old national labels do not wash off that easily.

IN THE ASHRAM

Being a third generation American, Bob,
who not even once had felt drawn to visit his
ancestral Viking Sweden, nevertheless was
pleasantly touched when thinking of his Swedish
neighbor, as my heart indeed sweetly melted when
I thought of the Russians on the frigate
"Pallada." Now what kind of a riddle is that?

As it was time for breakfast, we walked
Swen to the dining room where Gerald introduced
us to Betty and Michael Goldner, who had just
arrived from New Hampshire.

Michael's brown eyes were penetrating and
warm, his hair resembling a tall, caracul hat.
Betty smiled without a break, while Michael
played mute.

Another Kim and Swen, we thought.

Leaving Bob in the dining room, I walked
across the ashram lawn thinking about Natasha
Derujinsky back in New York. I had promised to
get her a subscription to Sat Sandesh Magazine
which was published somewhere in Sawan Ashram.
And to keep my word, I had to embark on a
safari.

In spite of the early morning hours, it
was already hot and humid. Keeping to shady
areas seemed to be a wise policy.

Knocking on the first door I came to and
getting no answer, I looked into the room but
found that all was empty and dead silent there.

Beyond Master's house a few Indians sat in
the shade of an awning eating chapatis* and

---

*Chapatis: flat Indian pancakes.

drinking tea. Two of the men got up and politely escorted me to the other side of the courtyard.

"That's the Sat Sandesh office," one of them said, pointing to an open door; "Please go in," and quietly walked back.

In the large office all doors were open. A twittering bird flew in through the window with obvious enjoyment of her adventurous life. Two lizards basked on the empty wall, their round bellies full of mosquitoes.

Beneath them on a wooden bench an old man with a long, white beard slept peacefully, letting out a snore once in a while. A pair of old, round spectacles adorned his large nose, while his turban slipped to one side.

The table in front of his bench was covered with an array of papers in utter disorder. Above them like an odd sentinel towered an ancient telephone.

Next to the bench a young man idled aimlessly with a half-eaten chapati in his hand.

To his left stood a bigger table with two Indians sitting on top, cross-legged, silently and unhurriedly sipping cups of aromatic Indian tea. Both were in long, white shirts and trousers. One wore a turban; the other had none. They looked at me inquiringly.

"Could someone here please help me with a subscription?" I asked.

As the young man understood not a word of English, he smiled in a pleasant way while both tea-sipping Indians on the table grinned happily. One of them, pointing to the sleeping old man said, "Gyaniji here will help you and take care of everything."

Eventually old Gyaniji awakened. Slowly getting up, he smiled; then smoothing out his silken beard with a flowing motion of the hand, he took off the turban and blotted down the perspiration from the top of his silvery head.

While he was putting back his turban I said, "Hello. Good morning, sir." Extending the scrap of paper containing Natasha's name and address, I added, "A subscription is wanted for Sat Sandesh Magazine."

Carefully, he studied the English writing, then said a few Hindi words to the aimless young man. "Acha, acha*," the man answered quietly and began a leisurely search.

First, he checked Gyaniji's table; next, the shelves on the wall. He looked into the pockets of clothes hanging behind Gyaniji's back, attentively peered under the table, while Gyaniji cordially explained to me, "This is the ashram secretary, and he is in search of a pen."

The time ticked along peacefully while the secretary continued his search.

The twittering bird flew out through the window. The secretary walked out through the doorway. And one could observe the young man crossing the courtyard and vanishing behind a flowering tree.

---

*Acha. O.K.

IN THE ASHRAM

Gyaniji sighed, then yawned sleepily and decided to take another nap. Stretching out on his wooden bench, he yawned once again and fell asleep.

Unconcerned, the turbaned Indian on the top of the dining table blew a fly that fell into his tea to one side of the cup, then continued sipping the fragrant liquid, unimpressed, blowing and sipping, sipping and blowing in silence and peace.

Good Lord! By what fantastic whim of fate was I cast into this blessed corner of the world where even the atmosphere itself is permeated with gentleness and tranquillity!

130 years ago in the legendary estate of idle Oblomowka*, the Russians used to live just like that in the good, olden times of the Czars. How dear and familiar was such a way of life to the heart of a native of old Russia, by now ruthlessly crushed and destroyed.

Never would I like to leave this room. Never would I want to change a thing here. This was certainly a place to stay and stay and stay!

With a dreamy smile on my face, suffused in pleasure, I wondered why the rest of the world lived a life of mad hurry and scurry. Oh why, dear Lord? What for?

------

*Oblomowka: Goncharov's Russian estate, famous for its sleepy, unhurried life, hospitality and idleness.

Finally, the secretary came back with a long pencil in his hand. Sleepy Gyaniji once again sat up on his bench, took the pencil, with his elbow moved the papers to one side, then unhurriedly copied Natasha's address and returned my note.

Picking up the old receiver from the old and rusty hook, he dialed a number and listened patiently, but there was no response on the other end of the line.

Slowly hanging up the receiver, Gyaniji waited for quite awhile, then tried again and again dispassionately with the same outcome.

After one hour of this effort, Gyaniji was still doing the same: picking up that old receiver from that old and rusty hook, dialing and listening, dialing and waiting, but the line remained mute.

The young, pleasantly smiling secretary, like a soap bubble, had vanished without a trace.

Gone like vapor were both lizards.

From the top of the dining table, gone were both tea-sipping Indians.

Only Gyaniji continued sitting, dialing and listening, and I, basking in beatific peace. As fate ordained it, someone answered, and the address was dictated to him. "Acha, acha," Gyaniji said listlessly and hung up for the final time.

"Everything has been taken care of. Sat Sandesh will be mailed to your friend," said Gyaniji in a most gentle manner.

Giving him the subscription money, I folded my hands in the Indian way. "Thank you so much for this invaluable lesson in patience, ahimsa* and tolerance, sir. It was needed and needed badly, so I am greatly indebted to you," and I bowed before him slowly, so very slowly indeed.

Walking back along the courtyard in a mood of elated joy, I noticed Bob running hurriedly.

"I was worried sick. Where were you so long?"

"In the heavenly oasis of Oblomowka," I answered dreamily in a quiet, unruffled voice. "In Oblomowka which vanished 130 years ago. And just now I have been lucky enough to visit that fine estate, and that is where I was!"

Looking utterly perplexed, Bob asked with concern, "Are you still all right upstairs? What happened to you?"

When the tale of Natasha's subscription was finished, I smiled placidly. "Such a simple, Oblomowka type of life, I believe, is conducive to meditation as nothing in it agitates the mind from without. It provides that necessary background of tranquillity without which single-pointed concentration cannot that easily be achieved.

Thus, one can sink with ease from one's circumference to one's own center of peace within and indeed progress in meditation with leaps and bounds! Don't you think that such a way of life is kind of idyllic?"

---

*Ahimsa: non-violence.

"I don't know," Bob replied. "By the way, there is no honey in the ashram kitchen at all. We'll have to do some shopping."

Back in our living quarters, Bob began an intense search for his misplaced billfold, while I went behind the wall of the guesthouse to find out what was going on there.

A long row of filthy latrines separated the ashram territory from the fields beyond, and a railroad track on which a whistling train was noisily rolling by.

The narrow corridor between the latrines and the ashram wall was paved with cobblestones along which a God-intoxicated Sikh in a dark, blue turban paced to and fro like a metronome.

Devotedly chanting hymns from Jap Ji, the morning prayer of the Sikhs, closing his eyes, he bowed reverently, then raised his head to the heavens above.

"If I may only please Him, 'tis pilgrimage enough.
If not, nothing—no rites or toils—avail.
None has won salvation without His Grace—
regardless of karmas*.
You can discover untold spiritual riches
within yourself
If you but abide by the teachings of your
Master.
My Master has taught me one lesson:
He is the Lord of everything; may I never
forget Him." (9)

____

*Karma: the law of causation.

IN THE ASHRAM

Leaving the ashram, we walked along a short, bumpy road, then stopped on the narrow bridge making way for a two-wheeled, wooden cart on creaking axles in which a whole Sikh family was sitting.

Up front, the man snapped his whip over the donkey's head, while his wife and daughter sat backwards, legs dangling, almost touching the road.

Both of them, calm and undisturbed, admired the colorful panorama before them: the sewer canal beneath the bridge, its smelly, aged stone walls, the peeling paint of the ancient homes and cow dung that lay all around.

At the end of the bridge we entered the same street on which Mira had driven us to the ashram, on one side flat-roof dwellings, on the other a tall wall with barbed wire on top.

The two white cows with humps on their backs still stood at the long wall. Dipping his brush in a waterpail, an Indian scrubbed one cow. Then, very cautiously, he wiped her curved, gilded horns, while the second cow chewed her green cud and brushed flies off with her tail.

Walking along the fence talking cheerfully was a group of schoolgirls. Lunch, copybooks and bags in their hands, they were clad in uniforms—pink outfits—the same for all.

In front of the houses, behind low white fences, people slept on rope beds, void of pillows and spreads.

'An Indian scrubbed one cow'
(Page 47)

"It's hard enough to sit on these rope beds. How on earth can they sleep all night long on them? How very uncomfortable!" exclaimed Bob, shaking his head in disbelief.

Families crouched on small mats on the pavement while having chapatis and tea. A skinny dog—all her ribs quite visible—wandered around sniffing busily in search of some food. Afraid to be late, people rushed to their work as they and their families also needed money for food.

It was just about 9 a.m., but it felt as hot as the fabled Russian sweat baths. Soaked with perspiration, Bob stopped and pleaded, "Let's go back. It's not wise to continue searching. In the room we have large fans working, you know."

"Indeed, you are right," I said, "but let's see first what's around this corner. Maybe, by a stroke of good fortune, we shall find a store there."

Turning left, we discovered a small black hole in the wall, an entrance to a store, hidden under a ragged awning.

It was too hot to ponder whether we did or did not possess the required unimaginable bravery to enter. Without wasting time, we walked into the hole and stopped in front of a bedraggled counter, but fortunately under a briskly rotating fan.

Everything in the store was unfamiliar, quite strange and unconventional to the Western eye.

IN THE ASHRAM

In unique disorder, goods were scattered over the counter. A collection of flies sat on the culinary products enjoying a bite to eat.

On the shelves, darkened by time, all sorts of eatables had been placed in transparent bags: nuts, dry peas, lentils and an unusual Indian product which looked like orange spaghetti.

Behind the crowded counter stood the beaming owner, his teeth seemingly whiter than white against his dark skin.

"Namaste," he grinned.

Pointing at the only jar of honey on the shelf, Bob said, "Honey, please."

To his delight, the proprietor spoke good English and a lively conversation ensued.

The fan from above mixed up the heat, humidity and the spicy, sharp smells of the little store into a fragrant, warm breeze which made it most pleasant to stand there.

As no other customers were in the store, the owner was in no haste and having no particular desire to leave our spot under the fan, we, too, were in no hurry, and thus spent a delightful hour chatting, shopping and just looking around.

"Who is this lovely, golden girl in the picture on your wall?" asked Bob, "and who is the prince she is presenting with this astonishingly beautiful flower? Why are his face and hands blue?"

"You see," said the storekeeper, "blue is the color of love, while gold is the color of highest spirituality. This girl is Radha, or the pure human soul, who is presenting the flower to Krishna, the prince of love, as God is love, you know."

We finally left the friendly little store carrying a jar of honey, nuts, orange spaghetti and fruits in a bag.

As we returned to the ashram from our hot safari, Mira and Elaine were already on the porch waiting and immediately introduced us to Donna and Stephen Hamilton, who had lived in the ashram for many years and were Canadians.

Donna, a ravishingly pretty blond with features reminiscent of the great works of Renaissance Masters of Art, was inwardly shy and demure.

Master's correspondence with the West was in great part her responsibility, while Stephen worked in the Canadian Embassy, bicycling to work through traffic and heat.

Swen, the Swedish-Canadian, also stood on the porch as a tailor had just finished taking his measurements.

"Kira, in Master's ashram bare legs are not appreciated," said Mira. "It would be good if, like Swen, you ordered an Indian outfit with long pantaloons."

Since Bob wanted Indian attire as well, the tailor was overjoyed to get the 2 additional orders. Not wasting a moment, he began measuring us from head to toe.

As the tailor worked, Bob, who was in the habit of speaking candidly and never let a lie adulterate his words, frankly shared with everyone present his first impressions of India.

IN THE ASHRAM

He thought it was of paramount importance
that India should change, as such a way of life
was quite uncomfortable. The whole country,
everyone and everything, should be Americanized
and the sooner the better.

"Why?" chuckled Mira, turning slightly in
Bob's direction, humor twinkling in her large,
doe-like eyes. "Why? Maybe in America you are
air-conditioned and comfortable, and you have a
lot of material things, but at the moment of
death all these comforts, conditionings and
things will be left behind, and you will go up
just a poor pauper. In India, many live in
exactly the opposite way. We amass the wealth
of parmarth and God-knowledge and leave the
material doll's play to the fools. At the time
of death, we go up wealthy in treasures
inestimable and eternal."

Elaine, sitting in the lonely straw chair
at the bare wall, lifted her delicate finger,
"Even if you become immensely wealthy and
powerful like the Mogul Emperor Shah Jahan, even
if you become a ruler of the whole material
world or even all the planets and suns in the
cosmos, you will have gained—nothing! As, if
your meditation is not done, nothing is done,
and if your meditation is done, and nothing else
is done—everything is done. So says our
Master."

"We do not want any change in India,"
continued Mira seriously. "It is a land of the
Sages, the cradle of spirituality. Eliminate
all that, and what do you have? Another
America?

Let America be America and India be India. Whosoever wants material things can go to America, and whosoever wants spiritual knowledge will come here. Didn't you come here?" She smiled disarmingly.

"Maybe you are right," Bob conceded. "Humanity has a choice this way.

By the way, why is the color of blue a color of love? We were told this in the grocery store."

"Well," answered Donna, quietly joining the conversation, "our Master tells us, that everything below and above in the Creation is the manifestation of Naam, Word or God-Absolute in action. This action is vibration of the very essence of God which expressed itself as Light and Sound principles.

As this conscious current flowed down, it formed spiritual planes. With its further descent, it became the source of Creation of the spiritual-material and the material planes. (10) The vibrations of this creative current, or Word, diminish in velocity as they descend creating the Creation. Thus, different rates of vibration create different universes, the material one being the lowest and the darkest."

"Some physicists these days," said Bob, "have also concluded that the underlying principle of the Creation is indeed vibratory energy."

"Looks like physics and metaphysics are about to shake hands," I observed.

While continuing to sit comfortably in her chair, Elaine added, "The Bible, too, says the same thing in different words, of course. You know the lines:

'In the beginning was the Word and the Word was with God, and the Word was God. All things were made by Him, and without Him was not anything made that was made.'" (11)

Swen leaned against the doorpost of his cell listening when the animal that resembled a mouse suddenly appeared from his room and scurrying past his legs entered the porch. Swiftly running along the walls, the little creature left through the open doorway.

Startled, I gasped.

"Why be afraid?" laughed Elaine. "This little thing is harmless. There are quite a few of them living in the ashram."

"So," Donna proceeded unperturbed, "in the Creation intensity and variety in the lights, colors and sounds are due to this difference in the rate of vibrations of the creative underlying current of Naam, the Word. Thus on the inner plane pure love is perceived as blue-colored light, worldly love as muddy red brown, crystal clear spirituality as white or golden light, and friendship as green. So says our Master."

Mira broke in to say, "The Holy Ones that have risen on the current of Naam and crossed the Creation from its lowest material end to the beginning tell us that the light increases in strength. And the Creation increases in splendor and perfection as one rises up and up until in Sach Khand* the soul of man shines with the strength of 16 suns.

We do not see these things, as our physical senses are quite limited. In the material world we have willy-nilly to go by these limitations, and that is why the East says, 'This world is an illusion, a dream.'"

"Indeed," smiled Donna, "if one did not go up, then anybody with strong, worldly logic will immediately instill doubt in his mind. On the other hand, for the one who went up and saw, no logic whatsoever is dangerous any more."

"Let me tell you a story about our Master," said Mira. "Once a pandit** accosted Him after Satsang. This pandit was an expert in the Sanskrit language.

'Why,' he asked politely, 'did you not describe Dasam Dwar*** according to such and such a Sanskrit word which means this and that?'

'Because,' answered our Master very lovingly, 'I describe that which I see with my own eyes, and not that which is written in your Sanskrit books, dear friend.'

---

*Sach Khand: the 5th plane of Creation.

**Pandit: learned man.

***Dasam Dwar: a region that lies in the 4th sphere of Creation which is called Par Brahm and constitutes the lower part of it.

Another Sanskrit pandit joined the conversation, and, addressing the first one, said that in another Sanskrit book the word mentioned means exactly what the Master had just described at Satsang.

Master chuckled and spread out His hands. 'You see, dear friends,' He said, 'this is exactly where the difference lies between direct perception and reading of books.'"

The tailor finished his job, dropped the tape measure into his pocket, bowed and said that all 3 outfits would be ready the next morning.

Swen disappeared into his cell while Bob exclaimed joyfully, "Back to the fan!" and walked toward our large room where both fans were vigorously working, but Mira stopped him, saying, "We have ordered a taxi. You will have to go to New Delhi as you will need rupees to pay the tailor. The taxi will take you to the American Express Bank. The boy went for it 40 minutes ago, so why not go to Master's house and wait there?"

We thanked Mira for her thoughtfulness, switched off the delightful fans and slowly walked through the courtyard, as, indeed, we had no rupees left.

At the cast-iron gate in front of Master's house, we waited in the shade of a flowering tree. All was serene around us. Not a leaf, not even a blade of grass stirred as the winged Zephyr himself was busy sleeping somewhere in the airy heavens.

IN THE ASHRAM

Like a pearl in a costly setting, Master's house looked magnificent. As we admired the tree growing through its roof, hollow sounds of car wheels rumbling over the bridge disrupted the silence.

An ancient taxi entered through the gate and ground to a stop before us.

Jumping out of the car, the driver, who wore a grimy, red turban, politely opened the door.

Comfortably, feeling like two real Maharajas, we settled into the ripped and soiled back seats. A soft breeze entered the windows, loud honking warned everyone of our approach and almost frightened the two cows with gilded horns that still idled at the long wall.

Skillfully working his way through the insane traffic, the driver speeded towards the American Express Bank near Connaught Circle.

We passed a large billboard where, in violet and red colors, huge faces were painted of men and women in rich, gorgeous attire.

"This is an advertisement of a new film," explained the driver. "Two very famous actors are in the top roles. One plays a dacoit* and the other a Maharaja**. I myself did not see the movie. I have much more important things to do than waste time in the company of dacoits and Maharajas."

------

*Dacoit: thief.
** Maharaja: king.

After a brief silence and some more loud honking, our talkative driver continued.

"You know what all these movies deal with? Lust, anger, greed, attachment and vanity in all sorts of combinations and degrees. And all that is no more than filth. As a fly is repelled by musk and sandalwood but is enamored of the refuse around which it keeps buzzing, so are the people of the world. If one starts to tell stories of dacoits and murders, of loot and war, of knavery and swindling, people will come and see such a movie and listen most attentively to you the livelong day; but change over to a sermon on the joys of solitude and meditation, and they will move away in utter indifference." (12)

We crossed a bridge over a muddy river and approached the historic Red Fort.

"This Fort," our chauffeur launched into his next subject, "was built by the Mogul Emperor Shah Jahan under whose reign the splendor of the Mogul court reached its zenith.

When Shah Jahan fell ill, his son Aurangzeb defeated his brother Dara Shikuh in the battle of Samugarh. After that he assumed the imperial title and imprisoned his father in the Fort at Agra until Shah Jahan's death in 1666."

It seemed that the red walls of the Fort in Delhi stretched endlessly into the distance. The destructive hand of time was collecting its toll, and the marks of deterioration were obvious everywhere.

On the tall watch towers, living black condors, the sinister birds of prey, were perched, their necks bald and long, their beaks thick and bent.

Fearfully, I watched them as we passed the red towers and was happy to leave the fabulous Fort of the Mogul Emperor Shah Jahan.

Deftly avoiding a two-humped Bactrian camel and his owner, who was perched like a condor between the camel's humps, our driver stopped at the American Express building.

Here, without too many delays, we changed dollars into rupees and decided to go on a shopping spree right away.

The chauffeur drove us around Connaught Circle where, over the sidewalks, a white roof was spread, delicately resting on graceful columns. In its protective shade, shoppers gazed at the merchandise in the stores and promenaded in both directions.

The stores were elegant, touched with enchanting flavor of the Orient, and seemed to be almost as fine as those back home.

We got out of the car and strolled, looking at the shops, while our taxi, a few beggars and a shoe-shine boy with a brush in a box suspended from his shoulder followed us. The boy demanded loudly and with some emotion that Bob let him polish his American shoes. One of the beggars pitifully stretched out his arm while holding a paralyzed, retarded child of tender years on his other.

In compassion, we gave him some change. The next moment, a wonderful metamorphosis took place. The paralyzed, retarded child of tender years jumped off the beggar's arm and started laughing and happily jumping around as any healthy, completely normal child would do.

Stunned, we stared at him in utter amazement, while the other beggars continued their pitiful pleas to share in any alms we were giving.

With raised eyebrows, Bob thought aloud, "This kid has a great future in movies," and dismissed the rest of the beggars rather impatiently with a wave of his hand.

We entered a store and bought a pair of open-toed Indian sandals as Bob's American footwear was not fit for this climate.

The shoe-shine boy had waited patiently outside. Following us once again, he resumed his loud demands.

Pointing at the new open-toed sandals, Bob exclaimed, "Dear friend, don't you see there is nothing left to polish."

"There's plenty left to polish," I sighed, "only all this polishing should be done within."

We stopped at the stores of the Tibetan refugees. Bob, having a passionate dislike for this kind of shopping, remained with the driver across the street while I slowly wandered in and out of the shops.

All sorts of goods were piled on the tables including cheap, blackened jewelry, some remarkably beautiful incense-burners, bronze figurines of Bodhisattvas and Buddhas and carved elephant tusks of most delicate design.

After buying several figures of Indian deities and a few hand-made copper burners with excellent silver incisions, I glanced quite accidentally at the other side of the street.

My dear husband was waving impatiently with both hands, making it quite clear that the shopping spree was now over, that it was time to return to the ashram and leave the rest of the intriguing wares there where they lay.

The driver in his grimy turban placidly leaned against the side of his car, hands crossed over the breast, observing the events unwinding before his eyes, and like a lizard on the wall, waited with calm unperturbed.

The heat became utterly unbearable as we once again drove alongside the walls of the sinister Red Fort this time from its other side.

Our philosophical chauffeur now tried to convince us to take a tour of this 5-1/2 mile long magnificent structure, as for a small additional fee he would love to be our guide.

"No, no," I said with a shudder. "No Red Fort, please. We feel close to having a heat stroke and would like to get back to Sawan Ashram before we expire."

However, our taxi driver, a competent tour guide, could not restrain himself, fee or no fee, and he narrated quite eloquently additional historic events connected with the existence of the Fort.

Bob listened with rapt attention, while I, taking no interest in history whatsoever, looked out the open window at the fleeting scenery.

When we had left the long Fort behind and passed over a bridge, the driver asked, "Did you see the famous Taj Mahal, sir?"

"Yes, a few years ago, when I was in India covering a news story. But my wife Kira did not."

"I saw a photo of the Taj Mahal, and it completely satisfied my curiosity."

"Oh, Ma'am Sahib, a picture is like a book, all dry and dead, compared to real life. One has to go through an experience to know the difference. You should take time and go see Shah Jahan's Taj. It is the supreme achievement of Indian architecture."

"Oh," I sighed, "Poor, poor Mogul Emperor Shah Jahan! With all these supreme achievements he achieved nothing. Everything was left behind, and up he went quite empty-handed. A poor pauper, indeed!"

Arriving alive in the ashram, we dashed to our room, instantly switched on both fans and laughed with relief.

After a brief meditation we leisurely strolled into the ashram dinette.

Surrounded by introverts, Gerald was already sitting at the table, beaming at us.

Right above his head on the wall a large sign was now prominently posted: "Simran!" and its message was as clear as clear could be: "Repeat Simran, the Satguru's mantra and keep inner and outer silence."

The introverts followed the commandment scrupulously, while the extroverts--Gerald and Bob--immediately engaged in a lively conversation, as a skinny cat yowled and mewed demandingly, rubbing her arched back on the kitchen doorpost.

"Before Master left for Rajpur," began Gerald, "a fakir came to the ashram, and he chewed up and ate a fluorescent bulb, a razor blade, a nail and a needle, too!"

"You saw it?" exclaimed Bob with fascination.

"Yes, yes, with my own eyes," answered Gerald. "This fakir showed us his tongue on which these objects lay in a melted condition. He probably could raise his body temperature to the degree necessary to melt iron and glass, I think.

As we stood around giggling, Master frowned, 'This man can do at least something. Can any one of you do the same? No? Then what is this giggling all about?'"

"Well," after a short pause, Bob thought aloud, "all these so-called miracles lie within the sphere of nature's laws as obviously nothing can stand outside of these laws. One man is aware of them, while the other is not, and for this other chewing a razor blade seems to be a miracle.

If a caveman were to pop his head out of the cave and see a whistling train passing by, what do you think he would say?

Western science is lacking in the knowledge that the fakir is aware of, and the West had better get with it."

"How can one make the West get with it, when they do not want to get with it?" I laughed. "Bob and I know a very prominent doctor, Gerald, who has written a few books and lives with his family in Connecticut. When such cases and facts are related to him, his answer is quite blunt.

'Maybe so, maybe not,' he says. 'One thing is clear to me. I've invested too much time and money in my medical trade and do not at all intend or have any desire to relearn or change.'

This, you see, is the reaction of the Western scientific pundits to things that do not fit into their materialistic theories and viewpoints."

The ashram jeep drove up to the open gate leading into the Western sector, and the sevadars* brought in packages, bags, boxes and baskets, all filled with food.

From behind the jeep, a tall, dark-haired figure emerged with a sack of apples in one hand and a travelling bag in the other.

The man was clad in an excellently tailored Western suit. His dark, rich hair was slightly ruffled by a windy ride in the open jeep, but his oval face glowed with delight while brown eyes smiled from under his soft eyebrows.

____

*Sevadars: workers.

IN THE ASHRAM

The groceries filled the ashram refrigerator to capacity, while the excess was delivered to his room next to the kitchen.

Within 10 minutes, he made his second appearance. The Western-style suit had been replaced with immaculate Indian attire, highlighted by silken flowers embroidered around an open collar.

Energetically and determinedly, he breezed into the kitchen. Following a thorough check of the refrigerator, he entered the dining room. Putting his hand to a non-existing peak of a non-existing hat, he saluted and clicked his heels in a manner reminiscent of officers' behavior in the army of old Kaiser Wilhelm.

"Werter Meinhardt from West Germany," he reported succinctly.

"Probably flew in on Lufthansa," muttered Bob while chewing lentils with rice.

"Hi, Werter," I smiled. "Welcome! We've been here for a few days, and if you need any help, being new, just ask as we have explored the place thoroughly. I do speak a bit of German, so if any translation is required, you know whom to turn to."

Radiant and buoyant, Werter joined our Western group behind the table. While swiftly peeling a banana, Werter informed everyone that he was a musical conductor, had his own orchestra in West Germany, and that he had just flown in from Japan where he obtained some music that he had sought for a long time.

He had been Master's disciple, he said, for 4 years, and this visit to the ashram was his second.

He went on to say that he couldn't control his mind, couldn't understand English too well and did not understand Master at all.

The latest model of a German cassette recorder hung from his shoulder. "Last year," he admitted candidly, "I recorded one of Master's talks on it but still can't figure out what He said there."

After a short pause, Werter wanted to know why people asked questions at darshan* when Master's books say that one has to be silent. He turned to Bob for an answer.

"What is darshan?" Bob asked in turn.

Werter, having no time to explain, hastily left the table, rushed out and stopped in the middle of the velvety ashram lawn. Then lifting his face towards the sun he smiled as he basked in the glowing stillness and bowed readily to everyone who passed by.

Gerald chuckled with amusement. "Doesn't Werter look like a true Indian?" he said.

Back in our room Bob decided to wash his dirty cup and spoon. Pulling at the handle of the bathroom door several times, he then listened carefully but all was quiet.

----

*Darshan: sitting before the Master and looking at Him.

"Swen forgot to lift the latch again," he sighed, standing in front of the closed door, a sour expression on his face.

Determined to enter the bathroom through Swen's room, Bob softly tip-toed past the Swedish Buddha sitting cross-legged on the floor, lifted the latch and washed his cup.

Now that the latch was up, our laundry could be done. Bob stretched a rope from one side of the room to the other right over the beds, and after this wearisome task relaxed on the mattress opening Master's book, "The Mystery of Death."

Through the 4 open windows, clouds of heat, blended with the moist smell of the sewer canal, floated in unhindered.

As I hung up our wet clothes, dirty wash water dripped on Bob's head. Unmindful, however, he continued reading silently.

"Listen to this!" he suddenly exclaimed and with emotion read aloud:

"Know thou, O Prince of Pandu, that there was never a time when I, nor thou, nor any of these princes of earth was not; nor shall there ever come a time, hereafter, when any of us shall cease to be, as the soul in due course of time will pass on to another body, and in other incarnations shall it again live, and move and play its part.

Those who have attained the wisdom of the Inner Doctrine know these things, and fail to be moved by aught that cometh to pass in this world of change. — To such, life and death are but words, and both are but surface aspects of the deeper Being within. (13)

The lamentable, horrifying and much-dreaded death is, in reality, a rebirth into a life which may be more joyous and more beautiful than known hitherto. Death, the awe-inspiring and heart-rending death, says Kabir, 'is to me a harbinger of joyous life, and I welcome it fully.'" (14)

"Isn't it wonderful?" Bob commented without taking his eyes from the book. "It's simply wonderful!" and continued reading further:

"Behold, I show you a mystery. We shall not sleep (in death), but we shall all be changed, in a moment, in the twinkling of an eye...raised incorruptible...putting on incorruption...and immortality....swallowing death in victory. (15)

And each and every one will go to his own appropriate place according to the law: 'As you sow, so shall you also reap.' Hence the exhortation of the Prophet of Galilee: 'Be ye perfect as your Father in heaven is perfect.'

Perfection then is the goal of human life which consists in self-unfoldment or evolution of the individual spirit by transcending the limitations of body, mind and intellect." (16)

The thought went through my mind that "Slavery to senses is certainly no perfection. We have to rise to that exalted state of freedom where senses are under our complete control."

Being an artist, I found it quite clear that beauty and harmony in colors, tones, shapes, forms and lines were dominating and relentlessly running my life. I was their bonded slave.

On the other hand, my husband was completely free of that kind of slavery. The mild chaos in his New York room was sufficient proof of that.

While Bob continued reading, I decided to conduct an experiment. Throwing wrapping paper from the recent purchases on the floor, I pushed the bronze figurines onto a shelf, head down, legs up, on the side, as the spirit moved them. Contents of the suitcases were dumped over the sofa and club chairs. Bob's left shoe rested on top of one pile while the right lay under his bed. Other paraphernalia were scattered in utter confusion everywhere imaginable.

A roll of toilet paper served as my centerpiece and was put in the most prominent place. With a sweeping glance, I admired the result of this demolition.

"Heavenly free! What a blessing!" I thought with jubilation. "One step towards perfection has now been mastered!"

Someone knocked and opened the door. Mira Ji* and Elaine stood on the threshold, appalled and speechless.

---

*Ji: an endearing syllable added at the end of a name.

Catching her breath, Mira Ji finally stammered: "Kira! What kind of a dump is this?"

After a brief explanation, both girls grinned, entered the room, cooperatively moved stuff from the chairs onto the floor and settled down comfortably.

Raising his head from the book, Bob looked around with interest and told the visitors, "Oh, we have completely turned Indian now. I feel quite at home in this mess."

"Why so many idols here?" Elaine wanted to know.

"Idols? Oh, these, you see, are our future memories. Memories, memories about our Master and our trip."

"The tailor will come in the morning," Mira Ji reminded us. Then she added, "Tomorrow is Krishna's birthday and for India it is just as big a holiday as Christmas is for the Christian world. Everyone will be fasting till midnight. The temples will be filled with people, music and the aroma of incense.

In the evening, please come to Donna and Stephen's apartment. We'll have a cup of tea together."

After both girls had left, once again I triumphantly admired the chaos of freedom in the room, and liked what I saw.

If one can be equally happy in order and disorder, I thought, then happiness is a state independent of the realm of senses and probably is the essence of one's own inner being, or soul.

IN THE ASHRAM

It was dark when we began our meditation in peace and quiet, when suddenly I shrieked, beside myself with fear.

Something was rapidly climbing up my leg sinking its nails deeply into the skin. Shaking the leg vigorously, I screamed, "Quick, quick, Bob! Light, light! A cobra, a cobra!"

Bob jumped up as if struck by lightning, overturned the lamp, but managed to switch it on anyhow. "Where is the cobra?" he yelled wildly, eyes bulging with horror.

Looking around, we found only a silent, pink lizard sitting on the floor. It was he who mistook my leg for the wall.

Mischievously, he observed us while rapidly blinking his beady eyes, then rushed up to the ceiling without admitting his guilt.

"Gee, sorry," I mumbled in shame-faced apology. "Pardon me. A mistake crept in somehow. It was a lizard, not a cobra. I beg your pardon, please."

Bob looked at me reproachfully. "Kira, you are just a second Captain Cafarelli, you know!"

"Well," I laughed, having recovered my equanimity, "at least the Captain and I admit our mistakes."

We listened to the sound of crickets cheeping as if intoxicated, while the crows, so vocal during the day, had now become quiet.

It was night.

As I lay on the bed with a protecting towel on my head against the buzzing mosquitoes, perspiration began streaming profusely down my cheeks, while various insects started creeping and crawling over my body. Petrified but silent, I waited for them to start biting.

As time ticked by, there were no bites. All these little creatures wanted was to crawl and not to bite.

In the morning festive Indian music woke us up as the nation began its annual celebration of Krishna's birthday. The sounds were exotic, the tunes hypnotic, holding us spellbound. The charming melodies completely ruined our meditation, and we decided to have an early breakfast.

In the empty dinette, flies buzzed around pleasantly, a bumble bee hummed busily over spilled sugar crystals on the floor while the sun flamed and sparkled in cascades on the slightly rusted handle of the refrigerator door.

We could see Gerald washing Sushila's diapers in his bathroom, and in the bedroom Sushila letting large, shiny bubbles escape from her mouth, accompanying them with unintelligible baby talk. Suddenly Jodi cried out in a voice filled with despair, "Gerald, Gerald, Sushila ate soap!"

At that moment, fresh as a daisy, Werter entered, all smiles, wearing his embroidered shirt.

Settling down at the table with a banana in his hand, he reported that the night passed splendidly, that he had been a member of all sorts of mystic groups and societies in the past, had also dabbled with the Self-Realization teachings, had searched everywhere and read a lot of metaphysical books.

But he always ended up quite disappointed. Everyone suggested and implied only that somewhere, something indeed existed, yet never explained to him how to get there and what he was supposed to do.

Bob's ears perked up as he sensed a kindred soul in Werter. "Exactly, exactly," he said fervently. "With the passage of time, our house in New York has turned into a veritable library.

After years of searching, we became disciples of Dr. Bhagat Singh Thind, but discovered that while talking beautifully about the Godman, he was not one himself.

Last year, though, after reading our Master's books, we immediately got initiated."

Mira Ji and Elaine entered the dining room. Elaine joined us while Mira Ji busied herself giving orders to Ramji in the kitchen.

Bob continued, "This search, you see, once started, does not end until the Ultimate Truth is found. Master says that the soul of man is so fashioned by its Creator that it will not find peace until it rests in Him. You know why? Because being a drop of the same Essence as that of God, the soul is Truth, is permanent happiness, bliss and love. She will not and cannot be satisfied with anything less than that, as birds of one feather flock together."

"How could it be otherwise?" added Elaine. "How could the soul, an exiled princess of royal blood, be happy in the lowlands of mind and matter?

This world is not her home. None is happy here. Did any one of you possibly find someone who was?"

"No, no, I did not," Werter quickly responded.

"Observe this world," Bob continued. "Each and every person in this world of ours in one or another way is engaged in a constant search for permanent happiness and love without even knowing why. They search instinctively, blindly, restlessly urged by the soul from within.

All that ceaseless, endless commotion in the world that one is part of has existed since time out of mind and is nothing less than the search of the soul for herself, or God. And to find that permanent peace and happiness of Unity with its Creator is indeed the task of every individual soul."

"As Werter said," Elaine pressed on, "none has found that permanent happiness so far. Because the soul, identified with the magic box of the material body, conducts her search in the material world outside, while the treasure lies hidden within."

Werter mused, "True. If one dropped a needle inside the house and then conducted his search outside, the result would obviously be nil."

Elaine offered an additional point: "As Heraclitus said, one cannot enter the same river twice. Everything in this world of ours is in constant change and flux, change itself being the only constant. The very essence of this Creation is in ceaseless vibratory motion, and where there is motion, there is change."

Everyone was listening attentively as she went on, "This world of matter and mind is a spectacular show of ever-changing, fleeting phantoms, objective or subjective, as the case may be, containing within her ever-moving folds no permanence of any kind whatsoever."

"Truly," the thoughts flowed through my mind, "today one is among the living, tomorrow among the dead. A moment ago one was completely healthy, then suddenly becomes quite ill. For some time one is immensely wealthy, then instantly loses everything. Today one is admired and respected, tomorrow utterly defamed. Today he is Czar N. Romanoff, next morning he is shot. One thinks that he has just acquired something, but in a second it is gone!"

I turned my attention back to Elaine who said, "Realizing that no permanent happiness can be found outside, man turns the direction of his search within, and if successful, achieves God-Realization through Self-Realization.

The search of the soul for herself then is finished. 'I and my Father are One,' she exclaims in jubilation, saturated by permanent happiness, bliss and love.

IN THE ASHRAM

Such a person stands there, perfect, soul-centered, rooted in the permanence of Truth, or God, unaffected, indifferent and free from all illusions amidst all these fleeting phantoms of the worlds of mind and matter."

Bob sighed, "But to change from a sensually outward-oriented being to one who is soul-centered requires time and a lot of hard work, as this is no small thing to do. It will not happen in one day."

"Maybe this is why Gyaniji is so composed," I wondered. "He certainly is unaffected, indifferent and free."

"Yes," said Werter finishing his banana. "Es ist ganz klar*. We now are on the right way."

Mira Ji interrupted and asked us to come with her as the tailor was waiting on the portico.

The Indian outfits were perfect, the thin material quite adjusted to the climate. The pantaloons and the wide shirt let the breeze through easily, and it became obvious why all of India was clad in a similar fashion.

In these pajamas, we now looked outwardly, at least, like anyone else on the street and could melt into an Indian crowd like a drop of water into the vast sea.

Since a few letters had to be mailed, we embarked on a new adventure--looking for a mailbox.

---

*Es ist ganz klar: it is quite clear.

IN THE ASHRAM

Leisurely, we crossed the courtyard, gravel grinding under our feet, while admiring the butterflies, who like dainty ballerinas in a pantomime danced over the flowers amidst the golden rays of the Eastern sun to the bewitching Krishna's birthday music rolling over the ashram.

We entered the office of Sat Sandesh Magazine and waited for several minutes observing that old-fashioned telephone still towering silently over the heap of deserted papers on top of the desk.

"It's useless to wait," Bob said. "Not even Krishna's birthday music can coax a spark of human life here today or break the spell of serene peace of this enchanted place."

We decided to give up the search and slowly began walking back. However, noticing an open door opposite the wrought-iron Western gates, we stood there indecisively for a moment and then stepping through it cautiously, found ourselves in a small, inner garden facing another door. Hesitantly, we opened it and peered in.

An old woman in a bright green saree was mixing food with a long spoon in a pot on top of a kitchen stove.

Seeing us, she folded her hands and bowed, while we did the same feeling quite Indian in our brand new outfits. The kitchen was so small that 3 of us had barely enough space to stand there.

"Is this the postoffice?" Bob asked.

Pointing to 2 low club chairs in the tiny, adjacent room, the old woman smiled and left, as she spoke no English.

Knees touching his chin, Bob sat patiently in one of the chairs and waited, while I admired a gold-framed photograph of a noble-looking Sikh that was lovingly placed atop a small, wooden table.

Suddenly, I realized that the face belonged to Gyaniji, when young!

Bob rose from his chair now as the old woman returned, a teen-age girl trailing her. We bowed again.

"Is this the postoffice?" Bob asked.

"Post office?" The girl's eyes grew large from surprise as eyebrows arched on her forehead. Quickly, I glanced at the photograph where young Gyaniji seemed to be smirking.

"No, no," she said. "It is a private house."

"We need to mail 3 letters to the United States," continued Bob, nonplused. "For quite some time we've been wandering around the ashram in search of a mailbox."

"India has no mailboxes. Please leave your letters with me, and I will take care."

"Is there a postoffice close by somewhere?" Bob pressed on, but with no success, as the girl's answer remained the same.

"Please do not worry. I'll take care."

We thanked her and left Gyaniji's house.

The problem of future letters could now be solved in one of two ways: either we stop writing altogether which would upset our folks back home, or begin a new search for the postoffice.

After a short deliberation, we bravely left the ashram and walked along its outside walls, then turned into narrow side streets, passing open, smelly sewer ditches running along the pavements.

Naked children laughed, cried and played in puddles, making chapatis out of dirt. The adults were relaxed on this holiday. Some stood around talking; others crouched on the pavement eating; and still others gazed idly at events taking place on the street.

Our simple question baffled everyone. Finally, we found one confident fellow who said, "Yes, yes, a postoffice in Delhi certainly does exist, though I am not sure what that address is. But do please believe me, without a bicycle a trip there is simply a dream!"

We then asked the same knowledgeable fellow where the ashram was, as after one long hour of this journey, we were completely lost.

The young man had no answer as he did not know, and neither did anyone else, no matter whom we asked. Now it was our turn to be baffled.

"Imagine!" Bob exclaimed. "Kim arrived from Hawaii and knew where the ashram was; Swen came from Canada and meditates in the ashram; Gerald and Jodi flew in from America and wash diapers in the ashram; Werter hails from Germany and eats bananas in the ashram; and these people who've lived here for years, maybe all their lives and just a few blocks away from the

Master, yet they do not even know that Sawan Ashram exists and that one of the greatest Saints ever born makes His home behind its walls! I can't fathom it. I can't believe it."

With the sleeve of his new shirt, Bob wearily blotted the perspiration from his face, then continued thoughtfully: "I think I know the answer to this strange riddle. It's hidden in the words of the Master: 'Whosoever has no strong desire to meet God will not meet Him.

If, on the other hand, one has a strong desire to meet God, God Himself will make the arrangements for him. One will be spotted, singled out, will have faith in the Guru, will get initiation, meet the Creator and be happy.'" (17)

"Knock and it shall be opened unto you," I interrupted.

"Yes, but one will not knock, unless the Creator wants him to," continued Bob. "Sawan Singh Ji in 'Spiritual Gems' says that if the Creator does not wish to bring a person on the path immediately, you may try your hardest, but he will not grasp the idea. And those Whom He wishes to give to, accept it without hesitation. (17a)

'Do not doubt,' says the Master, 'but go to the next plane and with your own eyes see this immutable law working!'

In other words, first God plants the strong desire for Him in you Himself, and makes you knock because He wishes so, and then He brings one to His own feet, to a Godman, the Son of God, where He is manifested fully. And then

He Himself, in the form of the Godman, as Gurudev, or the Radiant Form of the Master within, takes His chosen one Home to Sach Khand.

No wonder Christ said: 'Noone knoweth the Son save the Father. Neither doth any know the Father save the Son and he to whomsoever the Son willeth to reveal Him.'* And this is where the secret lies: God does not wish so!"

After a long and exhausting search for the ashram, sweltering in the scorching heat, inhaling odors of the spicy Indian kitchens and sewer smells, benumbed by the unending loud music rendering homage to Krishna, crossing narrow streets, unknown by-streets, lanes and backyards, we suddenly stood in front of our own deep sewer canal and once again beheld the narrow bridge over it.

Dazed but happy, we entered through the gates. Lovingly and warmly, the words: 'Be good, do good, be one,' greeted us from the wall.

Loud bursts of cannon fire were now added to the festive music. The holiday was at its peak.

In the evening at the Hamiltons' we sipped aromatic, sweet Indian rose tea in a lovely, cozy room. Little pieces of glittering, silver foil floated passively on its surface.

Our hosts lived a simple, uncomplicated life. The expression of kind hospitality never left their faces for a moment.

---

*Matthew 11:27.

'We suddenly stood in front of our own
deep sewer canal'
(Page 80)

As we talked about spirituality, books and libraries, Mira Ji turned her face to Bob. "Do you know," she said, "that Master read through 2 libraries before coming to a simple conclusion: 'Bookish knowledge is all wilderness, no way out. Intellectual reasoning, wrestling and wrangling is subject to error. Seeing is above all.' Master tells us, 'First see, then say.'"

Enjoying the tea and the silver petals, I asked, "And what if one does not see anything within?"

"Then don't speak," Mira Ji answered, "as it's morally incorrect to say something that you do not know to be true.

Surat Shabd Yoga is a path of inner, practical experience, the path of inner seeing and hearing, the path of direct perception, of knowledge that leaves no doubts. Go within; be convinced. There is no other way."

After six years of living in the ashram and observing Master, Stephen believed that the Satguru was the world's greatest dissimulator. "He is not what He seems to be," he said.

"Yes," Donna added. "Outwardly, Master looks like a Sikh in His white clothes and turban, but inside, He is Naam or Word, you see. Master told us Himself that He had no ego."

"No ego?" Bob wondered, "What does that mean?"

"Between the soul of man and God," Donna explained, "stand all the 4 layers of the mind. Ego, the sense of I'ness or separateness, is the fourth and most refined layer, and is dropped off last in the soul's journey towards its Creator.

Whosoever has no ego realizes that the soul and God are of the same essence. Further up, the soul merges into the Highest Divinity and becomes One with God.

While living on earth, such exalted Beings are nothing short of God descended into the human form. And that is exactly what the words of Christ mean: 'I and my Father are One.'"

"True," added Mira Ji. "A Muslim prophet says the same thing--in different words, of course:

'The place inside is so filled with my
Beloved
That there is no room for me; only He
is there.
In You, am I. Look in my eyes and see
the Oneness.
If you do not see, am I to be blamed?'"
(18)

After pouring more sweet Indian rose tea into our cups, Donna continued, "Every Saint is the embodied form of the Formless. He is the all-omnipotent power of God Manifest. And that is no exaggeration or hyperbole. You will find it to be true for yourself when your time comes."

"Yes," sighed Mira Ji, "for us little pieces of humanity, the only hope for salvation is a living Master. Listen to what Guru Nanak has to say:

'O Nanak: free yourself from worldly companions,
      And seek the friendship of a true Saint.
      They shall forsake you even in life,
      But he shall not leave you even after death.' (19)
      "Some time ago," she went on, "I consulted a palmist. 'Oh,' he told me, 'in your past life you tried unsuccessfully to get off the wheel of life and death. Again this life you are attempting the same, but you will not succeed.'
      In tears I ran to the Master and told Him the prediction. 'Master,' I sobbed, 'I did not cross the inner blue sky.'
      Master answered reassuringly: 'But I did.'"
      "Can you explain a bit more? How does it work? What does it mean?" Bob inquired.
      "It's very simple," answered Mira Ji. "Where you are attached, that's where you will go after death. If you are attached to the world, you will come back to the world. Your very attachment will draw you down. Thus, you will remain on the wheel of life and death.
      If, on the other hand, you are attached to God in the Master, you will go where the Master goes. You'll cross the inner blue skies and plane after plane till you reach the Highest Divinity in the Company of the Gurudev."
      With a smile, Donna passed a plate of Indian sweets to everyone. While eating them and sipping tea, we listened to Elaine: "As our Satguru says, 'If He is not to come back, then why should you have to come back? Thus, one is

off the wheel of reincarnation, returned Home and achieves Salvation.

And that's exactly why in the Bible it is said, 'Love the Lord thy God with all thy heart, with all thy Soul, with all thy strength, and with all thy mind.' (19a)

Once at a darshan, Master asked us, 'Don't you want to play the game of Love?'

Going Home, you see, is but a glorious game of eternal Love, where the Beloved is One while the wedded brides are many, as every human Soul is a bride."

"How does one get that kind of Love?" I wondered.

"Leave it to the Master," smiled Mira Ji. "The Satguru Himself will cut asunder your attachments to the world. He will separate you from everyone in His own mysterious way."

Bob summed up our conversation saying, "Gurubakhti* is the way to salvation."

No matter how wonderful the evening and fascinating the discussion, no matter how intoxicating the atmosphere filled with Krishna's devotional music, it all had to end.

We left the Hamiltons and leisurely walked back to our room, caressed by the warmth of the night, as the bright, full moon, like a petal of silvery foil passively floating in a cup of dark, Indian tea, glittered silently from the limitless space above.

---

*Gurubakhti: love of God in the Master and devotion to Him.

Bob sighed, "Did you notice how beautiful and orderly everything was in our host's apartment?"

"Bob is changing," I thought, just a shade surprised, "either for better or for worse. Who knows?"

Taking his delicate hint, when back in our quarters, I cleaned everything up. Beauty and order were restored, the roll of toilet paper on the shelf replaced with a bronze Bodhisattva figure.

Only the rope with the dripping laundry remained untouched, a faint reminder of my glorious freedom just lost.

I COME AS A THIEF IN THE NIGHT

TO STEAL AWAY YOUR HEARTS.

   _Hafiz

CHAPTER FOUR

MASTER ARRIVES

The morning, the long-expected morning on which Master was to return to the ashram had finally come. From the very early hours of the day, the population of the ashram had assembled in the courtyard.

In their white Indian outfits, they stood motionless as sculptures gazing longingly at the road on which the Master's car would make its appearance.

We sat cross-legged in the refreshing shade of a tree also looking without let-up at the road in front of us.

In the air--intense expectation, some kind of felt but not seen jubilation, quiet joy radiating from everyone's eyes.

Deep silence enveloped the ashram, as noone talked, everyone's attention absorbed in that one spot on the road.

The shade of the trees imperceptibly shifted as the sun moved up on its heavenly arch closely observing every inch of the ashram, inspecting the waiting people, carefully and generously pouring its glowing rays upon the scene below with increasing strength as time passed by.

"Maharaji is coming!"

The silence was broken as everyone rushed to the entrance.

Slowly, Master's grey car rolled through the gate, slowly crossed the backyard and stopped in front of His house. The chauffeur quickly got out and reverently opened the back door. Master stepped onto the ashram ground and straightened up.

Before me stood a superman, beyond description and beyond comprehension. The whole world blanked out as our eyes met.

In a moment my heart like a torch set afire blazed up with the Godman's own Love as the world and worldly pleasures, attachments to relatives and friends, fear of death, worry for the future of humanity, hatreds, inner unrest, the values of culture, its arts and crafts, its paintings, music and literature, the vanities of possessions, castes and creeds, all philosophies, rites and rituals of religions, all that and much more fell from the Soul like a dark, sinister spell.

The old world crumbled as values shifted and changed. From the ruins and smoke of those dying past values, the Master, radiant with the light of God's Love, emerged, becoming all in all.

Slowly, Master walked towards His house, His hands folded, greeting His disciples with the light of Love and a gentle smile on His silent lips.

One might think that royal majesty and humility could not blend in harmony in any man on earth. But as we watched and saw how Master moved, how Master looked with our own eyes, we realized that this blend of royalty and humility was the very nature of a Saint.

The gatekeeper flung open the gates and Master's peerless figure disappeared behind the door of the portico.

Speechless and dazed, not yet quite realizing what had happened to us, Bob and I stood there gazing at the open door.

As we recovered our senses, we immediately understood the words of the Satguru: "One lyrical glance of a Master is enough for the jiva's salvation."

I thought, "Even if I never again see the Master, all the sleepless nights, all the torments of a life-long search for Truth, all the painful arguments with opposing friends and relatives, all was rewarded, amply rewarded, more than rewarded by just this one life-saving glance of the Godman."

Someone tapped Bob on the shoulder. "Master wants to see you and your wife," someone's voice said.

"Us?" We gasped in disbelief. "Master wants to see us?"

"Yes, the newcomers. Please follow me," the voice invited us.

Hearts pounding with expectation, we timidly entered Master's house and once again beheld Him as He sat comfortably on a soft couch dressed in a white, immaculate Indian outfit.

A graceful turban adorned His noble head, a silken white beard fell softly over His breast, and from under heavy, dark eyebrows two silvery blue eyes shone quietly, drenched with divine Love. His glowing, inner splendor overflowed in a sort of spiritual radiance all around, captivating, magnetic and irresistible.

His face, serene and exquisite, was such that none would believe could exist among men. Master, this veritable lion of spirituality, was indeed a breath-taking sight to behold.

We fell silently at His Holy Feet while the Satguru smiled graciously. "So you have come," He said.

I vaguely remember what took place next.

We sat there at His Feet in kind of a fog through which Master's voice penetrated as from a distance. He asked about our trip and inquired whether we were comfortable in our room. He said that in the evening there would be a darshan and the following day—Sunday—a satsang. Thousands of people would be coming to the ashram that day.

Monday morning He would be giving initiation and in the afternoon leaving on a tour of the Punjab. If we so desired, He said, to our gratuitous joy, we would certainly be welcome to accompany Him on His trip.

Back in our quarters, elated and enthusiastic, I exclaimed, "We don't dare lose this golden opportunity. The remaining time is precious. Let us not fritter it away. Greater than He we will never meet!

For so many years we prayed and longed to sit before a Living Master, to be able to look into His Godly eyes, to listen to His words of wisdom, to bask in the Light of His holy Presence. What a stupendous miracle! Our wishes have been granted!"

We talked and philosophized trying to comprehend and somehow to grasp the significance of all that had happened to us just moments ago, yet remained at a loss to understand.

After an unsuccessful meditation filled with wonderful thoughts and impressions of our meeting, a cold fear gripped me, fear that all that will be over in just a few days and that maybe we will never see the radiant, love-drenched eyes of our Master and never hear His tender, kind voice address us again.

There will be no more ashram, no more sweet Master's disciples. Slowly, everything will sink into the fog of vanishing time and disappear without a trace, like a dream.

Once again, we shall be thrust into the calculating, heartless business life; again in people's eyes we shall read egotistical self-assertiveness, self-confidence, self-righteousness and deceit.

Again, the battle for the right to live and think in one's own way will commence and visitors will invade our home, who for one or another reason, are firmly convinced that our short life is at their constant command and beck and call.

What a nightmare! Tears rolled down my cheeks and sobs shook my body.

"Kira," Bob exclaimed with concern, "what happened? What is the matter with you now?"

"Oh, you really want to know?" I cried with a breaking voice. "I don't want my relatives. I don't want my friends. I don't

want the house.   I don't want America.   It is
not my home.

My Master is my father.   My Master is my
family.   My Master is my friend.   My home is at
His feet."

Sobbing and blowing my nose, I lay on the
bed, miserable and despondent.

At a loss what to do or how to help, Bob
decided to continue meditating, and eventually
all quieted down in our room as the time for the
evening darshan approached.

When we put our heads out of the screened
porch, startled, we could not believe our eyes.
The ashram was unrecognizable.

Gone with the wind was idle Oblomowka,
vanished lethargic sleep.   Everything around was
brimming with intense life.   People full of
vigor and energy worked every place.

A big podium had been erected next to the
Master's house, slightly to the left, and
covered with a white cloth.   Above it, a
colorful canopy, resembling a rug, was stretched
and gleamed in the rays of the setting sun with
colors of gold, rubies and emeralds.

A huge, multi-colored material was spread
like a big tent over the courtyard securely
attached with ropes to metal poles.

An incessant droning of hammers came from
the construction site.   Bricklayers efficiently
mixed cement and water while hundreds upon
hundreds of people were pouring in through the
gates and settling down in the Indian quarters.
Everywhere, everyone was occupied with
something.

What a metamorphosis; what a magic transformation! Even Gyaniji was walking briskly, a jug of milk in his hand.

As we approached Master's house for the evening darshan, the gatekeeper let us in, and we entered the crowded porch.

Indians were talking in a pleasant, foreign language that we couldn't understand, but one word chimed and rang without letup, "Maharaji, Maharaji, the Superior One," and we knew Whom they were speaking about.

Amidst our Eastern brothers, Swen, with his pale Northern face, sapphire eyes and flaxen hair, in spite of his Indian shirt, was an eye-catcher.

Gerald, holding Sushila on his arm, shared a few thoughts with Werter, who listened attentively, the German tape recorder draped over his embroidered shirt, while Bob and I did not at all know what to do or what not to do, until Mira Ji took pity on us.

She explained that Master teaches in 2 ways, one-third by word of mouth at satsangs, and two-thirds of the teaching is given out through radiation. And this was precisely the purpose of the darshan: one should sit in silence in a receptive mood and absorb the radiation of Love emitting from the Satguru.

"Mira, how do you become receptive?"

"By stilling your mind."

Not completely understanding what she meant, I managed somehow to work myself into the first row of the crowd, so as once again to have a good look at my Master.

Maharaji entered the porch. Slowly and gracefully, with His hands clasped behind His back, He moved in a stately manner past His assembled disciples, briefly resting His glance of Grace on each one of them.

As my turn came, the Satguru looked at me from the corners of His magic eyes and whispered, but oh so sweetly, "I told you so. I'll separate you from everyone."

Dumbfounded, I looked at Master's back. "How did he know?"

Maharaji continued moving on. A silver curl of hair was gently resting on His neck. After He had settled in a white, wicker chair trimmed with red standing against the wall, we sat down on the rug in front of Him, as silent darshan began.

Master's heavenly Love radiated to everyone with equal intensity. The Westerners, the Easterners, the pundits and the unlettered, the untouchables and maharajas, Mohammedans, Hindus, Christians, Jews, all basked in the same ocean of Grace divine.

A young girl bowed and reverently handed the Satguru a box of soft Indian candy. Quietly opening it, Maharaji distributed the pieces of this sweet parshad* among those present, accompanying His gift with a benignant smile, full of irresistible charm.

---

*Parshad: a present touched by Master's hand.

After a while, the Superior One rose. Darshan was over.

We walked through the soft heat of the Indian night back to our Western quarters following Werter and Gerald, who were continuing their conversation. Meanwhile, Swen lingered at the gates of Master's house, gazing silently at the empty wicker chair.

Once again, we enjoyed the crickets as they sang their evening songs, and sat in our room, at a loss to comprehend our Master. All our attempts ended in dismal failure.

"Verily, verily, He alone knows His greatness," (21) sighed Bob, as our day came to an end.

The ashram's noisy life continued on Sunday morning.

Everyone was now preparing to attend Master's discourse. Although most Indians were already sitting cross-legged on one of the many rugs covering the courtyard, a few were still lounging around, talking.

Appetizing smells came from the kitchen as chapatis were prepared along with other food to eat after satsang.

Three thousand men, women and children were present, the scene resembling a bustling, lively beehive.

A humble, skinny old man, Masterji by name, was standing next to the podium chanting. It seemed that it was his very soul that was singing the devotional hymns of the Sikhs.

A translator narrated Masterji's story to Werter who stood next to us. We listened in,

Satsang in Sawan ashram.

'The surface of the courtyard instantly
became bubbling, orange mud.'
(Page 96)

sitting relaxed in our Western-type chairs at a metal pole under the canopy.

In earlier years, Masterji used to sing at Sawan Singh's satsangs, and when that Great Master left His body Masterji, in grief, vanished and noone knew where he had gone or what he was doing.

The time drew near for Kirpal Singh to begin His holy mission according to the orders of Maharaji Sawan Singh. Sawan Ashram was nearly ready when our Master told one of His helpers to bring back the Patdi, the chanter, Masterji.

"But, your Holiness, noone knows where the Patdi is!" the man told Him.

Maharaji smiled, "But I do," and explained to His helper where Masterji had been staying all during this time. Noone, you see, can ever hide from a Saint as they know everything.

A hushed silence fell over the assemblage. Everyone's attention was now fixed on the Satguru as He slowly approached the podium, ascended the stairs and sat down in a Buddha-like posture, facing the audience.

After a few minutes, without gestures, His hands folded, Maharaji began to talk. He spoke as a father would to his children. The words, charged with magnetic power, overflowed from His loving heart and in turn entered the hearts of His attentive listeners.

Everything was enchantingly sweet when suddenly, unexpectedly, with powerful intensity, a flood of rain poured from above; jagged lightning tore asunder the sinister clouds and thunder cracked and rolled threateningly in the sky.

The surface of the courtyard instantly became bubbling, orange mud through which torrents of water rushed down the light slope.

"Surely," we thought, "Maharaji will order us to take shelter immediately."

Completely unconcerned, not even a muscle moving on His noble face, the Satguru quietly continued His heart-to-heart talk. The crowd kept sitting on the wet, muddy rugs in one inch of water, attention fixed on the Master as if nothing at all was going on around them.

We Westerners, however, lost our composure immediately and were the only ones moving restlessly around, not knowing how to cope with such a situation.

Werter promptly dashed off and hid under the protecting roof of the Indian quarters.

Jodi tried to pull her shoe out of the dirt but it was hopelessly stuck. Gerald quickly came to her aid and after some struggle pried the sandal loose.

Bob and I stood at a metal pole under the canopy trampling mud with our bare feet looking for safety from the heavy downpour while rainwater overflowed from the seats of our Westerntype chairs.

We noticed Swen on the edge of the multitude crouching in water, his shirt soaking wet and transparent, his pink body visible through it, both legs firmly stationed in liquid dirt, pants filthy. He was the only exception, the only Westerner who behaved like an Easterner.

He, too, was unaffected and unconcerned.

Unhurriedly, the Satguru talked, not a tremor in His voice. In a whisper the interpreter translated His words, "If on the impact of worldly events one loses concentration, then it is apparent that satsang has had no effect on him so far."

Momentarily, the rain stopped and then began again with renewed force. Lightning flashed and thunder roared over our heads.

Unaffected, the Satguru continued speaking as His audience remained motionless.

"This is a test for you," said the Master. "Your body will be wet, but your soul will remain dry. No rain will ever reach there. As you have forgotten your body now, so you have to forget it in your meditations. You have to rise to the seat of the soul, behind and between the eyebrows. When your attention is fully collected at that spot, the single eye, the shiv netra, the inner door will be opened, and you will receive that, knowing which, nothing else will remain to be known."

Another burst of rain came down like a flood. A couple of women with children and a few men got up, walked towards the Indian quarters and stood there, while the remainder of the Indians continued listening in silence.

With a smile on His beautiful face, the Master complimented them in a soft voice. "You are taking the test well," He said.

As He spoke, another downpour of rain turned the rusty mud into a veritable brown lake.

Unperturbed, the audience continued to hang on His every word. He told them, "Your test is over. You took it well."

Our translator's voice from the back happily informed us, "There will be no more rain. Maharaji just said so. 'Your test is over.'"

With his handkerchief, he obligingly wiped the water from our chairs. "Sit down; sit down. Master says the test is over."

Hesitatingly, we sat down and looked up at the menacing sky. Black clouds still roamed in the restless air, propelled by gusts of howling wind. Thunder and lightning blazed and roared just the same as before. But there was no rain. None.

An orange-clad sadhu mounted the platform and began talking into the microphone while the Master placidly listened, correcting the monk when he made a mistake.

Next, like a bewitchingly sweet nightin-gale, the Patdi--Masterji--started chanting, after which another sadhu rose and addressed the gathering.

There was no rain. None.

Satsang over, Master thanked everyone, descended the steps and with hands folded, greeted the people lining the road to His home.

The crowd dispersed. Some left the ashram; some had a bite to eat in the sangat kitchen. We, barefooted, dirty and somewhat bewildered, went to our room and stood pensively before the window, while the raindrops from our clothes splashed onto the floor.

"Your test is over. You took it well."
Master's words were ringing in our ears.

Verily, verily, it's one thing to read
about the Saints and quite another to enter
their holy presence. There was something,
though, that we finally understood and understood quite well. In comparison with our
Eastern brothers we completely flunked the test
of concentration and controlled attention. We
also flunked the test of faith without doubts.

But in spite of all these failures, we
appeared in the dining room right on time in a
change of clothes, dry and clean, although with
egos considerably diminished in size and luster.

Introverts and extroverts--all the
Westerners were at the table. The first group
ate their lentils with yogurt in silence, and
we, like agitated, buzzing flies, discussed the
events of the satsang and excitedly shared our
impressions.

Standing in front of the kitchen door,
wearing a long, Indian shirt, Gerald was
gesticulating animatedly as he spoke, "Did you
notice this guy in the crimson turban in the
first row? He had such a dark, black beard?
No? You did not see him? Well, I did. You
know his story? I'll tell you."

We perked up our ears eager to hear.
Werter stopped eating his banana.

"This happened," Gerald began, "when Jodi
and I had just come to the ashram. You were not
here at that time.

Master was talking from the podium and
everything was going splendidly, when suddenly

the Satguru raised His hand, and turning His palm toward us held it in that position till the very end of satsang.

After everyone left and the Sangat kitchen was closed when just a handful of us remained, we accosted Master on the porch asking Him why He had held His hand up all the time.

Master answered, 'One dacoit* wanted to shoot a disciple of mine who was going to satsang. I had to stop the bullet.' And with these words, Master pointed to a handkerchief in which there was a hole with burned edges.

How did Master do it? I don't know, but this disciple was the guy in the crimson turban, sitting in the first row today. Sorry you did not notice him. I certainly recognized him even though a month had passed since he was pointed out to me."

Ceaseless talking and story telling lasted till evening. Bob and I mostly listened, having nothing to tell in exchange, although we both loudly philosophized, little realizing that our voices were disturbing our brothers and sisters meditating behind the thin dining room wall.

Later on, Mira Ji invited us to meet her sister, the Princess of Jind, and her brother-in-law, an Air Commodore, who came to pay homage and their respects to the Satguru.

In the light of the setting sun, the ashram seemed to have an extra, special flair of

____

*Dacoit: thief.

charm, as if welcoming the high-level guests to its secluded grounds.

Flowers, these delicate children of the tropical sun, bright and magnificent, adorned the Western lawn, their velvety leaves in languor slightly bending towards the grass.

In the blossoming trees, tired butterflies slept, absorbed, no doubt, in some lovely dreams, feeling safe behind the solid walls of the white ashram buildings that stood watchful guard over their delicate life.

In a big, comfortable chair in the middle of the lush Western lawn, the Princess was sitting surrounded by a small group of people talking in subdued voices. In their begilded sarees and white Nehru outfits, they looked very attractive and picturesque.

"Is your mother a queen?" I asked Mira Ji with interest as we walked towards her relatives.

"No, no," she laughed. "An empress."

As we approached her sister, the elder daughter of the Maharaja of Jind, Elaine politely introduced us, "Your Royal Highness, may I present Kira and Bob Redeen."

We bowed and settled down on the grass among the others present and joined in the Royal conversation.

The Air Commodore asked Bob why America, producing so much more grain than she needs for herself, did not give India the surplus free of charge.

And her Royal Highness wanted to know what kind of material my black, wide pants were made of and whether they were indeed the last word in American fashion.

Respectfully, I answered, "Your Royal Highness, I do not know what material the pants are made of, nor do I know whether they represent the last word in American fashions. All that I know is that I bought them in the basement at Woolworth's on sale.

Our Indian outfits, you see your Royal Highness, were so dirty after the satsang that at this very moment they are drying back in our room on a rope stretched over the beds."

The conversation, as boring as a toothache, thus continued until we had a chance to sneak away and hide in the security of our ashram room.

Losing his calm, Bob exclaimed, "Why should America continue giving everything to everybody for nothing? The Indian Government owes us, as it is, billions of dollars and can't pay back a cent, and this guy wants more for nothing!"

The colors of the sky began changing, dimming in brilliance, then faded away as the sun set and the humid night fell.

Long ago, the Princess and her entourage had left the Western quarters. Above the secluded ashram grounds, the moon like a Royal Princess sat comfortably on her throne amidst the lawn of heaven. The stars surrounding her entertained her with their own unsurpassable show while the Milky Way, like a pale, silken train, lay content at her delicate feet.

Mira Ji and Elaine dropped by for a few minutes. Settling down in the club chairs, Mira began talking, while the rest of us basked in her fantastic tale of the East.

"One Saint, Guru Ram Das, who lived long, long ago, used to rise in his meditations to the supercausal region, which has the form of a brilliant, eight-petalled lotus, its vast space glowing with intense, enchanting radiance. (19b) There, in Dasam Dwar*, on the bright shore of the wondrous lake of immortality, the lake of nectar, or Amritsar, Guru Ram Das stood in silent wonder.

As you know," Mira Ji continued, "when the soul takes a baptism in its holy waters, the ego and even the very stain of sin dissolves. (19b) Shining in its pristine splendor, the pure self-realized Soul exclaims, 'Wahi Guru! All the glory is thine, Oh Master.' All Saints say thus."

"Interesting to note," Elaine interrupted, "that some Christians symbolize this holy baptism in the inner lake of purification--Amritsar--by dipping the baby into the waters three times. Other religions symbolize the same baptism in their own different ways.

---

*Dasam Dwar: located in Par Brahm, the 4th plane of creation.

With the passage of time, the Truth has been lost. Only the symbols remained, and by now the symbols are taken to be all in all. This outer baptism will not wash away the ego nor will it give Self-Realization nor purify the Soul from outer dross and make one whole."

Squatting Indian fashion on the rug and propping my back up against the side of the bed, I thought aloud, "Mr. Trilochan Singh Khanna was obviously right when he said that the frog would be the holiest creature in the world if that would be true."

Bob, sitting on the edge of his bed, against the backdrop of our drying Indian clothes, remarked, "The baptism in the inner Lake of Immortality is the only true baptism and to reach its splendid shores would be the only true pilgrimage, I think."

"Anyhow," continued Mira Ji, "this Saint beheld a heavenly white and gold temple there, shimmering and glowing all over.

Rejoicing, Guru Ram Das decided to build a replica of this immortal temple in the middle of a lake in the city now called Amritsar. He summoned the best architect, a Mohammedan.

But the architect refused the offer, explaining that unless he could with his own eyes see this temple, he would be unable to build anything.

Having no way out, Guru Ram Das took the architect to Dasam Dwar. Only then did the construction of the Golden Temple of the Sikhs begin.

The architect was so taken by what he saw that every day he would come to the Guru and ask to be taken up, as he could not recall, he said, this or that small detail of the immortal temple as its ornate walls were intricate, involving tall arches and magnificent staircases.

The building of the Golden Temple of the Sikhs thus went on until completed in the times of the next Master, Guru Arjan.

This magnificent structure rises amidst a pool of water in the city of Amritsar. The faithful Sikhs nowadays take dips in the Temple's symbolic lake, believing that the outer water does wash off the inner sins."

"It would be thrilling to see even this replica!" Bob sighed.

Before leaving, the girls informed us that all Westerners were asked to attend the next day's initiation into the mysteries of the beyond. So in the early morning hours, we took off for the initiation, carrying soft beach chairs, velvet pillows with and without tassles, scarves to prevent flies from sitting on our bare legs and all sorts of other necessary and unnecessary objects and began settling in the back of the initiation hall.

Bob reclined comfortably on a Western-type seat; Gerald opened his green, folding-back chair, while the rest of us sat on throw rugs and pillows.

Dressed in clean Indian outfits, we were well washed, well polished and well groomed. Interpreters on the alert sat behind us.

Intellect, interest in the events outside, understanding--although quite limited--and ego in different degrees of density shone clearly in our eyes. Barefooted, we quietly waited--a small, privileged, Western group.

The hall was long and still under construction. On one end a small podium was built with windows opening on both sides of it. The opposite wall, where we settled, was not as yet completed and the ground was not so far cemented.

Bricks, stones and dirt lay everywhere in disarray as they would be at any construction site in the world.

The future disciples of our Master entered the hall one by one. These were simple and humble people like those we had seen in the mud huts and washing cows. They came and sat down, right on the ground, straight onto the stones, bumps and sand, assuming the lotus posture, men to the left, women to the right.

All was hushed as Master entered, slowly approached the podium, walked up the steps and sat down observing the assembled group attentively and fondly.

Addressing them in Hindi, Maharaji said a few heartfelt words.

We noticed that some people could not comprehend these words at all. Unmindful, however, they just continued looking at His holy face, eyes glowing with sincerity, devotion and awe.

Descending from the podium, hands clasped behind His back, Maharaji slowly, slowly, head slightly bent as if listening to something, walked among the silent rows of people.

Suddenly, He would stop, lift His head, and pointing at someone far off or close by, motioned the person to get up and leave the hall.

Of a few others He asked questions, then either permitted them to continue sitting or told the person to leave. One fellow in a pale blue turban was hustled out by two sevadars who, holding the man at the elbows, walked him straight to the backyard.

Hastily running around the building, he stopped in front of the window behind Master's podium and we could clearly see his face and the pale blue turban as if framed in it. He bowed, and every time he bowed, his turban would completely vanish behind the window sill. Straightening up, hands folded, he looked into the hall, then bowed and bowed again.

"What happened, Mira? Why were these people asked to leave?" I questioned uneasily. "If something like that would have happened to us we would be too ashamed to return."

Mira Ji responded, "Our ego is big, and we are full of pride and that is what would have prevented us from coming back to the hall."

"Well," I said, "if so, then this fellow in the window is void of pride. His ego is utterly imperceptible and in this respect he is better than I. Yet he is out, and I am in. Why?"

Mr. Sethi, one of the interpreters behind us, instantly whispered, "This poor fellow is not yet ready for the initiation. His karma* is much too heavy."

While Master continued reviewing the candidates, another voice in back of us proceeded to explain. "Once our Master asked a certain woman to leave initiation. She left, but again was back for the next initiation. Immediately spotting her, Maharaji told her to leave.

A few friends of this woman begged the Master to accept her and give her Naam.

'She has a heavy karma. I would rather initiate a lot of other people than her,' replied the Superior One.

But the friends were persistent and did not allow Master any peace. At the third

---

*Karma: the law of causality or the law of cause and effect: as you sow, so shall you also reap, or an eye for an eye and a tooth for a tooth.

Every thought, word and deed, good or bad, constitutes karma that has to be paid either in this very life or in later lives.

As long as man thinks he is the doer, he is responsible for his deeds and collects karma. The law of karma is immutable and not subject to mercy.

By becoming a Conscious Co-worker of the Divine Plan (or making God's will one's own and seeing His will manifesting everywhere) one becomes Jivan Mukat, a free soul, not subject to the law of causation or karma.

scheduled initiation, Master permitted the woman to remain.

You certainly know," continued the voice, "that during initiation, Master not only connects the soul of the candidate with the Audible Life Stream or Naam, but also takes upon Himself the load of karmas of his new disciple which He Himself then has to pay."

"Vicarious atonement, yes," said Bob, as Swen nodded mutely.

"So during the initiation, Master turned yellow and left His body.

When the Satguru regained consciousness, He looked sternly at this woman, and in front of everyone asked, 'How many children did you kill?'

'4 or 5,' was the answer.

Turning to the assembled crowd, Maharaji then said, 'This will explain to you what happened here just now.'"

Mira Ji added a few words of her own. "Jaimal Singh Ji had a similar case, you see. After reluctantly initiating a certain fellow, the Great Saint fell gravely ill and suffered for a while."

After a short pause, the voice of our interpreter was back. "As you have witnessed here today, our venerable Master sees through us as if through a glass jar full of pickles and knows immediately whether the pickles are sweet or sour. Masters, you see, know everything—that which is visible and that which is invisible." (20)

Kirpal Singh Ji had now returned to the podium and addressed His audience thus: "At initiation, the seeker after Truth is consciously linked with the Holy Word*, the God-into-expression Power in the form of Light and Sound emanating from the vibratory motion in the depth of the Ocean of Love, as God is.

By attuning to the Divine Melody, the Soul is spontaneously lifted, as it were, in an electric lift, to higher and higher regions until it gets absorbed into the Source from whence it originated, the Absolute. (22)

You have not to do anything but simply to sit in a calm, composed and fully relaxed position with attention fixed at the eye-focus and engage in Simran or repetition of the charged names, which carry the life impulse of the Master through the ages and serve as passwords into the regions beyond.

This is where the spirit currents get collected and gain an entry into the Brahmand or the cosmic universe. This is the place where you have to knock." (23)

Giving them the Simran of the 5 charged words, Maharaji asked everyone to begin meditating.

165 people sat in absolute silence and motionless for one whole hour, withdrawn from the world and fully engrossed in the eye focus.

In back of us behind the unfinished wall, we heard workers talking as they mixed cement.

Holy Word: Naam, Divine Melody.

The moist heat beat mercilessly through the open windows, while the man in the pale blue turban looked into the hall without let-up.

"All right, leave off, please," said the Satguru. "Those who saw the Radiant form of the Master* within, stand up, please."

63 persons out of 165 stood up and were counted.

Checking on the experiences of the others, Master found 12 had entered the second plane of existence and the rest were on the way to this second plane.

One man, who was a Muslim, reported seeing not only the Radiant form of the Master within, but the Prophet Mohammed as well.

"Do you know how the Prophet Mohammed looks?" asked the Master.

"No, sir, I do not. But then whom did I see?" he wondered loudly.

Maharaji motioned to a sevadar to bring in a large portrait of Master Sawan Singh. Glancing at it, the man who thought he saw Prophet Mohammed within became so overjoyed that pointing his finger at Sawan Singh's portrait he cried ecstatically, "Yes, yes, yes, it is he; it is he I saw within!"

"We always keep the portrait of Master Sawan Singh** at initiations," explained our Satguru, "because such cases as this are plentiful."

---

*Gurudev: the luminous form of the Master.

**Sawan Singh: Our Master's Master.

Thunderstruck, we sat there, speechless and dumbfounded.

Regaining a bit of control over himself, Swen cried out, "Good Lord!" in an unrecognizable, hollow voice. "Verily, verily, I say unto you, except ye be converted and become as little children, ye shall not enter the Kingdom of Heaven.*"

Utter confusion and intellectual perturbation now reigned supreme in our small, privileged group, Werter being the only exception, the only one to retain his composure.

"When I was here last year," he said calmly, "at the initiation everything went just the same as today, so I'm not bewildered in the least. Rather, I'd be surprised if it would be any different."

Eyes bulging in astonishment, Gerald exclaimed, "What is the matter with us? What blocks the entrance into the Kingdom of God?" From intense meditation and high summer temperatures, Gerald was perspiring all over, wiping his neck with a silken kerchief and pushing his spectacles up his nose. He suggested, "Maybe they are fibbing."

"But the Mohammedan guy did not fib!" Michael asserted with indignation. "Why should he?"

"For God's sake, what is the matter with us?" Gerald moaned again in exasperation.

---

*Matthew 18:2-3.

"That's exactly what is the matter with us," continued Michael. "We do not believe anybody. We sometimes even dare to doubt the validity of Master's words. You know, we always drown in the swamp and morass of intellectual reasoning.

Even if we see something inside, right away we subject it to scrutiny, to vivisection. We take it apart, bolt by bolt, and our intellectual fuss never stops: 'What do I see? Where does it come from? Maybe it is from outside; maybe from within; maybe it is my imagination. Why do I see so little? Why not more?'

Unending mental ripples and oscillations eclipse even the little that we do see, and this precious little gasps and expires right in front of our inner gaze."

"That's true," said Gerald, quieting down. "All of us are over-educated, over-stuffed with all that learning."

"Well, friends," exclaimed Bob, his chair squeaking accusingly under him, "we should be greatly ashamed of ourselves."

Master had left the hall long before. Our new brothers and sisters were departing one by one, yet we still remained sitting in the almost empty hall, talking and intellectualizing.

Mr. Sethi offered to repeat to us a story that Master usually narrates at satsangs, and we listened eagerly.

"Two disciples came to a Saint. One was an intellectual and the other an illiterate person. Before them stood a long ladder.

'How will you go up there,' asked the Saint, 'as from the upper step you will behold the sun.'

The intellectual answered that from the brain an impulse would go down to the leg and contract the muscle, which in turn would lift the foot onto the first step. There was no warranty, of course, that the foot would remain there as the step might be wet and it could slip.

The illiterate man did not answer the Saint's question, but quickly climbed up the ladder and shouted from the top to the old pundit still talking on the ground, 'Oh, God! The sun is really bright.'

'Now,' said the Saint to the pundit, 'I will charge you a double fee and the illiterate one a single fee.'

'And why is that?' asked the astounded pundit.

'Because I have first to teach you how to unlearn everything that you have learned so far, and then teach you how to go up.'"

Sadly, his wide shoulders drooping, Swen muttered, "Jesus Christ also collected pupils among fishermen and simple folk, and certainly not among the pundits."

"And that's where the secret was buried," Gerald sighed loudly, pulling the coffee-colored scarf from his bare legs and lifting up the green beach chair. "We live and have our very being in the intellect. We live like these old pundits on the ground, yet in the turbulent waters of the mind, the sun of spirituality does not reflect.   Finally, I have understood something."

"This punditism,"* I thought, "has served its purpose after awakening an interest within a man, yet may indeed turn into a fatal sickness if not checked in time, as there is a vast difference between talking about walking and practically walking, and mama mia, what a difference that is!"

Eventually, we got up from the throw rugs, left the empty hall, slowly dragging our feet towards the Western quarters, carrying with us a load of velvet pillows, coffee-colored scarves, photo cameras, tape recorders and beach chairs.

We noticed Master sitting in the wicker chair in front of His house. With all our belongings dangling about us, we hurriedly approached the small Indian group that was settled in a crescent around the Satguru listening with complete absorption to a woman crouching at Master's feet.

She talked loudly and excitedly, constantly raising her hands in the air.

Master listened with amusement and chuckled softly.

"What is going on, Mira? Why is she yelling at the Master? What has upset her so much?" we asked.

Punditism: learned talking on metaphysical subjects without having a practical experience thereof.

Slightly drawing her head into her shoulders, Mira Ji laughed to herself, then explained, "She is reprimanding Master, saying that in the astral world He looks so splendid, gloriously breath-taking, utterly ineffable and fantastic, while here on earth He just resembles an old patriarch in a white turban and not a notch more, and that's what upsets her so much."

With fascination, we continued standing, watching what was going on until everyone left and Master Himself rose from His chair and walked towards His house. He lovingly motioned to us to join Him.

Back in Master's room, we sat on an Indian rug in front of a white couch where against the background of light blue curtains that fell in simple pleats to the floor, our Satguru rested. The white walls were bare with no decorations any place. To the left of the couch stood a matching club chair.

Subdued light entered softly through the screened windows that faced the portico, from where a melodious song of a bird floated in to the room.

Leaning slightly forwards and folding His hands on His knees, Maharaji looked at us.

In the shining stillness of Master's gaze, we rejoiced as sparrows might in the warmth of the early, clear, spring sun. Indeed, sitting on that simple Indian rug before the Satguru felt better than if we had sat on the famous royal peacock throne of Emperor Shah Jahan.

Although Bob wanted to ask a few questions, he was doubtful whether it was the right thing to do, and restrained himself.

"Yes?" Master gently broke the silence, His arm stretching gracefully towards Bob. "Any questions?"

Seizing the opportunity, Bob asked, "Why do some see more inside and some very little?"

"Ego* is in the way, pride, the sense of I'ness and my'ness, and not before one becomes a Conscious co-worker of the Divine Plan** will the ego completely disappear. Clean up now," Master smiled. "Keep your self-introspection diaries; weed out all imperfections; meditate while there is still time.

You see, one's face may be very much beautiful, clean and white, but inside the man is all black. Did you read 'The Mystery of Death,' my last book?"

"Yes, sir."

"Then you must have read that in the astral world noone can play a hypocrite, as one's true nature is displayed there in blazing colors. If a man goes through the door from one room to another, you think he is changed?"

------

*Ego: sense of I'hood.

**Conscious co-worker of the Divine Plan: a person who practically sees that only He is the Doer, He is the only controlling power and beholds himself as a puppet dancing to His Will.

After a short pause, Bob asked another question. "Do Masters ever make mistakes by taking on someone like us?"

"No, Masters make no mistakes. They see, I tell you."

"Master, I think we are not worthy," Bob suggested with a worried tremor in his voice.

"How do you know?" Master chuckled.

"I don't know."

"You see, initiation is pre-ordained. There is a mark on the forehead of each and everyone so destined."

"On the physical forehead?"

"No, on the astral," answered the Satguru, and, looking at Bob with His penetrating eyes, said simply, "I certainly can see it."

Returning to our quarters in a most elated and jubilant mood, we began packing our suitcases for the trip to the Punjab. Next door we could hear Swen moving around and sneezing.

In the evening Mira Ji and Elaine entered the room, informing us with some concern in their voices that Maharaji had postponed the trip for one day.

"Do you know what kind of a job it is to prepare Master's tour? Everything has to be exactly coordinated, day by day. It takes more than a month to do it. And just now Master delayed the departure for one day. The cause must be grave," Mira Ji said pensively.

"Why," I wondered, "today or tomorrow, what is the difference? We shall just unpack again."

"Mira, do you think Master would consent to an interview," Bob inquired. "We brought a cassette tape recorder for this very purpose. Is it feasible, do you think?"

"It is not difficult to ask," she replied. "I will have the answer for you tomorrow afternoon."

Both girls settled down in the chairs. Behind the ashram wall, a train whistled while passing by. When its sounds had died out, we heard soft chanting coming through the windows as the Sikh in the dark blue turban was again pacing the cobblestones in front of the backyard latrines singing the hymns of Guru Nanak.

Peacefully, the water dripped from the bathroom faucet into the sink. The lights in the windows were dimming as the sun prepared to set into the gold and crimson of the lacy clouds.

"My daughter Veera was 7 years of age," Mira Ji began. "For her birthday she asked me to give her a very special present. 'Mommy, I want Master to be at my birthday party.'

'Veera,' I pointed out, 'Master is on a tour. He is not in the ashram, so He cannot come.'

'I'll ask Him,' she said. Next morning the child happily ran up to me saying, 'Master promised to come. I have seen Him myself. He was made out of light. His eyes were out of light. His beard, His feet, His clothes-- everything was light. There is one thing, though, that I cannot understand. Who was the tailor who made such splendid clothes for the Master?'

I paid no attention to her childish prattle, believing that she had related a dream to me. But how great was my surprise on the evening of the birthday party when the door opened and Master entered the room. Stretching His hand towards Veera, He said, 'I canceled the rest of my tour and came to you, just as I promised.'"

The sun had been hiding behind the horizon for quite a while when Mira Ji and Elaine left our room.

Next day, as the Satguru did consent to an interview, Bob settled down on the soft ashram lawn way ahead of time with all the recording equipment scattered around him jotting down his introduction in a notebook.

Mira Ji and Elaine stood on the second floor of the Western quarters leaning their elbows on the railing and observed the activity below.

Next to Bob, Gerald was teaching Sushila to walk. Lifting up both her small hands she would promptly fall right on her diapers after taking two steps.

Watching her strenuous baby efforts, I thought, "She is just like us, spiritually speaking, of course, as we all fall back on our diapers every time we try to take one inner step ahead. Hard as it is for everyone, thank God there is bright hope for all."

Werter hastily passed us by walking towards the dining hall or maybe his room adjacent to the kitchen, his embroidered shirt flapping all around his athletic body, while Bob counted loudly, 'One, two, three, one, two, three,' adjusting the volume of the sound on his recorder and then started taping the introduction.

At a distant corner of the lawn in the shade of a building, Swen sat cross-legged and meditated away from the oppressive heat of his room although the crickets disturbed him, cheeping loudly all around.

In the evening we assembled for the darshan at the portico. To our left towered the trunk of the tree that grew straight through the roof of Master's house. We settled down in a half-circle around Satguru's empty wicker chair.

Above that chair, a bird fed her squeaking offspring in a small nest tightly affixed to the wall, as a few pink lizards lurked silently, blinking their beady eyes.

Cassette recorders were placed on the rug and checked by Bob and Werter, as everyone got ready for the interview. Sushila in a fresh diaper slowly crawled past everyone.

Gracefully, Master entered, sat down and smiled at Bob. "Yes?"

Werter immediately switched his cassette recorder on, as Bob began the interview.

"You teach of a tenth door at the back of the eyes," Bob started, "where the Master takes His initiates. Why don't Masters take everybody in the world through that tenth door?"

Master started talking but Bob discovered that the machine was not recording. The Master was holding the mike in His hand, but the switch was not on.

Undaunted, however, Master agreed to begin all over again, and the talk turned out to be a most powerful exploration of the role and mission of the Living Master, as Kate and Malcolm Tillis wrote later in the editors' preface to 'Heart to Heart Talks.'

Replying to Bob's question, the Satguru said, "The Master comes for the sinners. He takes those who come to Him up for a while. But to stay up there requires purity.

So to even the most sinful, the Master gives a boost and takes him above body consciousness. When a man peeps through that Door, he sees Light.

Whether good or bad, sinful or virtuous, the Master gives them all first a boost to come up. Then, if they are not attached to the world too much, they will be able to remain there. For that reason they must become pure.

So, He gives His hand to everybody, even the most sinful. He loves the sinner, but hates the sin. He gives all who come to Him a boost and something to start with. Unless a man is raised, taken up, how can he see the Light?

So, when he reaches It, it is just like a man who has gone onto the roof by going up the stairs. When he gets near the roof, he sees Light. When he is withdrawn from outside and rises above body consciousness, he comes nearer to the place where that Door is, the Tenth Door.

Only then is he able to see the Light. This the Master gives to everybody. But the point is, if a man is attached too much to the world, naturally he must be changed. For that reason he is asked to lead a virtuous life.

I will give you an example. Nowadays we have dry-cleaning, but previously the washerman used to strike the clothes against stones to take out all the filth. Even if it was the filthiest cloth, he did not mind. He never refused. He took it. He just cleaned it. It was his job. He was the washerman, you see.

Now, the times have changed. In the old days it was arduous work, but nowadays the Master does the dry-cleaning by sweet ways, by inducement, by loving words: 'All right, please come up. Leave all this filth behind.'

And the spiritual diary that the initiates are asked to keep is only meant for that purpose. But first the Master gives a boost to every man. He accepts everybody. He comes for the sinners as well as the virtuous."

Bob observed, "Quite a few of us here saw You give a boost to 165 people the other day at their initiation. And of those, 63 saw the Master inside, and others—in fact all of them— had experiences of one kind or another. Would they all have had experience like that had it been a group of non-Indians?"

"All get something," said Master. "Whether they are non-Indians makes no difference. When I went to the West, you know, those who had been given initiation—even those who were never given initiation—all received something.

My system has been to give free talks. Then after that there was an hour of questions. Then all were invited to come to the meditation sitting which was usually held the following morning. And those who came--even those not initiated--had some experience.

One lady came to me. She said, 'I don't want to learn any theory. Just give me an experience.' It was given.

It is the giving of a boost which helps the soul to withdraw from outside and go up. So this happened in the West also."

Bob recalled, "There have been some who have described the Path that You teach as a science. And, of course, most of us think of a science as something that can be repeated if you follow the exact instructions. But apparently here there is an added element, namely, the Master. Now, doesn't the addition of this added element take it out of the realm of pure science?"

"What is the Master," Kirpal Singh asked. "He is not the man body. It is the Power working through Him that gives the boost.

A small child learns something from his father and mother and from his brothers. In school he learns from the teachers. Similarly in this way, those who are adept on the way give a little way up. Not everybody can do it.

Of course, there is nothing lost in nature, but sometimes things are quickened, just as a young fruit tree if left to nature will take about 7 or 8 years to bring forth fruit, but if in a scientific way it is given some scientific food, it will bear fruit in 2 or 3 years. So the way up is something given by a higher, competent Soul to help another Soul to have that experience.

So this has been given in the West. I went to Athens where I gave a talk, but I did not know the Greek language. Professor Halas interpreted. Then after that there were questions and answers. At the end I told them, 'All right, come to the meditation hour in the morning.'

So about 50 or 60 people came. They all got an experience. Then, people ran up like anything.

So Professor Halas has written a book telling how Pythagoras used to teach the same thing, how Socrates said such and such.

They have put my photo in the book and told how I have revived this ancient science. So this is something still given out, you see. But to maintain it, that's the point now.

We must not be so much attached outside. However, we must live a normal life. If you are attached too much to outside things, you cannot concentrate inside. They will be dragging you outside. For that reason the diary is to be maintained.

As regards a Master, you see, He is Someone Who just gives you a boost. That's the God in Him, not the son of man."

Changing the subject somewhat, Bob asked, "On a less high plane, do initiates who propose others for initiation take on part of the karma of the people they propose?"

"No, not in the least," said the Master. "It is only God who sends. They become only the medium.

Those who are ready, God sends them, brings them in contact through some source. They come to know through somebody, or through a newspaper, anything. They are brought in by Him. They are brought in contact with the Master.

He sanctions their initiation through somebody over there. That Master Power works everywhere. So with a little thought He sanctions, gives them a boost over there.

They get their experiences. Most of them get something. If not, it is because they are either in a hurry or they come very tired. I then tell the group leaders to give them another sitting when they are buoyant and fresh.

So that Master Power works all through. That's the Christ Power, God Power, Guru Power or Master Power."

Since our arrival His Holiness Kirpal Singh had used the term 'Conscious co-worker of the Divine Plan' several times. Bob now asked Him what it meant.

Master replied, "When the man sees that He is the Doer, He is the Controlling Power, he sees that Power working, manifest in all. When he sees he is a mere puppet, that means he is a Conscious co-worker of the Divine Plan."

"And there," Bob noted, "we get right back to where we started. In order to see that Power, we have to go through that Door we talked about."

"Surely," Master replied. "A lift is given. The lift is given by the Master to come up there, to experience something to start with. If a man tries to remain there, he must be up to that level. Each man is in the make.

Hitherto, in the old days, men were first prepared. Only when they were ready did the Master give them something.

Those days have passed. Nobody can now live with a Master for years and years and years. Now they must give something and be told to come up to that standard by self-introspection. Times have changed."

"What happens," Bob wondered, "to initiates who are given initiation and then fail to keep Your instructions and fail to meditate?"

With sympathy and understanding in His voice Master said, "That seed is not lost. No power can spoil it. That will grow, grow and grow sooner or later when convenient circumstances arise.

So such-like people when they suffer some sickness, some untoward circumstances, naturally they say, 'Oh God, what have I done?' If a man turns, then he comes around. I have seen cases like that.

My Master used to say, 'I give a long rope. Let us see how far he goes.' Then with a little tug, he comes and answers.

Even if he does not do anything in this birth, that seed is not lost. He will reincarnate at a level of man, not below, because the seed cannot grow anywhere else.

Man is in the make, as I told you. Some are ready. Some are not so ready. So a man who has got this seed and has, perhaps, done something in the past, that counts to his credit.

Suppose a man leaves a school in the primary class. In the next school he won't read from the first primary. He'll start ahead.

But there is one thing very definite. Love is a great force. If you have love for the Master, even if you are a sinner, you will be drawn like anything.

What is sin? To let your attention be attached to the outside things—maybe good or bad things, excuse me. Even if it is attached to right things, it is an impediment. You are attached! You must withdraw.

Those who have love for the Master, where will they go? Where the Master goes. But that should be the ruling passion with love and full faith—only in that case. That is rare, of course.

But for those who have done a little work, it is like a canker in the wood which sometimes eats the inner wood itself. Outside, it appears all right.

Those who are given initiation, that works like a canker, I tell you. Outwardly, they appear worldly. Then, slowly, slowly, slowly, they are detached. Towards the end they say, 'Oh God, lead me on.'

Help is also coming from within. The
Master is there always. We must turn our face
to Him, that's all. The more receptive we
become, the quicker results we will have." (24)
"Thank you, sir."
"All right, I also thank you for your
questions," Master laughed inaudibly, as Bob
switched off the mike, his face glowing with
joy.
(In the following year--1970--Bob recorded
14 more interviews. Still other question and
answer sessions were added to them--81 in all--
and on August 21, 1975, 2 volumes of "Heart to
Heart Talks" were published.)
The holy darshan continued, sweet and
silent, till the Indian sky got pitch dark.
Back in our room, Bob sat on the bed,
diary on his knees and wrote with absorption:
"September 10, 1969. With Master's clarifica-
tion of the term 'Conscious co-worker of the
Divine Plan,' I think that I now begin to under-
stand what Professor Hilton Hotema meant in his
poem, 'The Supreme Illusion.'
'God and I in space alone,
And nobody else in view.
'And where are the people, O Lord,' I said,
'With the earth beneath and the sky o'erhead,
And the dead that I once knew?'
'That was a dream,' God smiled and said,
'A dream that was never true.
There were no people, living or dead,
No earth beneath and no sky o'erhead.
There were only Myself and you.'
'And why do I feel no fear,' I said,

Meeting you here this way?
'For I've sinned, I know full well,
And is there Heaven and also Hell,
And is this the Judgment Day?'
'Nay, those were dreams,' the Great God said,
'Dreams that have ceased to be.
Fear and sin are the products of mind,
And you, yourself, you have never been,
For there is nothing at all but me.'"

September 11 was our departure day. In an elated and happy mood, we milled around the 4 cars which were to make up Master's caravan to the Punjab.

With a contemplative look on his face, Werter stood among his many belongings as Bob deposited our own travelling bags, pillows and suitcases on the ground next to him.

Mira Ji told Gerald, Jodi and Sushila that they were supposed to travel with the introverts in the station wagon, while the rest of us got a white Indian Ambassador car that a Mr. Kapoor had loaned to our Master, together with his young chauffeur.

Silently, the introverts loaded the station wagon. Werter efficiently stuffed our own luggage into the trunk of the Ambassador, while I loafed aimlessly, holding a blue, plastic container filled with ashram water.

Gerald, with Sushila on his arm, spoke to Donna while Bob listened. "Why can't the whole world live like we do in the ashram? We have so many people from all sorts of countries here, and we live like one close family in love and peace, ready to help each other anytime it is necessary.

If the people of this planet could live like this, no wars would erupt between nations. In the countries themselves there would be no need for police, lawyers or jails, as there would be no place for hate and revenge."

"What can I tell you," Donna said thoughtfully. "The Garden of Eden or the higher form of life cannot be lived or understood on the earth plane unless one is reborn.

Master says in 'Mystery of Death' 'to come to the better understanding of this higher life, the life of the spirit, one has to actually cross the trans-frontiers of the earth life and pass through the gates of what is called death and be reborn in the ethereal, unearthly world beyond.'

Master often quotes the Bible, 'Marvel not that I said unto thee ye must be born again.*'

Only then a complete change in the nature of man comes about, a marvellous change. And that's why Christ said, 'Learn how to die so that you may begin to live (in the living spirit.)' If all humanity could change like that, the Garden of Eden would be upon us."

Gerald grinned, "And meanwhile, let Sawan Ashram be our oasis, our Garden of Eden!"

A messenger came with an invitation from Master to Bob and me asking us to join Him immediately.

---

*John: 3:6-7.

In the large living room, by now so familiar and dear to our hearts, people were carrying luggage and fussing around, while we sat at Master's feet placidly, silent and unconcerned, just looking at Him.

"You will meet some difficulties on this trip," He said. "Bear them all for the love of the Master."

An elderly but still quite beautiful woman, rather on the heavy side, in white widow's attire, put a few shawls of different colors and two red books on the club chair next to the Master.

Picking up the books, Master handed to each one of us this precious parshad gift. On the red covers our names glittered in gold letters.

"Jap Ji!" I gasped in disbelief, as this was my favorite of all the books that Master has written. "What a coincidence," I thought.

Meanwhile, Bob, opening the cover of "Godman," beheld on a front page a lovely picture of the Satguru Himself, and the words in Master's own handwriting, "With love, Kirpal Singh."

Speechless with joy and gratitude, we continued gazing at the Master, all smiles.

Picking up a shawl, Master kept it for awhile in His hands, then lovingly held it towards me.

The thought crossed my mind, "What a muddy and unattractive color!"

Master's outstretched hand froze in midair. "How do you like the color?" He asked most gently, and looked at me point-blank.

In utter confusion, fidgeting on the Indian rug, I mumbled unintelligibly, like a toothless, senile, old chap through his dense whiskers. "Whatever comes from Your holy hands is endlessly precious."

Master chuckled, a touch of amusement twinkled almost imperceptibly in His silver-blue eyes, then gave me this muddy, unattractive colored shawl.

Many years have passed since this unforgettable moment. The priceless parshad shawl invariably lies on my bed next to the pillow. Every time I touch it I relive this sacred episode over again while Master's words clearly resound in my memory, "How do you like the color?"

Satguru's presents in our arms, we returned to the courtyard.

Mira Ji was now pushing heavy blankets on to the top of our car, while Werter gallantly assisted her.

"One young Westerner could not sit cross-legged yesterday," she told him. "He complained that the floor was slightly slanted, while our Indians sit for hours on pebbles and gravel intoxicated with the love of God. Westerners are weak people. They cannot cope with difficulties."

"You really hit the nail on the head," Bob laughed as he climbed into the middle back seat.

The caravan started on its trip, our station wagon leading the way. In its wide back window sitting cross-legged in the luggage compartment we could see Swen and Kim opposite each other, eyes closed in meditation.

FROM THE GALLOWS TO A PINPRICK --

SO MUCH CONCESSION IS GIVEN . . .

_____Kirpal Singh.

CHAPTER FIVE

LUDHIANA

As soon as Master's car leaves the ashram, we suspected, everything and everyone there will slowly sink into an endless sleep and once again nothing will stir and nothing will disturb the peace.

Only the crows will fly high over the beautiful gardens. Pink lizards on the walls will lazily blink their eyes, and the train will whistle loudly as it thunders by.

Mira Ji, Elaine and the young driver from Mussoorie sat in the front seat, while Werter, Bob and I were in the back.

As the "Ambassador" left the ashram, rumbled over the sewer canal, and passed the two cows at the long, white wall, we were facing new adventures.

Who knew what the veiled future held in her secret vault, what unknown triumphs or tragedies, what kind of encounters?

Thinking thus, we passed the Red Fort. Leaving the City of Delhi, we drove up a narrow, smooth asphalt road which wound its way amidst trees and fields. The distant hills were covered with dense woods or possibly they were wild jungles, and we dreamily wondered--feeling safe in the car--whether tigers, cobras and hyenas were prowling there on the loose.

As noone had any answer, I changed the subject. "So strange, such an unbelievable coincidence," I said, and the tale of the parshad book and shawl was related to everyone.

"There is nothing strange and there is no coincidence in this event," Mira Ji said merrily, turning her smiling face to us. "Master knows every thought that passes through our head, whether you are sitting in front of Him or are hidden behind the walls of the ashram or separated by oceans."

"What? Every thought?" gasped Bob incredulously. "How can that be?"

"Yes, every thought," Mira Ji repeated, "and you will have ample proof of it as your visit with the Master is not yet over, you know. Master and God are one. God is omnipotent and omniscient, and so is the Godman."

It was drizzling lightly outside. The sun played hide and seek, appearing for a few moments pouring its bright rays on the road and fields and then vanishing behind the dark clouds.

We gazed out of the open windows. Werter chewed a banana. The driver honked loudly. Everything was fine and normal when suddenly the car quivered.

The driver immediately reduced speed and stopped at the roadside. We had a flat tire.

The third car in which the Indians followed us, halted instantly. All doors opened at once and they hurried out, rushing over to help. Within a few minutes the tire was changed, the doors closed once again, and we were back on the road as if nothing had happened. Werter finished his banana as we continued looking out of the windows at the scenery.

"Who was the elderly woman who brought the parshad shawls to the Master?" asked Bob.

"Her name is Taiji," Mira Ji replied. "She is Master's housekeeper, a widow. Her husband was a very, very wealthy businessman who helped to build the Satsang Ghar in Beas for his Master Sawan Singh. Taiji was quite young when her father married her to the elderly Raja Ram.

On his deathbed, Raja Ram weakly whispered to his Master, "I am worried about Taiji. What will become of her?"

"I will take care," promised Sawan Singh Ji.

When Master Sawan Singh in turn was dying, He ordered our Master to take care of Taiji, and that is how she became Master's housekeeper.

Taiji, you see, is not an ordinary woman. Once, she asked our Master to show her hell as she had already seen the spiritual realms. 'All right,' the Master consented, and Taiji went to hell.

Taiji's father was a worldly man. He liked to drink and to be merry. In hell Taiji saw her father in loathsome and sinister surroundings, his face distorted with fear.

When back in her body, she asked the Satguru with concern, 'Is that so?'

'Yes.'

'But he is still among the living!'

'Our deeds prepare the place for us in advance.'

From that moment on, Taiji gave her father no peace until he agreed to get initiated.

Shortly after, he became ill. His sick bed was placed in the middle of the ashram lawn where he lay unconscious. Breathing his last, his wrinkled hand was moving rhythmically in the air as if beating time.

Frightened, Taiji and I looked at him. 'It seems that he is back in hell,' shuddered Taiji, when unexpectedly the old man opened his eyes, fully conscious.

'What happened?' we asked him fearfully. 'Why are you beating time with your hand? Are you in hell?'

Taiji's father smiled, tears streaming down his hollow cheeks. 'The Radiant form of the Master met me in the beautiful world beyond,' he said. 'There are no limits at all to my happiness. Dancing from pure joy, I am beating time with my hand.' Then, he closed his eyes and died."

Looking out our car's window in the twinkling of an eye we could slip back in time 2 thousand years and then return to the 20th century in a flash. Enough to look at the cement road, where trucks, motorcycles and cars moved noisily in both directions to be immediately reminded of the present century's bustling life, but in the pastures and fields, the eye basked in biblical antiquity and the soul rejoiced in complete peace.

What kind of human life lay hidden behind this antiquity we did not know, but on the surface everything seemed to be an idyllic pastoral setting taken from some ancient saga.

The more we observed, the less we believed our eyes, as it seemed that the pages of the Bible yellowed by time rustled one by one while turning, magically coming alive right in front of our eyes.

On the rolling green slopes among the pristine beauty of nature, sheep and goats peacefully grazed, watched over by shepherds with staffs in their hands resembling wise, old men of yore. Dark faces were framed in white beards. Their eyes shone serenely. In their movements one detected nobility. Lean bodies were wrapped in loincloths or time-worn rags. Traditional turbans adorned their heads.

We passed a few camels trotting steadily along the road towards the North, the same way they trotted in the time of the Prophet of Nazareth, and a few buffaloes that rested in cool, liquid mud reaching up to their black bellies. Here and there, we noticed an ox pulling a wooden plow, the tiller slowly walking behind it.

"Look at those wheels out of the stone age." Bob was astonished and leaned to his right to see better the ancient, wooden oxcart that we were passing. "Who would ever think that such fantastically large wagon wheels still exist. It's mind boggling!"

Following a sandy path which wove among the pastures, an old man trudged along in a torn shirt, his only other belonging a rope bed balanced on his head.

All these variegated scenes, verily, were a feast for one's eyes and unwittingly we got lost in their ancient charm.

We reached, at last, the suburbs of Kurukshetra located not too far away from New Delhi where the famous ancient battle, so magnificently described in the Bhagavad Gita took place. And it was here that Prince Arjuna carried on a conversation with his beloved Guru, Lord Krishna. We halted near the battlefield in the backyard of a large, roomy house belonging to one of Master's disciples for a brief rest.

A simple breakfast of chapatis and tea was served to everyone. Later, some of us toured the premises; some investigated the house; others enjoyed what they were told were the historical sights of Kurukshetra visible in the distant blue mist.

Meanwhile, like Arjuna with Lord Krishna, Bob carried on a conversation with Gyaniji, who accompanied our Master on His tour up to Kurukshetra. On his wrist, Gyaniji wore a silver bangle to remind him not to forget the Lord even for a moment.

Bob discovered that Gyaniji himself was quite a pundit in his own right. In his head like in an ancient Egyptian trunk, all sorts of answers were hidden. No question put to him remained unanswered. And Bob had a lot of questions.

Gyaniji explained that at initiation Master takes over the Sanchit Karmas of his new disciples or Karmas that had been accumulated in the disciple's innumerable past lives while the present-life Karmas, called pralabdh or fate Karmas, Masters do not touch or the life of the body would be severed immediately. "Through this present Karma," said Gyaniji, "one has to go willy nilly although from the gallows to the pinprick, Master gives so much concession.

You see," continued Gyaniji, "there are two laws that work in the Creation, the law of justice* and the law of mercy.** The disciples of the Master are under the law of mercy or positive power. How very, very fortunate are the disciples who are under the shadow of Master's holy wings as the Satguru is the fountainhead of grace and compassion.

Strange and unfathomable indeed are His Godly ways. Should He in His pleasure place His blessed hand on the head of a jiva,*** the latter wishes for no other blessing. (30)

Different is the fate of the non-initiated. They remain under the law of justice, untempered by mercy."

Nearby, Sushila lifted her little head in an attempt to better hear Elaine who crouched next to her talking lovingly while Mira Ji observed both of them with a smile.

---

*Negative power: the downpouring ray of Creation going into manifestation.

**Positive power: the returning ray of Creation going back to its Source.

***Jiva: embodied soul.

Gerald and the silent majority had settled down on a large rope bed and were staring into a room where Master was sitting. Winding up his movie camera, Werter asked, "What is going on here? Why is everyone staring?"

After grasping the idea, he placed his foot firmly on the side of the bed, crossed his hands on one propped-up knee and also began looking intently into the room.

This loving effort did not go in vain as the Master leaving the devoted host joined His disciples and everyone of us enjoyed a short, blessed darshan.

After Master left, we hit the road again and proceeded on the way to the Punjab.

"Driver, please close the window. It's blowing in too much. Last year we all got flu from this wind," Werter pleaded. Our practical chauffeur, however was adamant and refused, as he had to signal constantly with his hand through the open window.

A real, professional virtuoso, he dashed along the road without fear, firmly convinced of his own unsurpassed skills. To avoid crashing into oncoming vehicles, he would swerve the car sharply and abruptly to the left at the last possible moment.

"He is playing chicken!" Bob lamented.

"Chauffeur," Mira Ji calmly addressed the young man, "chauffeur, you are driving too fast. Lessen the speed immediately!"

"Don't make me nervous!" the driver quickly replied while fidgeting on his seat and

'Like Arjuna with Lord Krishna, Bob carried on
a conversation with Gyaniji.'
(Page 140)

'Sushila lifted her head in an attempt
to better hear Elaine.'
Page 141

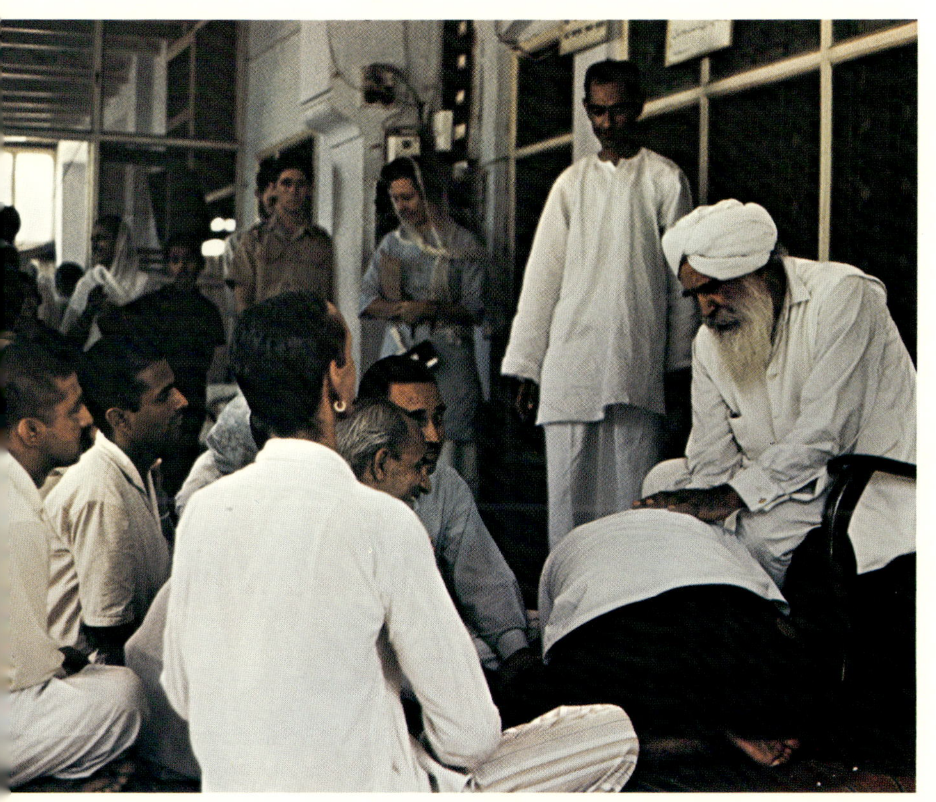

Master's darshan

'Werter placed his foot firmly on the
side of the rope bed.'
Page 142

'Mira Ji, slightly bending forward,
walked right under his arm.'
Page 144

'His face a picture of peace and tranquillity.
Page 144

'Bob and Gerald with Sushila on his arm,
enjoyed a hearty philosophical conversation.'
Page 170

honking vigorously as an enormous truck approached us head-on at full speed.

Realizing that there were just a few seconds left before death would pick us all up, our daring young driver turned the steering wheel to the left with such speed that, like a weightless leaf, the car flew off the wet pavement up into the air as Mira Ji reached over and switched off the ignition.

The white Ambassador overturned and crashed on its left side down a slope, the wheels spinning with a screeching noise right over our heads.

The chauffeur, this virtuoso, like a veritable monkey dodged out of his open window, while we lay one on top of the other in a twisted heap inside the car. Dead silence reigned supreme, in spite of the droning wheels above.

In shock, one of Werter's eyes stared at me from below, while the other was covered with Bob's head unnaturally turned to one side.

Time passed and passed. Finally, someone fearfully inquired, "Is everyone alive?"

As noone was even hurt, our voices once again sounded loudly inside the car. Cautiously untwisting ourselves, one by one we left through the open window, Bob crawling out last.

On our bodies, not even a scratch, just a small bruise here and there including one from the doorknob to the top of my head.

A concerned Indian crowd already surrounded the overturned vehicle, eager to help in every possible way, talking excitedly among themselves.

One curious man was leaning his elbow on the front wheel that was suspended in the air; the other in a bluish turban, propped his hand on the car's headlight, while Mira Ji, slightly bending forward, walked right under his arm, and someone else held the door which opened straight up into the sky.

A rugged farmer, who left his plow back in the field, along with others helped the chauffeur in his effort to turn the car over. The farmer, addressing everyone, talked animatedly, "I saw the accident from the beginning to the end and had absolutely no doubt that not a single soul would leave the car alive. It is beyond my understanding that noone was even harmed."

Werter, meanwhile, back in good spirits, enthusiastically took movies of the whole event. The blue plastic container of ashram water stood solemnly by the side of the road.

Master's grey car slowly approached the scene and stopped in front of the overturned Ambassador. Serenely and unhurriedly, the Satguru walked towards us. Attentively, He surveyed the whole situation, His face a picture of peace and tranquillity. Waiting patiently until the car was finally back on its wheels, He then turned to our unhappy chauffeur and looked at him silently.

"Surely," I thought, "Master will bawl him out, but good!"

The Satguru smiled warmly, then blessed the young man with a piece of parshad caramel and told him very softly, "From now on, dear friend, please follow my car wherever you go."

The frisky chauffeur gazed at the Superior One with boundless gratitude as a faint smile slowly began to enliven his ashen face.

Quietly, Master's glance turned to us, and again the world with its countries, people, flowers, skies and accidents faded away into naught as His saintly Love and deep compassion filled our souls to the brim.

When, after a while, the Satguru left, the world came back: the road, the flowers on the slope, the people, the Ambassador car, but for a moment all seemed to be tinted with the oneness of Love as the shift in values continued deepening and widening.

We got back to our seats and waited for Mira Ji who had followed the Satguru up the road. On her return, Mira Ji said Taiji had told her of an explanatory comment that Master had just made. "On Monday, September the 10th," the Satguru said, "the cosmic conditions were such that some of them would have been killed, and that is why I postponed the trip for one day."

"Verily," gasped Bob, stricken with amazement, "from the gallows to a pinprick, so much concession is given! Gyaniji was indeed right!"

Our adventurous driver maneuvered rapidly following Master's car like a shadow, while the placid pastures and fields swept quietly past on both sides of the road.

"Miracle!" Werter exclaimed suddenly and ecstatically, "absolute miracle! Nothing happened to us, not even a scratch. Nothing happened to the car. Not even a window was broken and the dent on one side was insignificant. Not even a drop of ashram water was spilled from this blue plastic container. Unglaublich! So was!"

And energetically wiping mud from a large apple that he picked up from a puddle of water next to the overturned car, Werter munched it with gusto.

Mira, turning to us--face radiant with joy--said, "As you have now witnessed, Master can postpone death anytime He so wishes. Let me tell you a story that Radha Krishna Khanna, Master's lawyer, once told about a lady initiate.

Her doctor predicted that she would be dead within a few hours. This lady expressed a wish to see her younger son and added that she would not die in peace unless she met him as that desire would linger.

Maharaji said, 'The doctor is right. She has to go this evening, but now that her wishes have been conveyed to me, I think I'll have to intercede. How long will it take for her son to come and see his mother?'

'It will take 2 days.'

'All right, I'll send her by the next train to the other world. Let today's train go with other people.' (25)

146

And so it indeed happened. She died 2 days later after meeting her son."

"When the Guru is thy shield and buckler, millions of hands cannot strike thee down. (27) He is a guardian angel in both the worlds, and there is no friend greater than the Satguru," (28) Elaine added with a smile putting her shawl back around her head.

"I cannot understand all this with my head," mused Werter, "but with my heart I see and realize that it is so. Our blessed Master does not leave us even for one moment, and we are under His protective wings. Greater luck I cannot imagine myself, although being only a spiritual embryo, all that I understand is that I understand nothing.

But if we could scrupulously follow all Master's instructions, we could certainly understand something eventually, I think."

"I see; I hear; I witness; I comprehend it not." Summing up Werter's frank admission, I chuckled, turning my head to look at his happy face.

"Werter," exclaimed Elaine, eyes flashing with delight, "it seems that you are ready to embark on the path of Self-surrender..'To such a one, the Lord grants the blessings of Sahaj.'" (28a)

"Sahaj?" Raising his eyebrows in surprise, Werter asked, "What is that?"

"It is a state when the turmoil of the physical, astral and causal worlds with all their enchanted panorama are transcended, and the great principle of life is seen within." (29)

"Exactly," smiled Werter in complete agreement. "Anybody want some bananas or nuts?"

Our car slowed to a halt as a large crowd blocked the road. It was a group of Master's disciples who had come from the surrounding villages to get His blessed darshan.

Above the sea of heads, we could see Master's towering, white turban. We noticed a wrinkled old man, poor and not too clean, who stood in front of the Satguru, tears flowing from his eyes.

Folding his hands in adoration he pleaded with our Master. "Blessed Satguru," he wept, "your saintly feet so far have not stepped on the soil of our little village. Please sanctify our land and people with Thy Holy Presence." A faint smile made the man's white beard quiver while crystal clear tears continued streaming down his cheeks.

After the road darshan was over and we were just about to continue our trip, Mohan, Master's driver, brought a silver goblet full of water to our car. "Master's orders!" he said cheerfully. "Master's orders! You have to drink up the water. Parshad! Parshad!" And he grinned widely.

We divided the clear liquid so that everyone could have a sip and decided to keep Master's goblet for a little while, till Ludhiana at least.

Further up the road, we were stopped by another crowd of Master's disciples and again the Satguru gave them His blessed darshan.

LUDHIANA

We halted in a suburb of some unknown city where Mira Ji invited us all to join her and have a cup of tea in a small roadside cafe. Inside, the Eastern flavor of the tearoom with its strange uneven walls, ten or so round tables standing where the spirit moved them without order or system of any kind, with no table-cloths, utterly bare, but with a lot of reminders on top left there by previous patrons, different style chairs, exotic, strange smells, buzzing fans, darkened lights, soft background music that the loose planks of the floor provided in abundance, and people with unusual faces sitting around, all that like a gentle breeze passed over our souls slowly awakening vague, latent memories of a deep, deep, forgotten past, enlivening dreams and imaginings that vanished or perhaps never were.

Comfortably, we settled around a splattered table in this tiny, dark room. The delightful Indian tea steamed in our cups as— over puris and orange spaghetti—we emotionally discussed the accident just past.

Suddenly, bright light flooded the dark tearoom as the outside door swung open. Startled, we looked up. On the threshold, as blinding sunlight streamed and flowed around His tall, and stately figure, stood the Master.

We hushed, immediately rose and reverently folded our hands in happy greeting as our Satguru majestically approached. We stood there before Him in reverent silence, just gazing, just looking, when unexpectedly Mira Ji, pointing her finger at me, cried out, "Oh, Maharaji, she has a bump on her head!"

"Yes?" Master turned to me.

Taken by utter surprise and flustered, I repeated Mira Ji's words, "A bump on the head."

Master drew nearer, and in His Infinite Grace put His hand on top of my head. In the radiant stillness only my heart pounded loudly.

The words came back to me, 'Should He in His pleasure place His blessed hand on the head of the Jiva, the latter wishes for no other blessing.' (31) "Thank God for the bump," I thought.

Pulling a tiny box out of His deep pocket, Maharaji presented each of us with a small, white homeopathic pill. "Take them," He said simply. "And now," continued our Satguru, "everything is well that ends well. Learn to live in the present moment. What is past is past. Forget it. Forget the accident now."

Once again He looked us over carefully, then turned around and left the room as we quietly followed Him and watched how Master walked towards His car, got into His seat, closed the door and drove off.

Hurriedly paying our bill, we swiftly got back to our Ambassador. The frisky chauffeur had already turned on the ignition and off we went following Master, as our steaming cups, puris and orange spaghetti remained forgotten back in the roadside cafe.

How difficult it is to abide by Master's simple commandments! "Learn to live in the present moment," He said. "What is past is past. Forget it. Forget the accident now."

Yet all we did was continue talking about that accident, over and over again with absorption and gusto. More than that, when our long trip was finished and we returned to Sawan Ashram, the first thing that Mira Ji told Donna was, "Oh, Donna, you know what happened to us? We met with an accident. The car overturned!"

An unexpected stop interrupted our lively chattering. "This is Ludhiana," Mira Ji informed us. "We shall stay here for 2 days."

The Ambassador was parked in the large yard of an agricultural college. Looking around in surprise, we could not comprehend how in such a short time we could have once again reached the familiar shores of America.

Everything was recognizable here: the modern, square, glass buildings reminiscent of motels, cement sidewalks, neatly cut lawns.

"Americans built this University," Elaine explained.

We walked along the wide, empty corridors of the student dormitories and entered our assigned room enjoying its American flavor and especially the sight of the American mattresses as to us that meant "heavenly soft."

From his bed Bob exclaimed in jubilation, "America! No doubt, America it is. The Yankees have finally come home." And he laughed in quite a patriotic manner.

Completely forgetting the Russians on that frigate "Pallada," I felt indeed quite American on my own American mattress. In perplexity, I wondered aloud, "Who are we? Swedes, Russians, Americans, Indians, Westerners, Easterners, earthlings?"

"You see," Bob said after some thought, "we should rise above these hampering cultural, historic and geographic badges of nationalities among which we feel familiar and comfortable. We should even rise above the unifying badge of 'earthlings,' or 'citizens of the planet Earth' as even that viewpoint, being only from the bodily angle of vision, is narrow and limiting.

Man, being soul, is 'a citizen of the cosmic empire of God with its home in Sach Khand;' yet to live up to this lofty ideal is surely quite some task."

"True, it's difficult to become such a citizen," I sighed.

"Yet that's what is wanted," laughed Bob. "Before becoming perfect, we shall experience many a fall as the time factor is a necessity-- even Rome was not built in one day. Man is in the make, in the process of becoming. There is hope for everyone including us. So why be disheartened? We shall have to be brave and persevere. That's all."

With another sigh I said, "No wonder our Master constantly emphasizes that while Truth is above all, yet even higher is True Living as practice alone will make the man perfect, a cosmic citizen of the empire of God."

Deciding to stop playing pundits for a while, we went to explore the American University practically and in doing so discovered

that dear old India had touched the institution
with her fairytale Eastern hand.

Everything was not as clean as back home,
not as opulent. Something was missing everyplace, and we especially missed the toilet
instead of which we found only a dark hole in
the floor.

Undaunted, however, we once again sank on
our comfortable mattresses just as if back in
New York. Finally, our bones and tired muscles
had a chance to rest in peace.

This appreciated interim did not last long
as at 8 o'clock sharp our spirited chauffeur
honked loudly in the yard. It was time to drive
to the evening Satsang. Our energy, although
not so far completely restored, was, nevertheless, sufficient to allow us to climb wearily
onto the Ambassador's seats, lean back and
relax.

Again Mira Ji and Elaine sat in front of
us, heads covered with white shawls. To their
right, the chauffeur energetically pushed his
horn. Werter busily peeled a spotted banana and
Bob asked his next question.

Only the American University with its
brick, steel and glass walls vanished into the
nebulous past as we continued speeding on in the
ever-living present moment.

"Time," I thought, "high time to learn the
art of living in the present moment as where did
the past go? Where is the future lurking? And
where is this present fleeting moment?

Is it in that dot between the past and the future in this small, imperceptible, still dot? And does this dot contain the secret of a successful meditation and perfect concentration?"

Having no answers, I gazed outside as scenes changed almost with kaleidoscopic speed. Houses, streets, people, temples appeared for a moment and then vanished into the all-engulfing past while my thoughts continued unabated in this living present moment: "Is this dot the door of escape from the goading whip of Time or Negativity, rooted in which we begin to live in timelessness in spite of fleeting time?"

Bob interrupted my reverie with his own thoughts, renewing the conversation that we had started over the steaming cups in the roadside cafe. "The past and the future are an open book to the Mahatmas. So I have read in one of Master's publications. That means that the past and the future are already there, invisible to us, because we are yet spiritually undeveloped, but they are accessible to the Saints, who live in a universe of timelessness, where there is no past or future, but everything exists in the eternal now."

"Yes," said Mira Ji, "the divine script is all written."

"And that's how Master knew about our impending accident," I thought. "He simply saw."

"And noone can change God's script save the Godman as our Master did today by postponing our departure for one day," continued Bob. "We are still among the living instead of among the dead as we should have been according to the divine script.

Then the idea of free will is certainly an illusion and obsolete just as Master told us at the interview back in Sawan Ashram. God is the Controlling Power; God is the Doer; and man is a mere puppet dancing to His bid."

Mira smiled as she looked at Bob. "Do you know what is written in Jap Ji?

'You have no power to speak or be silent,
No power to ask or to give.
You have no power over life and death,
No power over wealth or state for which
you are ever restless.
You have no power over spiritual
awakening,
No power to know the Truth or to achieve
your own salvation.
Let him, who thinks he has the power, try.
O Nanak! none is high or low but by
His Will.'" (32)

"True," I thought. "Master Sawan Singh presents the same ancient wine but in a different goblet: 'From the top of the creation it looks as though the Creator is all in all. He is the only Doer, and the individual seems like a puppet, tossed right and left by the wire-puller. There seems to be no free will in the individual. It is all His play. It is the manifestation of His Will. It is all Oneness.'" (33)

Moving my cramped legs slightly, I relaxed in the soft corner seat as Master Sawan Singh's words continued drifting through my mind: 'From

the bottom of creation it looks differently.
Everybody appears to be working with a will of
his own. The individual believes he is the
doer.

From the top of the astral plane the same
individual sees the mind actuating all forms.

From Dasam Dwar he will see the Spirit
Current working everywhere and will see how the
mind gets power from the Spirit.

And from Sach Khand, or the 5th plane, the
whole creation looks like bubbles forming and
disappearing in one spiritual ocean.' (33)

Mira Ji went on to say, "Guru Nanak
proclaimed that:

'By His Will is matter quickened into
life.
By His Will are men's joys and sorrows
ordained.
By His Will (the pious) obtain Salvation.
By His Will (the impious) wander in
endless transmigration.
All exist under His Will,
And nothing stands outside.
All things are manifestations of
His Will.' (35)
All Masters say so."

"Do you think you could describe this Will
to us?" Werter inquired.

"No, it is an impossibility," said Mira
Ji. "In Jap Ji Master wrote: 'Hukam, or Will
Itself, is something which no words can
describe. It baffles all description. The real
understanding of the Divine Will comes only by
direct revelation to every Soul. (34)

The touchstone by which such a Soul could be recognized is the absence of ego as knowledge of the Divine Will means destruction of the ego." (34)

"It seems that the illusion of free will begins with the sense of separateness or ego," I observed.

Everyone fell silent. Werter leaned back with an absorbed, thoughtful expression on his face, half-eaten banana in his limp hand, while Bob after considerable thinking said, "Apparently there is no individual free will, as to have an individual free will, we would have to have an individual in the first place.

Yet in Dasam Dwar the Soul of man realizes that 'I and my Father are One,' and always were one and that the delusion of individuality and free will started with the sense of separateness, ego or I'hood. Further up the illusion of individuality is completely lost. He alone remains the only Doer and Controlling Power while His Creation appears as the manifestation of His Will.

Not only the Masters say so, but even Hilton Hotema in his poem 'The Supreme Illusion' states this. If we can accept this conclusion, and I can't see why we should not, the complete surrender to His Divine Will becomes inevitable. Am I right?"

"Yes," answered Werter, "we all should surrender to His Will and live a life of perpetual resignation, as there is no other choice anyhow—or so it seems to me."

Bob's face beamed with pleasure, "And if nothing stands outside of His Will or can stand outside of His Will because there is nothing but His Will," he continued, "then where is the reason for worry? We should all live unaffected and serene, no matter how high the waves of the Ocean of Life might rise."

Elaine, lifting her finger up, added, "Do you know that discipleship truly consists in unswerving devotion and resignation to the Will and Pleasure of the Master, (36) the God in Him, of course."

We continued now northwards along a beautiful road with trees on both sides, enjoying the refreshing breeze and the soft warmth of the Ludhiana night.

"Do you know the story of the perfect disciple by the name of Bhai Bhikari? You see, he surrendered his will completely to the will of God," and Mira Ji began the story:

"In the time of Guru Arjan, the fifth in line of succession from Guru Nanak, there lived a model Sikh, Bhai Bhikari by name.

A man once asked the Guru to introduce him to a Gurbhakta, or a devoted disciple. The Guru directed him with a letter to Bhai Bhikari and asked him to stay with the Bhai Sahib for a few days.

Bhikari received the man, who was his brother-in-faith, very warmly and entertained him to the best of his means. The day he arrived, his host was calmly sewing a piece of cloth which looked like a coffin-covering.

The disciple, after spending a few days happily in his company, proposed to go back, but Bhikari requested him to stay on for some time more and to attend his son's wedding which was due shortly. At the loving insistence of the host, he agreed to do so.

The wedding day came. There were festivities in the house, but Bhikari was as serene as ever. The visiting disciple, like all the rest, accompanied the wedding procession, witnessed the merry nuptials, and escorted the bride's procession back to Bhikari's house.

The following day, as ill-luck would have it, Bhikari's only son, the newly-wedded youth, took ill suddenly and died. Bhikari quietly took out the cloth that he had prepared on purpose a few days earlier, wrapped the dead body of his son in it, took it to the cremation ground, and performed the last rites with his usual equanimity.

Bhikari's steadfast attitude of composure all through this varying panorama of life struck the disciple dumb with astonishment, for in Bhikari there was no trace of joy or sorrow, but perfect resignation to the Will of the Lord, which he knew right from the beginning; and he had acted accordingly without exhibiting any personal feelings or emotions in the least." (37)

Driving through the City of Ludhiana, we realized that it differed little from Delhi as its architects had chosen the same flat-roofed design for the dwellings.

The little stores and the noisy traffic were quite familiar to us by now, but since it was already night, filth and uncleanliness disappeared in the velvety darkness while hundreds upon hundreds of candlelights flickered festively in front of all stores, each one creating around itself a trembling, living aura, out of which long, gleaming rays reached courageously into space.

Enchanted, we silently gazed, absorbed in this ravishing sight.

Fifteen thousand people were already assembled as we drove up to the place of Satsang and were settling down under a flowery canopy. The multitude resembled a vast, heaving sea. Brilliant spotlights from different sides illumined the crowded arena and one could see no end of the turbans as the last rows were eclipsed by the veils of blackness.

Master was not yet present, as we had arrived way ahead of time. Standing in the back of a large speaking platform, that was covered with white cloth and adorned with bright, multi-colored, tiny lights hanging under its marquee, we noticed that more and still more people were arriving and like streamlets poured into the vast human ocean.

Mira Ji filled us in, "Our next stop will be at Ferozepur. Maharaji will visit a murderer there. This murderer was caught and sentenced for life imprisonment and is now incarcerated in the Ferozepur jail.

Somehow, you see, this criminal found out about our Master and began meditating in his cell. The Radiant Form of the Master appeared to him within and now this murderer conducts a satsang for the inmates over there."

"Good Lord! Even a murderer is better than I am," Gerald sighed, kicking the gravel with his foot.

We were asked to sit on the podium. Master was due any moment.

Settling down cross-legged in the shape of a new moon, right behind the spot from where Maharaji would address the multitude, we realized that inventive Gerald has discovered a new method of propping up his knees.

Pushing a plastic, air-filled balloon under each of them, he concealed his efforts with a light, coffee-colored scarf. Then, he sat immobile, eyes-closed, an impressive American Buddha with spectacles.

Right on time the Superior One made His appearance, walked to the place in front of us and sat down, leaning forward slightly observing the silent crowd. And like the sun in so many drops of water, He reflected in the soul of each member of His audience.

For the last time the microphones were checked and then the tape recorders were switched on.

For 2 beautiful hours Master spoke in a pleasant, foreign language while we enjoyed the sound of His voice and sweet tranquillity within.

On the way back considerate and thoughtful Mira Ji conveyed to us the gist of what Master had just said: "Everyone has, as a matter of course, to die some day--man, bird or beast, rich or poor, healthy or diseased, young or old. The soul which takes on the physical raiment has to shed it one day. Death alone is certain and real, while life in this world is uncertain.

We seldom pause to think about the long journey which lies ahead of the inner being in us. We usually lament the death of others, but are not wise enough to care for our own end and prepare ourselves for the final journey into the great unknown that lies beyond life's end.

With the process of withdrawal of sensory currents from the body, the death process commences.

Death is not a dreadful incident. In reality it opens new vistas and new horizons of life beyond the grave. The flames of the funeral pyre engulf, entomb and extinguish the mortal remains. 'Dust thou art and unto dust returneth' was not spoken of the soul.

The life principle in us or in fact in any other living thing never dies. It is only the elemental parts that go through a process of change which we erroneously call death, and wrongly understand it to be an extinction." (38)

Arriving exhausted at the American University, we sank instantly into a deep and dreamless sleep.

Mira Ji and Elaine, as Gerald told us later, were the first ones up in the early morning hours. Having a splitting headache, Mira could barely hold up her eyelids or stand on her legs. Elaine pleaded with her to rest and not to go shopping for breakfast food at the Ludhiana bazaar.

Near to tears, Mira Ji rebuffed her. "How can you say such a thing! Master entrusted the welfare and comfort of His Western disciples to me. I am responsible! Migraine headache or not, Master's trust is above everything else in the world." So both girls drove off to the bazaar.

With the sun already high in the heavens, we woke up, stretched and yawned. Our breakfast, warm and fresh, was waiting for us in the dining hall. Appetizing odors assailed us from the bowls filled with rice and mashed potatoes in lentil sauce. We settled down at the table as Mira Ji poured delicately scented tea into our cups.

Lifting his eyebrows in surprise, Bob asked, "Oh, Mira, where did you get those blisters on your hands?"

"From peeling potatoes for breakfast," she said briefly. "Please do not wait any longer before eating as the tea and rice may get cold. How did you sleep, Kira?"

"Terribly! My eyelid is swollen from mosquito bites and that's why you see me wearing these sunglasses to hide my unsightly appearance. Bob said he was fighting them off all night long."

"Oh, how very unpleasant!" Mira Ji exclaimed with regret.

Embarrassed, I thought, "How stupid of me to complain about such trifles. Now look at Mira Ji, a pampered princess, a Royal Highness, a daughter of the Maharaja of Jind—for the love of the Master she got up at an early morning hour, a splitting headache not keeping her from driving to the bazaar. She prepared our breakfast as painful blisters developed on her hands. She did everything that lay within her power and would do even more if she possibly could.

She tells us stories about our Master so that our inadequate comprehension of Him could be increased at least a little. Without hesitation she caters constantly to our smallest and most insignificant whims.

And just to think that all was done without complaint or grumble whatsoever and in a sweet and grateful mood.

'What is the matter with us?' Gerald's words came to mind. 'Wherever we turn, we are not up to the mark!'"

"No toilet paper!" Werter's excited voice droned and echoed in the hollow corridor. "How terrible! No toilet paper! No toilet paper anywhere!"

We listened transfixed as his Indian slippers loudly clapped and resounded in the empty, long hall. Closer and closer came the clapping, then abruptly the door flew open. Like a framed picture, Werter stood there, clad in his white, embroidered shirt, in loose pants, slightly ruffled by the events of the previous day and with a fixed stare in his brown eyes he repeated in panic, "Mira, there is no toilet paper! No toilet paper anywhere!"

Immediately, Mira Ji joined him at the door, and her voice was like soothing balm on Werter's raw wounds. Without delay both drove off to the Ludhiana bazaar to buy a roll of toilet paper.

We continued sipping tea while talking to Gerald.

From the plate with the palm of his hand, he picked up rice and mashed potatoes, put them on top of the table, while Sushila standing full height on his knees, uttered a delighted sound, grabbed some food in her fist and stuffed it into her mouth.

Sushila's face and shirt were smeared with mashed potatoes, her diapers hung heavily down the little body and between the shirt and the diapers, a round, full belly stuck out.

"I heard your car overturned down a steep slope. What happened?" asked Gerald.

As Bob began repeating the story of the accident, Sushila uttered another loud exclamation and lay down on top of the food, mashed potatoes, rice and lentils sticking fast to her naked, round mid-section.

Meanwhile, both Mira Ji and Werter who looked quite disappointed, returned to the dining hall, as no toilet paper was sold in the Ludhiana bazaar.

After breakfast, we were scheduled to visit the head of the Jains who was a secret disciple of our Satguru, so we were told. Master wanted to obtain permission from him for Muni Sushil Kumar to accompany Him on His impending world-wide tour.

Like birds of passage with not a care in our hearts, we joyfully got into the seats and twittered ceaselessly while rolling along the familiar Indian city streets paying no attention whatsoever either to the views of the city or the suburban landscapes, as everything seemed to be quite the same no matter where we had been so far.

Bob was curious about the way of life led by the Jain gurus nowadays and Mira Ji obliged him with information. "This Jain guru," she said, "has a spy living in his house appointed to keep watch over him and report to the main body of the Jains if this guru breaks a rule, and the rules are two thousand years old, you know!" She giggled merrily.

"And what if he breaks a rule?" Bob inquired.

"Well," Mira Ji replied, "the organization throws him out and appoints another guru instead."

Our car stopped suddenly. We looked out the windows, and to our amazement we beheld nothing but buffalo snouts—black, phlegmatic muzzles with and without horns and shining wet noses surrounding us on all sides. We were stuck in the midst of a large herd.

One buffalo stuffed his enormous head and horns into the open window, then dully eyed us all while his green cud mixed up with saliva dripped onto Werter's embroidered shirt.

Startled, Werter blurted out, "Bitte, fräulein*, don't put your face into my window!" And with both hands he energetically pushed the wet nose, mouth and horns, trying to get the snout out of the car.

After a considerable struggle, he finally succeeded, quickly ground up the window, let out a sigh of relief and, leaning forward, continued attentively listening to Mira.

"This guru," she went on, "is the leader of the Jains. Ahimsa** is their law. To kill even a microbe in considered quite a crime, and that is why they wear this white gauze in front of their mouths, so that, God forbid, some invisible insect does not unintentionally get crushed and swallowed."

"Das ist doch schön ubertrieben!" said Werter in disbelief, and added, "Translation, please."

"That is definitely extremism," I quickly translated as best I could from Werter's German.

"And what if a mosquito bites him?" Bob wanted to know but remained without an answer as we had already arrived at the large 2-story high dwelling of this Jain guru.

Entering through a tall, arched gate, we were greeted by two black buffaloes that belonged to the guru and lived with him in the same house.

---

*Bitte, fräulein: Please, miss.

**Ahimsa: Non-violence.

Avoiding the animals and taking off our shoes, we mounted a narrow staircase leading to the upper floor.

In a large, empty room stood a small platform. A handsome fellow in white attire with white gauze under his nose sat next to it and quietly read a book.

Not knowing whether he was the guru or the spy, and just to make sure we did not offend anyone here, we bowed with folded hands.

He happened to be the spy.

After a little while, the real guru entered head shorn bald like a Buddhist monk. A long skirt dangled around his thighs; a light scarf hung down one shoulder; while a soft broom balanced artistically on the other. His face was glossy, the stomach over the frock considerable, and his bearing betrayed a touch of inner pride.

"This guru has a big ego," Mira Ji secretly whispered from behind our backs.

With his soft broom, the Jain swept the floor as he approached our Master, who in turn rose up and embraced him with love and kind words of greeting.

The guru climbed up the steps, settled down on the podium cross-legged, and began talking confidently while the Superior One and we sat on the floor.

There was an inborn nobility in our Master's bearing, graceful and dignified, yet tempered with boundless sweet humility. With admiration we observed our humble, perfect

Master as He listened attentively to the words of the Jain.

"Verily," we thought, "humility is the adornment of a Saint."

"All of you should have walked over here," the Jain guru continued talking, lightly shaking his head in disapproval. "We, as you well know, do not sanction traveling by either cars or airplanes."

Master sweetly chuckled. "But dear teacher, the 20th century is already upon us," He said.

"Not all Jains think like that," whispered Mira Ji. "Only the monks still adhere to the way of life that vanished long, long ago."

The Jain continued speaking for quite some time while our Master once in a while translated to us some of what was said, and when the guru ran out of words, Maharaji smiled softly, His eyes emitting nothing but flawless love, and rose to His feet.

While the Jain accompanied our Satguru downstairs, both exchanged a few words in private.

Master's driver Mohan had already started the car.

The Superior One thanked His host warmly for his cordial hospitality and drove off.

The handsome spy accosted Mira Ji in a small back room and asked, "Why did your Master sit at the feet of our guru when everyone knows that Kirpal Singh Ji Maharaj is the greatest Saint in India?"

Thoughtfully, Mira Ji looked at him and wisely kept silent.

Obligingly, the Jain showed us his big house, then swept the floor for Werter's movie and stiffly held the broom on his shoulder for Gerald's endless photos as the rest of us leisurely loafed on the top of the roof, gazing at the views of the city.

Thanking our host and wishing him well, we drove back to the dormitories. As there was still a lot of time left until the evening Satsang, Bob and Gerald with Sushila on his arm, enjoyed a hearty philosophical conversation while promenading around and trampling down the plush American lawn of the Indian University.

I slipped away unnoticed and fell asleep on the heavenly soft Yankee mattress back in the silence of our room.

The sun hid behind the roofs, then sank below the horizon as darkness fell, warm and soft.

We drove to the place of Satsang at night. Again thousands upon thousands of flickering candlelights were lit up in front of all the stores, this glittering show competing with the heavenly stars that shimmered and glimmered, hot and bright, as they tried to outdo each other in their own spectacular game.

In the deep, black splendor of the night, summer lightning blazed up on the horizon, and it seemed that some unseen creative forces were working triumphantly and invisibly everywhere you gazed.

'We gazed at the views of the city.'
Page 170

Again we sat in lotus postures forming a semi-circle behind Master's back as He addressed 15 thousand silent people who had assembled to bask in the words of the Greatest Saint of India, Param Sant Kirpal Singh Ji Maharaj.

Master spoke in Punjabi to the spell-bound audience, explaining to them for two glorious hours the purpose of human life on this our planet earth.

While driving back to the College, Mira summed up Master's words thus: "With all its seeming imperfections, this world serves a useful purpose in the Divine Plan, just like an apparently insignificant cog in the machinery of a great powerhouse. Nature, the handiwork of God, is not the least extravagant in its design and plan.

This world is a penitentiary, a house of correction, a sort of purgatory, a plan of expiation, a training ground where souls get chastened by experience. It is a half-way house between physical planes and spiritual realms.

The powers that be of the earth are hard taskmasters, believing still in the Mosaic Law of 'an eye for an eye and a tooth for a tooth.'

Here all kinds of third-degree methods are employed and hard knocks are administered, rendering less than justice, untempered by compassion and mercy, so that one should take his lessons seriously and by degrees turn away from the way of the world to the Way of God.

Life on the earth plane, then, is a dreadful thing, dark with horror and fear, and we are long-lost children of God in the labyrinthine wilderness of the world. (39)

The way of escape from the material world, the way to get off the wheel of life and death, and to achieve the aim and purpose of human life on earth, which is God-Realization, is through communion with the Holy Word, or Naam.

Yet this noble aim cannot be achieved without the help of a Living Master, Who Himself had traveled the whole ray of Creation from the beginning to the end."

"O NANAK, ON WHOM HE BESTOWS

HIS GIFT OF THE SONG CELESTIAL

IS THE KING OF KINGS."

_____Jap Ji

CHAPTER SIX

FEROZEPUR

After packing our suitcases with goods and chattels, we reluctantly bade adieu to the American University and the Yankee mattresses, and once again luxuriated in the soft Ambassador's seats.

In the wide, back window of the station wagon, we could clearly see Kim and Swen meditating, until we lost sight of them some distance up the road.

Turning her radiant face to us while getting comfortable in her seat, Mira Ji began talking. "What do you think? That I came to Maharaji just like that? No, no! I tested the Satguru in so many different ways, as if the Master is not perfect, then all that such a Master can do for you is take you up to his own level of inner achievement and not any further, and if he is not out of Brahmanda, how will you get out of Brahmanda?

You see, after crossing the 3 regions of mind and matter or Brahmanda, the Soul enters Par Brahm, where in the region of Dasam Dwar, as you know, lies the Lake of Immortality, Amritsar.

Passing the great, black void, or Maha Sunn, the Soul enters Sach Khand, her eternal home, in the fifth plane of Creation.

Still higher, there are 3 more planes: Alakh, Agam and Anami, or the Nameless One, the seat of the Formless Absolute. The Grand

'Bob and Kira Redeen on the way
to Ferozepur.'
Page 173

Dissolution does not touch Sach Khand, but it does engulf Par Brahm."

"Yes," added Bob, "it is so. Even Western science has concluded that our Cosmos first expands and then contracts in dissolution. It was thus before and will be in the future."

"The breath of Brahman, inhaling and exhaling," commented Werter knowledgeably.

"So," Mira Ji continued, "there is no salvation below Sach Khand, and if one's Master is not a Param Sant--an 8th plane Saint like our Master, or at least a Saint who reached the 5th plane of creation--then our salvation is doomed.

I tested our Master, and He stood all the tests splendidly. One last test, I thought, and if He passes that, I will get initiated.

I went to the lovely city of Mussoorie which spreads placidly over the hazy, Himalayan slopes and stopped at a little bazaar in front of a fruit stand. 'If Maharaji finds me here and talks to me, my tests will be over,' I thought.

Taiji later told me that at that time, back at His home in Rajpur, Master was very busy but suddenly He dropped everything and asked the chauffeur to prepare the car immediately as He had an important and urgent matter to attend to in the City of Mussoorie. In a few minutes He was on the way.

Worried, I waited at the fruit stand as the time slowly passed by, when a grey car appeared from a narrow side street, approached the bazaar and came to the very spot where I stood.

Voiceless, I gazed at it, while through the open window I beheld our Satguru's face. Smiling, He waved His hand and asked me, 'How are you doing today?'"

"Mira," I wondered, "is there any logical answer behind all these things? We'd like to understand how they work."

"Logic?" She laughed merrily. "In the science of the beyond, logic and reasoning have no place. (40) Logic and reasoning are no more than blind life in the brain.

How could logic and reasoning, for example, explain the events that took place some time ago when we stayed in Master's house in Rajpur." And Mira began the story.

"Once, I walked up the road toward Mussoorie, feeling sad. Darkness fell as it was past midnight. As I started on my way back, I noticed a bright light coming towards me. Suddenly I realized that this light was Master Sawan Singh and that a boy with folded hands followed Him.

Just as I wanted to touch His feet, He turned towards the boy and said in Urdu that great work had to be done in the future. As Master Sawan Singh did not speak Urdu I thought that He must be someone else. He looked straight into my eyes. 'He is Sawan,' I felt as my heart missed a beat.

Rooted to the ground, I watched them pass by. Then Sawan Singh Ji turned around and looked at me once again. I wanted to run after Him but instead fled back to the house and

'Once, I walked up the road toward Mussoorie'
Page 175

straight to the room where our Master was sitting.

'Yes,' He said, observing me.

'Was it Sawan?' I asked Him breathlessly.

'Yes,' He answered, 'you were in danger of dacoits at that time.'

Once before, I was quite alone in the Rajpur house at night on Master's business, while Master Himself remained in the ashram in Delhi. There was no door in the room, and through the open doorway I watched the path leading to the street.

'What if dacoits come in from the street, find and kill me?' I thought. Trembling with fear, I crouched in the darkest corner of the room transfixed, watching the moonlit path.

Suddenly, a tall man turned in at the gate and walked up that path, his staff sounding loudly on the dry ground.

Speechless, petrified and closing my mouth with both hands, I watched in horror as the figure approached the doorway and then listened as he slowly walked around the house, his staff monotonously hitting the gravel. This nightmare seemed to come to no end.

Then in a flash, his tall figure appeared in the doorway, lifting a lantern.

'Master! Oh, Master!' I shouted, beside myself with joy.

The figure vanished. I saw Him then just as clearly as I see all of you right now."

Smiling dreamily, Mira Ji rejoiced in her memory, while Werter swiftly glanced at us with an expression of boundless astonishment on his glowing face. Hurriedly blotting the perspiration with the edge of his embroidered shirt, he leaned forward so as not to miss a word of Mira Ji's next tale.

Bob commented, "Bi-location is a well-known fact to the mystics."

But, absorbed in Mira's fascinating experience, the remark went unnoticed by us like a pebble sinking in deep waters.

"Iqbal Kaur lived in Lahore and had 2 brothers. One of them was suddenly struck by pneumonia, took a turn for the worse and died.

Omi, his 10 year old younger brother, beside himself with grief, wandered out of the house and failed to return home that night.

The family was in distress, when late at night someone knocked at the door, and Maharaji Kirpal Singh walked into the room. After getting an explanation He said, 'Don't worry about Omi. Have faith in Hazur. The boy will be back home safe at 5 in the morning.'

And so indeed it happened.

Omi had a strange tale to tell on returning home. After wandering for a long time, he said, he had boarded a train at a railroad station. There he met a group of men whom he took to be sadhus. In their company he entered a jungle where they lived, and suddenly Omi realized that they were thugs in disguise. It was time to sleep and they placed him in their midst so he could not escape. Aware of his danger, Omi prayed and a light appeared. Within it stood the glorious form of Kirpal Singh Ji, ordering Omi to get up and follow Him.

'How can I? They are all around me and will catch me.'

'No one can stop you,' he was told.

Following Maharaji's bright light, Omi sped barefooted along through the jungle. At 5 in the morning, as predicted, Omi opened the door of his home." (40a)

"Verily, verily, India is a land of miracles!" Werter exclaimed and sank back into his seat looking bedazzled.

"Scheherazade! One thousand and one nights!" I cried out with complete delight.

Tucking a shawl around her head, Elaine turned around in her middle seat and looked at us for a few moments, obviously enjoying our high emotions, then said, "Masters do not do miracles in public, but for their disciples there are miracles at every turn!"

"Indeed, your statement is correct, Elaine," Bob said fervently. "Since our initiation in 1968 we found it to be true. What are these so-called 'miracles' but a superior knowledge of nature's immutable, universal laws working in the hands of a superior man?

The entire Creation is subject to these imperial divine laws working without error in the worlds above as well as in the worlds below, in the East as well as in the West, yet we in our dense ignorance never fail to be perplexed or amazed."

"How true!" I exclaimed, as we drove past a small Indian village drowning in rich foliage. In its deep shade a few cows sleepily rested on the ground, and a white puppy yelped at the

children who were unsuccessfully trying to make
a big kite reach the sky.

"When Eastern eyes look upon the West, the
same events happen there, too," I continued.
"Let me tell you the story about Mrs. Gordon
Hughes, who lived in Kentucky in the U.S.A. in
1928.

She was, you see, on her deathbed.
Suddenly, a luminous brightness appeared in one
corner of the room. It grew brighter and
brighter. Within the center of this radiant
light a form appeared, the most glorious being
she had ever seen.

He stood there, tall, slender, magnificent. His beard was white and glistening. His
vivid blue eyes were filled with divine,
compassionate, flawless love. His glance was
penetrating, inspired and keen.

His robe and turban were white and pure
and emitted a myriad scintillations of light and
color. The palms of his beautiful hands were
clasped together and held against his heart.
She thought that it must be God!

It was the Radiant Form of Master Sawan
Singh Ji. She looked at Him with amazement.
Then, He walked slowly toward her and passed
into her emaciated body.

The next morning her family was astonished
as she rose from her sick bed entirely healed
and every whit whole.

On her trips to the inner planes, Mrs.
Hughes met the Radiant Form of Master Kirpal
Singh, and being an artist, painted a portrait
of astounding likeness of this Glorious Being.

She met our Master physically only 20 years later." (41)

"This is no new thing," said Mira Ji. "To many a disciple, Master in His Luminous Form appears before initiation. Our Satguru Himself met Hazur Baba Sawan Singh in the inner planes 7 years before He met Him physically.

Our Master used to cross the inner planes in the company of a luminous, glorious Being, taking Him to be Guru Nanak.

Once He got off the train at Beas where the station attendant approached Him asking, 'Have you come to see the Beas Saint?'

Master, Who was very fond of rivers, told him that He had come to see the Beas River, but most certainly would want to see the Saint.

Great was Master's astonishment when, entering the courtyard, He saw on the podium the same glorious Being that He was so familiar with in the worlds beyond.

'Why has it taken so long, Sir?' our Satguru humbly asked Master Sawan Singh, His hands folded in adoration.

'This was the most opportune time,' smiled Master Sawan Singh."

For awhile we drove silently along a highway just enjoying the cooling breeze. As we entered a rather dilapidated suburb of a city, Werter, turning to the back window, picked up the blue, plastic container, unscrewed the lid, poured the warm ashram water into our cups and we happily sipped the liquid.

MASTER SAWAN SINGH

Considerably invigorated after this drink, Bob felt inspired to continue talking. "Notice," he said, "in India the people speak about death and life beyond death, about the geography of the next worlds as one might refer to an old, worn-out hat that one has owned all his life. Why is this so?

Because they have practically explored the next world. They went there and made it their home.

Imagine if in my office in New York I would open my mouth and say that there are Masters in the world who know. What do you think would happen?"

"What," I exclaimed with a grin. "Surely the same thing that happened to Carl F. in 1963. We met him, if you remember, later on.

Being a Christian minister, he was devoted to Jesus heart and soul and had built 5 churches during his ministry.

When Master came to Florida, Carl decided to expose Him and destroy the Satguru in a verbal dispute. He began asking questions all day long, and next day, too.

Finally, Master suggested to him that he take initiation on a trial basis which Carl did. And now, in Carl's own words, 'In a split second the microcosm became the macrocosm, and 20 years of seminary study went down the drain.'

His wife filed for divorce and put him into an insane asylum from where Carl wrote a letter to Master complaining about his plight. Master replied, 'Glad to hear you're having a good rest!'

The insane asylum released Carl shortly after, and he became a factory worker to raise his two sons."

"So was!" Werter said with consternation.

"The East stands humbly with eyes and ears open," philosophized Bob, "while the West, blind and deaf, menacingly swings her scientific club in the dead-end street of materialism, and by now is ready to blow up the whole of humanity."

As we entered the city, Mira Ji reported, "This is Ferozepur. The city lies next to the Pakistan border."

On the street a small crowd of people carrying slogans on long sticks as well as a big, red flag was loudly singing, creating a bottleneck. We were forced to halt. "These," explained Mira, "are communists, the hopelessly deluded materialists."

With a shudder, I looked out of the window. "Oof, how awful! This type of philosophy has already cost Russia one hundred million lives, you know."

Because we had stopped, the pleasant breeze that had cooled us all the way died out instantly, and it felt as if we had entered a sweat bath. Perspiration streamed down our bodies in rivulets and our faces got as red as the communist flag.

Not even Bob talked any more. We sat silently, waited and inhaled the scorching air with difficulty until the singing communists turned off into a side street and their slogans vanished from our sight.

FEROZEPUR

"Ignorance and delusion, whether political
or spiritual, will some day prove to be fatal,"
I sighed with regret.

Ferozepur reminded one of a partially
demolished medieval fortress. Some streets were
so narrow that the neighbors could have shaken
hands out of their windows if they wanted to.
But quite a few roads were wide and large
squares were in abundance.

We passed a few impressive houses where
past beauty was still quite visible in spite of
the peeling paint, fallen-out plaster, rust and
leaks that disfigured their walls. Some of the
windows were covered with rotten straw mats,
some closed with aged shutters hanging here and
there on a single hinge. Glued to the brick
walls were scraps of torn-up posters, their
ragged edges fluttering in the weak breeze.

Neglect and decay could be observed almost
every place, but in all this wretchedness there
was something very attractive, captivating and
thrilling to an artist's eye.

We noticed a number of young boys whose
hair in a knot on top of the head was covered
with a small kerchief tied with a string. These
were future Sikhs. As soon as they matured, the
kerchief would be replaced with the turban of a
grown-up man.

We stopped on a small square and followed
Mira Ji into a narrow street about 10 feet wide
festively decorated in honor of our Master's
arrival.

'We passed a few impressive houses where
past beauty was still quite visible.'
Page 183

Foil, both silver and gold, glistened above in a unique looking living arch. Flowers were plentiful, and so were the curious faces smiling out of each window.

We turned to the left stopping at a large, roomy house belonging to a medical lieutenant-colonel, now retired. It was quite apparent that the family lived well.

A brick patio serving as a courtyard was surrounded with colorful materials. Along the flimsy walls, a variety of tables were placed filled with kitchen utensils and food.

The same material that made the walls was also stretched above protecting the inhabitants from deadly sun rays.

In the middle of the patio on a wide rope bed, our frisky chauffeur already sat cross-legged and smiling. As a local servant had joined him, they lit a small kerosene burner and started preparing a meal.

This mansion had many rooms and corridors but only 2 bathrooms. The one upstairs was in such condition that both Werter and Gerald immediately came down to investigate the second one. They said noone could enter the first bathroom even with the best of intentions.

The walls and the floor of the second bathroom were covered with sticky slime and rusty spots. It required extreme caution to walk there if one did not wish to fall and break his neck.

'They lit a small kerosene burner and
started preparing a meal.'
Page 184

No tub was available but under the ceiling something strongly resembling a showerhead dangled from a metal pole. This contraption produced water when one pulled a skinny rope.

Many, many years ago the toilet had probably been white, but now it was a dismal black, either from rust or from something else even less palatable. From a defaced faucet that could not be completely turned off, water dripped methodically into the ancient sink.

"Yes," Gerald exclaimed with sincere delight, rubbing his hands with joy, "what a marvelous bathroom! Now I will be able to wash Sushila's diapers once again."

A 2-story high room of considerable proportions was assigned to us. Through its small windows placed high under the ceiling, the blue sky was visible and dull light filtered in.

At the distant wall on a flimsy spider-legged table a clock ticked with a shade of old age in its sound. Two metal beds covered with mattresses no thicker than a human finger were placed opposite each other at the empty walls.

The upholstery on the solitary armchair standing at the bathroom door was admittedly somewhat the worse for wear, but it was never-theless a splendid chair that mewed like a kitten as one sat on it providing a musical finishing touch to all this simple decor.

"What more is wanted?" We laughed as we sat down on the beds. Then, aghast, realizing that they were procrustean we uttered a few emotional comments when a loud knock at the door and a voice informed us that Master was expecting us for darshan.

We entered a second large room, so huge that it resembled a temple hall. Through the stained glass windows high above, the multi-colored sunrays tenderly and cautiously flowed in to this chamber faintly touching the sculptures in the hollow niches and recesses of the walls, playing delicately on the patterns of the Persian rug, the walls and furniture. We concluded that twilight—cool and mysterious—never left this peaceful abode.

Maharaji sat in a low armchair talking quietly with the host and his family. Eager neighbors poured in through the open door and settled around Him on all sides.

We paused, observing the lively scene, when Master lovingly motioned to us to join our brothers and sisters from Ferozepur on the soft Persian rug.

The divine, beautiful darshan continued until interrupted by the pitiful sobs of an old, old woman. Despondent, bowing and touching the rug with her dark wrinkled forehead she was crying and begging for something from our Master.

With boundless sympathy, our Satguru looked at the woman as He leaned slightly forward, then firmly said a few words in Punjabi.

Startled, we asked, "What happened, Mira?"

"What happened? She said, 'I am old and tired. Please let me go to the next realm. All

I ask of you, Oh Satguru, is mercy. Please let me go!'

'No,' Maharaji told her, 'your body is priceless. You have to reach illumination in it. Meditate and meditate again and again. Outside of that, your life is of no value.'"

The old woman gradually quieted down, and the darshan continued sweet and enrapturing until Master silently rose from His chair, smiled and left the room.

In the open corridor along the side of the wall facing the patio, tables were set, benches put behind them, and a meal served for all. Exuberant and in high spirits, we settled down, ate puris with appetite, drank warm, sweet tea and philosophized ceaselessly. Werter rapidly peeled a spotty banana, face glowing with pleasure.

The door to the bathroom was open, and we could hear Gerald struggling with the faucet that gave out first a loud gasp, then began making slow, undecipherable noises before shooting out some water of dubious purity.

Not wasting any time, Gerald started cleaning Sushila's diapers, the wash water bubbling in the filthy sink.

Suddenly, his voice, somber and deep, came out of the bathroom. "Tomorrow, we all go to a leper colony."

Instantly, dead silence fell, as abruptly our chatting stopped in mid-sentence. It became still as a morgue.

Petrified, Werter quit peeling his banana, as Swen's sapphire eyes became bigger than big.

The tea steamed from our untouched cups. We looked at each other with poorly concealed trepidation.

Gerald continued cleaning the diapers vigorously in the colonel's aged sink. Once again his grave voice resounded in the bathroom. "Why should I be afraid? I am a spiritual leper myself!"

Although his courageous words did not at all comfort anybody, at least they brought us all out of a state of shock. Silently, we began sipping the dark Indian tea, each one quite alone with his own conscience as there was certainly a great deal to consider.

A hot kettle in her hand, Mira Ji entered the corridor and asked, "Anybody want more tea?" but remained without an answer.

With deep anxiety in his voice, Werter instantly questioned, "How does leprosy start?"

Mira replied, "The fingers get numb, and it itches under the nails."

"And how contagious are these lepers?" Bob asked with alarm.

"I don't know," laughed Mira Ji. "Does anybody want more tea?"

Noone wanted anything as we rose and went back to our respective quarters. Mira Ji alone remained in the corridor, bending over the patio sink, washing the dishes that we left behind.

Gloomily entering our room, Bob sat down on the solitary mewing chair, sighed grimly a few times as a dry, stale smell of disturbed dust spread from his seat, then began meditating.

From there on, no matter how cheerful or joy-filled we were, the menacing ghost of the impending visit to the leper colony, like a bugbear, invariably hovered in the back of our minds.

Meditation was not successful as nauseating thoughts struck us from all sides like cobras without stop or hindrance. Realizing that no matter how long we sat there, a peaceful, thoughtless state of calm--the prelude to a successful meditation--would not be achieved that day, we decided to rest on our beds which had apparently been built for Spartans.

After a short while, an acute pain wracked my body, as my back fell out of joint. Bob pulled me up, as I could not make it myself. Then he left.

Perching on the edge of the bed, aching, morbid and frustrated, I was at a complete loss.

The chain of depressing thoughts was interrupted when, triumphantly displaying a broad smile, Bob returned, the host and a servant right on his heels carrying a thick quilt and another thin mattress in their hands. Both were piled on top of my bed. Gratefully we offered our thanks, and the host and his servant left the room.

The mood improved as we discovered that although I could not get up from bed any more, at least there was no pain when standing or walking.

A bit later, as if nothing had happened at all, both of us stood in the corridor eager to find out what was going on there, who was talking about what, and whether anybody was doing anything.

We noticed that the corridor entered the street on one end and observed that the heads of curious neighbors still continued sticking out from all windows as they tried to find out what was going on in the medical colonel's house, who was talking about what, and whether anybody was doing anything there.

The other side ended at a staircase which led to the second floor where we could distinctly hear Gerald's soft baritone mixing up with Sushila's childish prattle.

In the middle of the corridor, the best German electric razor in his hand, Werter was searching for an electric outlet, while Mira Ji, holding a timetable in her hand, informed everyone that tomorrow at 4 a.m. we were supposed to be present in a Hindu Temple, later visit a colony of blind people, in the afternoon go to the lepers and finally to satsang late at night.

Turning to Werter, she pointed with her timetable at a man in a white shirt and a turban. "Do you see him?" she asked.

"Yes," interest kindled in Werter's eyes. "Yes, he is very handsome. What about it?"

"You see, he had another guru before he was initiated by our Master. His guru taught him a different way of meditation. This fellow meditated for years in that fashion and could not meet his Master within.

Once the Radiant Form of Kirpal Singh Ji appeared to him on the inner planes. 'This is not my master,' he thought, and continued searching for his own guru but without success.

Finally, his guru appeared to him on the inner planes and told him to go to Kirpal Singh without delay, which this fellow did.

He arrived in Sawan Ashram and falling at the feet of our Master in reverence said, 'Venerable Satguru, I understand what you have done for me. In the form of my imperfect master, you yourself appeared before me in the Radiant Form, and it is you who has ordered me to come here. So I have come,' and once again, he bowed before the Master, touching the ground with his head.

He now lives in the ashram and all his free time he spends in the company of the Radiant Form of the Satguru on the inner planes. He arrived just now on the early train to Ferozepur as yesterday our Master ordered him to come."

"Yesterday?" Werter wondered. "How could that be? Did Master send him a telegram?"

Mira Ji burst into laughter. "Werter," she exclaimed, "for a Master and His advanced disciple, there is no need for a postoffice, a mail box or a telegram. Master told him so within!"

Werter stared at the inspired face of this advanced disciple with admiration and respect.

There was indeed something to look at with amazement. The disciple's face was pale and exceptionally handsome, framed in a black beard

into which soft whiskers melted. Under his
heavy eyebrows shone a pair of dark eyes full of
inner strength. A white turban crowned his
noble head.

Thinking of his own spiritual shortcomings, Werter sighed from the bottom of his
lungs and plugged the electric shaver into a
socket. The socket was dead as the Ferozepur
powerhouse had suffered a short circuit and
momentarily in the lieutenant colonel's mansion
there was no electricity.

"So was! Unglaublich!" Werter muttered.

The handsome disciple approached us humbly
and clasping his palms in greeting, said warmly
and cordially, "I am very happy to meet you
again, as I have seen you both in the ashram
back in Delhi. It is so good that you are safe
and well.

Our Beloved Master asked me yesterday to
join Him in Ferozepur, and so I have arrived
just a few minutes ago as ordered."

We looked at him goggle-eyed, as if he was
the 7th wonder of the world and folded our hands
in reciprocal greeting.

He bowed, then melted into the Indian
crowd milling around in the corridor.

"Is he handsome!" I gasped, not believing
my eyes.

"Handsome?" Now it was Mira Ji's turn to
be surprised. "Just an ordinary face," she
said. 'It seems handsome to you from want of
habit. You are not accustomed to such faces,
yet to us, your faces seem to be extremely
beautiful."

"Extremely beautiful!" It was now Werter's turn to be astonished, and not crediting his ears, he burst into spontaneous laughter.

"Everything is relative," Bob remarked soberly.

"Don't you realize what is going on here?" asked Mira Ji, pointing to the Indian crowd. "They want to see that which is strange, unknown and beautiful to them—the Westerners."

With a bit more understanding, we now looked at the Indians. A lot of children of all ages had filled the hall to capacity. The chauffeur, the host and Mira Ji took turns chasing them out, but it was wasted effort, as in a few minutes the hall and patio were full once again.

Staring without a break, they looked at us as if it was we who were the 7th wonder of the world!

"What is your name?" a little voice asked. Bob looked down, his blue eyes seeking to locate the curious one and met 4 dozen delighted brown eyes peeking at him from below as well as 2 dozen lovely smiles.

"Bob," he said.

"Bob!" The little exotic crowd twittered and chirped like a flock of rare Asiatic birds. "Bob! Bob! Bob!" There was no end to their exuberant joy.

The chauffeur once again turned them all out of the house onto the street and closed the door.

We decided to inspect the progress at the construction site on the square where Master's podium was being put up for satsang and invited Werter to join us.

Werter's long shirt dangled loosely on his lean body, falling below his knees. His wide pants, rumpled and creased, bunched up on his slippers. "It is Gerald's outfit. I borrowed it from him, and it is the wrong size," he explained. "My shirt is so filthy from all the green buffalo cud that I can't even put it on, and as you well know, there is no decent place to wash it in the medical colonel's house."

In Werter's company we left the house leisurely and unhurriedly entered the street. The little children who just a moment ago had been driven out by the chauffeur immediately surrounded us. Many grown-ups joined them, and we became the center of a tight and impenetrable ring of people.

No matter which direction we looked, from every place friendly, smiling faces gazed at us with fascination. Old and young bearded men in multi-colored turbans, beautiful girls whose heads were covered with the ends of their sarees, rhinestones glittering in their nostrils, ruby dots of vermillion decorating their foreheads, and children--delighted children--everywhere.

The chauffeur, who had just thrown another mob out of the colonel's house, noticed our plight and swiftly dashed to our rescue, his shining eyes emitting sparks as he yelled at the top of his voice in a most ferocious manner, thrashing his hands in the air.

The crowd gave way and as a narrow passageway appeared, we slipped through it and continued walking towards the square.

For some time our persistent admirers followed us. Soon we realized that in a few moments we would be encircled once again with the chauffeur far away this time. So, deciding to forego the square and podium, we turned around and began walking briskly towards the colonel's house, as the thought of being mobbed to death by a friendly crowd was less than appealing.

While the Indians remained in pursuit, Werter laughed heartily. "This is reminiscent of the German story," he said, "'Der Mäusefänger.' Are you familiar with it?

A man, der Mäusefänger, was playing his flute so enchantingly sweet that all the mice and afterwards all the children followed him, and he led them away."

The crowd began catching up, and we turned to jogging. Racing ahead and at the same time fanning his hot face with the edge of Gerald's shirt, Werter continued talking, "If only my wife could see me in this outfit and in this situation, she would no doubt immediately faint! I look like a persecuted patient escaping from the insane asylum! Das ist doch schön ganz unglaublich!" And he burst into laughter all over again.

Hurriedly turning in at the door of the colonel's house, we at last were able to catch our breath.

"Fantastic!" exclaimed Bob, settling down on the rope bed in the middle of the brick patio and propping himself up with both hands, while Werter, standing in front of him, continued fanning his face with the edge of his long shirt listening to Bob with full attention.

"What an invaluable lesson was taught to us by God's strange and unfathomable ways. Like these little children in the colonel's house and in your story, Werter, the soul should behave thus and pursue the Lord constantly, steadily, persistently, seized by wonder, adoration and awe, without ever letting go for a second the enchanting sound of God's flute, the entrancing melody of Naam, until the soul, now forgetful of her origin, achieves complete identification with Him and merges into the Ocean of Oneness with her Source or God."

Entering our 2-story-tall barn-room, we stopped in surprise. Out of the colonel's bathroom strange sounds emitted, the noise reminiscent of loud gnashing, gritting and gnawing of teeth.

Full of curiosity, Bob peeked through the slightly open doorway and silently motioned me to quickly join him.

In front of the black, polluted toilet in the filth and slime that was covering the floor, Elaine was kneeling, sleeves rolled up, her long pigtail restlessly swaying from side to side on her back, as she scrubbed and scraped with all her might and main the stinky inside of the toilet, a coarse, hard brush in her hand.

"It is simply wonderful!" I whispered. "Here is Elaine, an English girl who of her own volition does the work of an untouchable. Even the wife of Mahatma Gandhi did it only after considerable persuasion and that, too, just as an example to India."

Closing the door, Bob said, "It is not the work that graces the man, but indeed it is the man who is gracing the work. With one scrub of her brush, Elaine questions the rightness of the whole caste system."

After a little while, Bob added, "True are the words of our Master, 'There is only one caste, the caste of humanity.'"

As the day melted into dusk, and shadows became deep and dark, the monarch of the night made her royal appearance and shone like a fiery crest jewel amidst the scintillating stars. Her bright rays peacefully rocked and swayed on the leaves of the trees as we approached the square.

Many rugs covered the floor of the plat-form where Master was already sitting in front of a few Ferozepur potentates.

Bright lights illumined the square, pouring their rays into the neighboring side-streets. Out of one a jeep, clattering loudly, crammed with beturbaned Sikhs, drove up full speed. Noticing the dense crowd filling the square, the jeep stopped abruptly, then quickly backed up as a muffled bark of a dog accompanied its hasty retreat.

We sat just 3 feet away from a house wall. On my right lay a few fresh, smelly cow-droppings, to the left Bob fidgeted on the ground as he could not cross his legs, try as he might. Ahead, Gerald perched on the green beach chair with Werter next to him in Gerald's wide shirt which hung like a lifeless sail from both of his shoulders.

Master began to talk, and His words, like precious parshad, melted sweetly into the hearts of His listeners.

"In India," He said, "Diwali Day (the Indian Festival of Lights) is celebrated by lighting candles. The people usually gamble, and if you ask them why, they will tell you, that by gambling on that day, one's birth and death will cease.

There is a kind of gambling that finishes up the incarnations, but what kind of gambling it is, very few really know. The true gambling lies in sacrificing all other things—body and its environments—for the purpose of enkindling the Light within.

The greatest aspiration of human life is to realize God: the God Which expressed Himself into Creation, the Maker of Khand and Brahmand (astral and causal planes), the Sustainer of all things. In the language of the Saints that God-Expressed is called Naam through Which they say the Soul can gain salvation, irrespective of religion.

Listen to the Master's true words. He speaks of what He sees. While the senses are not controlled, the mind and intellect not stilled, the soul cannot open the inner eye to see the Manifestation of God.

By repeating the Naam, the light of millions of suns will manifest. In the Naam is the light, and light is the form of God, and in that light there is Sound--Udgit, Nad, the Music of the Spheres.

So the true meaning behind the Festival of Lights should be practised, and that is to enkindle the light, the True Light of the Lord, within. (42) Light and Sound are the direct way back to the Absolute God."

Around 10 p.m. my back gave out, and propping both hands on the ground somehow trying to relieve the pain, I stirred and shifted. Immediately, Gerald turned around, gave me his beach chair while whispering, "Are you going to faint?"

At 11 p.m. satsang was over, and we rushed to our beds as the next day promised to be strenuous.

In darkness at 3 a.m. we rose. The monarch of the night still shone like a fiery crest jewel amidst the scintillating stars above the sleeping city. Her delicate rays fell through our high window on to the top of the splendid chair, then slipped down to the floor in a glowing, erratic pattern.

Leaving the room, we noticed Werter on the brick patio exercising vigorously as his soft shadow faithfully reproduced all his movements under the moon's silvery light.

Later on, through the narrow, sleepy by-streets, we followed Mira Ji as she led us toward the Hindu Temple that was just a brief walk away.

Passing by sleeping figures on rope beds, recumbent cows on sidewalks, stray dogs that fearfully scrambled out of our way, we marched. In the silence of the dark night, only the clicking of our Indian sandals amplified by the emptiness of the street sounded loudly and commandingly over the ancient cobblestones.

Eventually, from the side streets, like thin rivulets, people began trickling out and the further we went, the larger became the crowd, until at last a whole, tumultuous river of humanity poured into a huge square.

Turning towards the garish Hindu Temple distinctly towering at its end, making our way through the crowd and what seemed to be a herd of cows, we approached the innumerable steps that led to the temple gates clogged from top to bottom with men and women.

A sea of shoes left behind at the entrance door presented a mind-boggling sight. Above the portals on the wall a flimsily affixed loudspeaker protruded through which the voice of the priest boomed, rolling over the whole neighborhood.

Somehow by a judicious use of our elbows, we squeezed ourselves inside the temple where in the stuffy heat, men sat to the right and women to the left.

There simply was no spot where one could crouch as heads seemed to touch heads, it was that tight. A few women squeezed tighter than tight so as to make a tiny space available. I settled down; who knows how!

The inner decor was more garish than the architecture outside. Amidst the living flowers and faded silks stood idols. On the walls painted deities were illumined by flickering candles. Multi-colored lights reflected and glittered on an extravaganza of gold and silver ornamentation.

On top of an embellished podium, drowning in the invisible fumes of the heavy aroma of incense, a priest, clad in a bright orange robe, spoke passionately into the microphone. A red dot decorated his forehead.

On his turban stood a proud cocks-comb from which a short piece of orange cloth fell lightly down the back.

The priest accompanied his vehement sermon with ceaseless, agitated gestures that made the garlands of flowers hanging over his breast dance, jerk and quiver. At times his voice would rise in frenzy, then drop to a lower pitch.

Drums were beating loudly, trumpets blared, large bells droned and small ones jingled in support of his words. A large fanfare blew directly into Bob's ear almost deafening him as he sat on the only available spot on the floor, facing a decorated pole.

People clapped loudly and sang in chorus.

Like a chiseled holy statue, our Master sat at the end of the orange podium, clad in pure white, silent, immovable.

As the whole procedure and the Punjabi language were utterly beyond comprehension for a novice, I thought it was a perfect time to put in a little meditation. Closing my eyes, I switched off the show.

Immediately, someone gave me a startling knock on top of the head. In Punjabi with the help of energetic gestures, my dear neighbors informed me that it was quite disrespectful to close one's eyes in the temple, and they could not and would not tolerate such uncouth behavior.

"Sorry. Pardon me," I replied in confusion.

Willy nilly, one was forced once again to observe the incomprehensible events going on until at last came the final blast of the trumpet, the drum died out and the preacher stepped off the podium.

Only then, Master rose silently and slowly moved forward settling in lotus posture before the assembled crowd, hands folded in His lap.

In a tranquil voice the Satguru spoke thus: "No amount of hand-clapping and singing, no amount of drum-beating and bell-ringing will help you, even if you clap from now on till the end of the world. It will give you no salvation. You will have no illumination. Outer sounds will keep you out, and in bondage. 'They take one to a state of forgetfulness both of one's self and God.' (43)

On the other hand, the inner music will take you in and give you freedom. This Godly music helps us in breaking through the bondage of the world and while remaining in the world, we cease to be of the world.' (44)

Listen to the Voice of God within yourself. Only Naam, or the Voice of God, will give you salvation.

It is through Shabd or Word that the Creation came into being with its various divisions and sub-divisions. Each division has its own peculiar musical notes which one hears as one rises from one higher plane to another. All the Saints have given detailed accounts of these Sounds and in Gurbani particularly we have an elaborate exposition on the subject. (44a)

The scriptures of all religions contain references to the ringing sound of bells or the blowing of horns and conches, the reason being that this is the first experience of the Soul as it rises above body consciousness and enters the Temple of the Most High, the Way which begins from the root of the nose behind the two eyebrows.

In the same way, countless melodies greet the Soul as it proceeds onward on the Path, but five of them are generally considered and accepted as of immense value in leading and guiding one on the journey Godward.

These melodious tunes interchangeably lead from plane to plane until one catches the native melody and reaches the Home of his Father with the proper help and guidance of some Master Saint. (44c)

Khawaja Hafiz, a mystic poet of great repute, says, 'Listen ye to the heavenly orchestra with notes of dulcimer, flute, zither and guitar.' (44d)

Truth is not so difficult as some of us have made it, and most have come to believe it so. All this is because of the lack of practical experience. We presume and assume many things of which we have no real knowledge.

Masters do come, not to destroy but to fulfill. So, stay in your religions. Just understand a little more, that's all." Master finished His talk.

At 7 a.m. it was already daybreak and after leaving the Hindu Temple, we walked back through the same corridors and caverns into which human figures going home from the Hindu service now turned in, vanishing like spectres into the twilight fog.

Parshad was plentiful on the table back in the colonel's house. Chapatis and tea were waiting for us as we sat down for breakfast.

The extroverts discussed the Varnatmak and Dhunatmak Shabd, or the outer and inner music.

"Our Master once said, 'What is this outside music if not noise of material objects?'" Elaine said, joining our conversation. "Is it not so? Man puts these noises into harmonious or disharmonious tunes as the case may be, then calls it music and deems himself cultured.

All that, as Master just said, keeps attention out, whether through the ears or eyes, as painting does. There is no difference between the two, in this sense, as the same damage is done. God Realization becomes an impossibility. God is inside, and if one is constantly groveling on the outside, then how can the two meet?"

"Imagine," I thought, "if the lifeless noise of dead, material objects can be so fascinating to the human ear, then what unimaginable power would the music emitted by Life itself have over a human soul!"

Elaine proceeded, "Master tells us in Jap Ji that only by listening to the inner Sound one rises above physical consciousness, comes into Cosmic Awareness and achieves the status of a True Saint.'" (45)

Looking as beautiful as an early spring day, Mira Ji smiled radiantly. "Use your trade for the purpose of making an honest living, but do not be attached to it. Don't make it your life, as the devices of negativity or the power of mind and matter are tricky."

As we left the colonel's house, trailing behind Mira Ji into a narrow street, we took a deep, pleasant breath of the fresh morning air and realized immediately that the air in Ferozepur was never, but never, fresh!

"We are now going to a party," said Mira Ji waving off a few children who started in pursuit. "An in-law of Mr. T.S. Khanna celebrates his youngest daughter's birthday, and he begged Maharaji to cut the cake. Master kindly consented and all of us were invited to come, too."

Entering an impressive three-story high building just a few blocks away from the colonel's house, we noticed our Satguru in the living room sitting on a plush couch engaged in cutting a big cake placed before Him.

We settled on the floor amidst the people present.

The birthday cake cut, Master handed pieces of this unusual parshad to the members of the grateful family and their guests. Master's eyes overflowed with Godly, powerful Love that shone bright and strong like the sun at its zenith.

As we happily ate this creamy parshad an old woman sitting next to me was blotting tears that silently trickled down her cheeks with the edge of her saree.

"Did you ever see so much tender Love at any place on earth?" she whispered.

"No, never. Nowhere did we see and feel such Love, nor did we ever even fancy that such Love indeed exists!" I whispered back to her.

She added, "God is all dazzling Love, you know. God loves us, and we love Him!" And she gazed at the Superior One with adoration, her smile pure and gentle, while the tears of Love continued running ceaselessly down her face.

We left the room quite reluctantly as our places were needed for other brothers and sisters from Ferozepur.

We crowded into the neighboring room, parshad in each of our hands. Werter smiled while chewing vigorously. "Very, very tasty parshad," he said. "From such parshad, noone can get sick! I firmly believe it to be so. I have no doubts whatsoever, and what do you think?" A piece of silver foil from the birthday cake glittered faintly on his chin.

"Thinking, you see, presents no problem," Bob said. "We believe in a lot of things, but can we live up to them? That's the question."

Meanwhile, more people were coming up the stairs, hoping to have at least a brief glimpse of the Master. Avoiding the traffic, we clustered in a corner of the room engaged in eating a lot of parshad, its silver foil, hot stuffing, burned crust, everything inside and everything outside believing, as we did, in the preventive powers of the cake as the visit to the leper colony was fast approaching.

"Tennis and other sports are also good for one's health," stated Werter. "Not only do they strengthen the muscles, but make a man take a lot of fast, deep breaths."

Bob asked him, "Don't you know that the number of breaths allotted to everyone is pre-determined by fate? If one plays tennis and breathes fast, he uses up the fixed amount of his breaths quicker and thus shortens his life."

"Oh!" Werter looked at Bob with astonishment and stopped eating. "How can that be? The amount of breaths is fixed? Hat der Meister so gesagt?*"

----

*Hat der Meister so gesagt?: Did the Master say so?

"Did you ever meet a professional sportsman who lived a very long life?" Bob queried.

"No, I did not, but then again I am not
acquainted with any. Oh, I really understand so
very little in all of these matters!"

"Do hatha yoga for 10-15 minutes in the
morning. Your muscles will be well exercised
and breathing will not be increased," advised
Bob finishing up his slice of birthday cake and
wiping his hands with a handkerchief.

"Take the Indian yogis and yogishwars, for
example," he continued, "who spend almost all
their lives in meditation in which breathing
becomes, as you well know, very slow. They live
long, long lives. Maharishi Raghuvacharya Ji is
over a hundred and ten years old by now."

Werter became pensive, and it was obvious
that even the thought of giving up sports was
painful to him.

As Master's short visit was over, He rose,
descended the staircase, and everyone crowded
right behind him. On the street a throng of
people was waiting for His holy darshan.

Folding His hands, the Satguru greeted
everyone, and then drove off to the colony of
the blind.

Mira Ji led the way for us as this colony
was supposed to be just a couple of blocks away.
Stepping on little stones and filth lying on the
cracked pavement, we briskly followed her.

"Walking must be good for you as it
certainly does not increase one's breathing,"
Werter mused. Then after a little while he
asked, "Mira, who is this Raghuvacharya?"

"Raghuvacharya?   He is a yogi by now 110 years old.   When Master Sawan Singh died, our grief-stricken Master went to the foot of the Himalayan Mountains near Rishikesh and spent half a year in seclusion.

Rishikesh is well-known for the many yogis living there, but none of them at that time rose above body consciousness except Maharishi Raghuvacharya.

This Maharishi then came over to pay respects to our Master, having learned about His arrival spiritually, that is from within.   He was a follower of a different path, the path of Patanjali, through which one eventually leaves the body and goes up.

When Maharishi Raghuvacharya died, out of love for him our Satguru in His limitless mercy returned him back to life, initiated him and warmly advised him to meditate in the Surat Shabd Yoga way from then on.

This Maharishi obeyed Master implicitly and now does exactly what he was told."

Bubbling over with laughter, Mira Ji continued, "Once, you know, in 1967 when Satguru visited Rishikesh, Maharishi Raghuvacharya asked to see Master's palm.   As he traced his finger along it, he said, 'Never have I seen such a palm in my life.'   He then became extremely animated, dancing around in ecstasy, exclaiming in rapture, 'You have the hands which belong to God!'" (46)

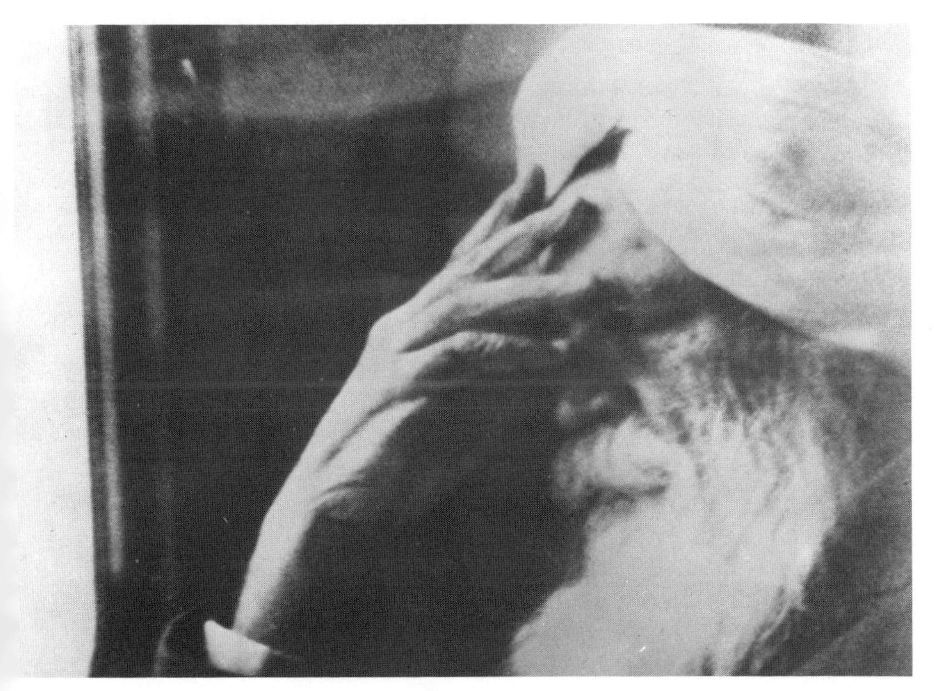

MASTER KIRPAL SINGH

Arriving at our next stop, we entered through an arch in a long wall and found ourselves in a large area where approximately 200 blind people were gathered. To our surprise all of them were children.

Hand outstretched towards his young audience, Master spoke from a white podium, kindly and fatherly.

Some of the children listened to His words with rapt attention and interest, some with curiosity, others not at all. A few boys in the last row turned around and looked at us wide-eyed.

"Mira, why do these blind children look at me wide-eyed?" asked Werter in astonishment.

"Because they are not blind."

"Not blind? Then who is blind?"

"The one whose third eye is not opened, and he does not see the light of God within."

As we chuckled in confusion, Mira Ji continued, "These are school children. We shall visit the blind people later on."

The school children, who, as it so happened, had eyes to see, sat cross-legged on the ground. The local teacher with a long, thin, wooden pole in his hand, walked among the rows giving a reminding slap with it to everyone who did not listen, or fidgeted around while Master explained to the pupils how they should behave in society.

He told them that one had to respect, love and obey his parents, that they had to abide by the laws of the country they live in, and that the aim of human life on earth is to meet God eyes to eyes and face to face.

Said the Master, "God, like a precious jewel, is locked and hidden in the treasure chest of the human body, and to find Him, you have to learn how to enter within. There, God is waiting for you patiently with His arms wide outstretched as He wants to hug you in a warm and loving embrace.

God's voice is like many, many melodies and is a beautiful fairy-tale song. He is constantly calling you, ceaselessly calling you, 'Oh, my little children, please, please do come back home.'"

Our next destination was located rather far away. After driving for quite some time, we stopped in front of a magnificent house resting impressively amidst trees and flowers at the end of an enormous lawn.

"We are invited for dinner here," said Mira Ji. "This mansion belongs to a Ferozepur judge."

"Sometimes unexpected things are most welcome," Bob smiled, feeling hungry.

Meanwhile, Werter, with keen interest, put his head out of the window and observed the long rows of tables covered with white cloth where all sorts of Indian dishes were laid out in abundance and arranged in excellent taste.

"Looks like a feast," he thought aloud, gorging his eyes on fluffy puris, hot steaming samosas, heaps of spiced biscuits of different forms and shapes, moist orange spaghetti, delectable fruits in inexhaustible supply, and sweet, yellow ladoos, resembling tennis balls covered with honey.

"Splendid!" I said eagerly, getting out of the car and joining others already settled comfortably in the shade of a flowery bush.

The mayor of the city, a general, the local librarian and all the cream and aristocracy of Ferozepur society, rich and famous, their wives clad in costly, silken sarees, embroidered with gold and silver, covered with diamonds and other precious stones, feet dazzling with golden rings--all were assembled here, sitting, standing, talking on this soft, lush lawn.

Well-dressed servants, trays in their hands, offered Coca Cola, a highly valued drink in India, to everybody who wanted one.

As the dinner went on, a few middle-aged Indians surrounded Kim. They wanted to know who his father was and what his father did for a living, where his family was and what country he called his home.

Looking at them lovingly, Kim sat silent for a while thinking, then answered quietly, "My Master is my father. My Master is my family. My Master is my home." With a sweep of his hand, gesturing towards the Satguru, he then added, "This is my Master." And no matter what the guests asked him, Kim's answer remained the same.

The Indians were soon bored and gave Kim up as a hopeless case, while quite unimpressed by their opinions he continued looking at the Satguru with an expression of awe.

"His physical father is a banker in Hawaii," Elaine quickly explained. "What Kim said just now was from the spiritual angle of vision only."

Four young men in immaculate white outfits, a la Nehru, wearing jeweled clasps on the front of their turbans, sparkling sandals on their feet, observed us with intense interest as we sat there on the grass, unwashed for 2 days, clad in Indian outfits that were rather unclean and by now considerably rumpled.

They briefly surveyed Bob's dusty sandals, then carefully looked at Werter, still unshaven and dressed in Gerald's long, ill-fitting shirt. Barely holding back their laughter, they whispered among themselves.

With limitless compassion, Mira Ji glanced at the four young men, her face presenting a picture of grief and sorrow. Lowering her voice, so as in no way to offend these fine fellows, she told us, "These are not the disciples of our Master. They are rich, proud and beautiful people with big egos which do not let them see the Truth."

Unaffected and quite unconcerned by this small episode, Sushila, in a dirty, heavy diaper, slowly crawled past eight sparkling sandals.

"Truly," remarked Bob smiling wryly, "how relative is everything. To some, we are the 7th wonder of the world, and to others—clowns from some circus."

Silently, Mira Ji got up and left, then settled down on a small knoll away from everybody, and there she remained all alone, barefooted in her white, humble widow's attire, engrossed in her own silent thoughts, unassuming and modest.

How true are the words of the Master, we thought. "There is only one aristocracy, the aristocracy of the Soul," He said, and Mira Ji is a princess of the bluest blood indeed.

Master was sitting on a velvet couch embroidered with red and golden stars. Our host, the lieutenant-colonel, in a blue turban stood behind Him. Holding a microphone with his hand, slightly bending over, he addressed the assembled guests with a few cordial words of introduction.

Next to the Master was seated a noble-looking Sikh in a black jacket. He strikingly resembled the Bronze Boddhisattva on our shelf back in Sawan Ashram.

"This is the local leader of the Radha Swami group," Elaine explained.

Master began talking. The voice of the translator diligently repeated His words in English as Master was speaking in Punjabi.

"The first thing is," said the Satguru, "we should observe truthfulness. What we mean, we should say. What we say, we must mean. Our hearts and tongues and brains should all agree with what we give vent to. This is what is called Truth or truthfulness.

'Master was sitting on a velvet couch.'
Page 214

Next comes humility. Water stays in a place which is low. It may be raining cats and dogs, in torrents; but the water will not stay on a steep place. It means that all good resides in a heart which is lowly, in those who are meek. St. Augustine was asked, 'What is the way back to God?' And he said, 'First humility, second humility and third humility.'

When you are humble, you learn something. When you know you know everything, you are naturally stuck fast in your own self-assumed ignorance, which may be taken as truth.

The third thing is chastity. 'Chastity is life and sexuality is death.' Chastity opens the door of meditation.

The Scriptures tell us that marriage means taking a companion in life who will be with you in the earthly sojourn. You should help each other to know God. One duty may be of begetting children, but it is not all of our duties.

And further, whatever kind of food you take should be a helping factor spiritually. It should be food that does not go to flare up passions within you. You will find that this is generally fruits, vegetables, grains, milk and any products thereof. All meat, fish and eggs should be avoided. All Masters come to advise this.

And last comes selfless service, love for all and love for God.

Man is truly one who lives for the sake of others. If you don't share with others and go on congealing or holding things for your own self, what will be the result? If there is a well from which no water is drawn out, it will give a bad smell. It will not even, I think, be good for drinking. But the water of any well from which the water is taken out profusely is always fresh, and fragrant, too." (47)

As Master rose from the couch, the translator enthusiastically added a thought of his own. "A blueprint for living! That's what Master's talk was all about!"

After a short drive we arrived at a long one-story high building in the shape of a horseshoe surrounding a large courtyard.

Blind people were cautiously leaving this building, checking the path with their canes and slowly walking towards a small podium erected especially for this occasion at one side of the area.

A tall Sikh gentleman talked to our Satguru as both stood in front of it.

We noticed a young woman dressed in a topaz colored saree trimmed generously in silver with a long pigtail falling heavily down to her waistline. She strolled past while inquisitively looking at us.

Carefully observing the blind and not trusting his eyes any longer, Werter questioned her, "Are these the blind people?"

"Yes, this is the colony for the blind," she answered. "My father, who at the moment is talking to Maharaji, built this sanatorium himself. He is director here.

The buildings that you see around you," continued the director's daughter, "are dormitories where the blind live and work. They are taught different trades here. To the right is the main hall, and to the left a hospital."

"Ja, ja, I understand. Es ist ganz klar!"* Gratefully, Werter thanked her. Then his movie camera began shooting the scene as the blind slowly assembled around the podium.

Mounting the few podium steps, Maharaji addressed them thus: "We can see out, but our inner vision is closed. What are we if not blind? The outer ears are open and they hear, but we are deaf to the inner music--the Music of the Spheres. The nectar of Naam is flowing within us, but man is drunk with the taste of the world.

Shamas Tabrez said, 'I have blessed thousands blind from birth with the sight to see God everywhere.'

Many people that lost their sight have been initiated and with such joy they tell how they have seen the rising of the sun inside. If you can see within, it matters little if the outer eyes function or not.

It is unfortunate that very few people are acquainted with this science. It is the oldest of all ancient knowledge, but man has forgotten.

------

*"Ja, ja es ist ganz klar."--Yes, yes it is quite clear.

Whenever the Masters come, they renew the old, old Truth, but when they go, again man forgets until another Master comes to renew the teaching.

The world has never been without a Perfect Master. The law of demand and supply is always at work, and there is food for the hungry and water for the thirsty."

The director thanked our Master and reverently followed Maharaji to the gate as his daughter and staff walked behind him.

The Superior One stopped for a second. "Do the blind have bad karma?" Bob questioned immediately.

"Why?" the Master asked in turn. "They are being helped." And He quietly left the premises.

"Bob, I did not understand Master's reply. Do they have a bad karma?" inquired Werter, but remained without an answer as Bob was following the Master, hoping by chance to ask another question and did not hear Werter's query.

"Ja, ja, bad karma; es ist ganz klar." Werter confidently answered his own question, wound up the camera and climbed into the car ready to go to the leper colony.

Sitting comfortably in the backseat of the Ambassador, Bob prophesied like an ancient Greek oracle in a deep voice, "Be prepared as unavoidable difficulties are hanging over our heads.

I have asked the Master whether there will be any difficulties on the way, and the Satguru said, 'very insignificant ones.' So that means we have to expect something."

Werter glanced at Bob with a feeling of inexpressible fear in his eyes while Mira Ji smiled appreciatively saying, "You've changed, Bob. Indeed, Masters see and know, while we live blindly in subjective worlds of maya."*

The frisky chauffeur followed the Satguru's auto up front. Through the back window we could see Maharaji's head, His white turban and a silken lock of hair resting gently on His neck.

Suddenly, Master's car quivered, proceeded ahead lamely and came to a halt. The back tire was flat, and all the luggage on the roof careened, the ropes tore and the suitcases and bags fell to the ground with a bang.

The spare tire with unimaginable speed crossed over the road to a field and proceeded rolling and jumping ahead as a frightened cow dashed aside, the bell loudly jingling on her thin neck.

Master's chauffeur raced after the tire with such a burst of speed that even sportive Werter himself watched Mohan completely spellbound. Mohan's shirt resembled a sail filled out with a gust of strong wind.

---

*Maya: Delusion.

Hastily leaving the car, Werter pressed one eye to his camera and began taking movies of the Satguru. Hands clasped behind His back, Master stood there tranquilly observing Mohan as he was catching up with the tire.

We joined the introverts, who rested placidly on a plush side knoll, above a ditch, enjoying this unusual darshan as a tall, fragrant bush provided the needed shade.

Tire caught, victoriously Mohan returned and energetically unloaded the trunk in search of a wrench. Blankets, suitcases, bags with food were strewn on the roadside, presenting quite a sight, while a donkey, pulling a creaky cart filled with hay, passed by, the farmer disinterestedly walking next to him.

As Werter's film ran out, he joined us on the hillock while Taiji lovingly distributed flat chapatis to all.

Eating this dry bread, we thoroughly enjoyed the peace of our brief interlude.

Skillfully and quickly changing the tire, Mohan loaded up the trunk as the muffled jingling of the cow's bell again sounded calmly from the silent field.

We drove on, following Satguru's car, and through the back window again we could see Maharaji's head, His white turban and a silken lock of hair resting gently on His neck.

Unexpectedly, the road ended and disappeared under a shallow pond. In its muddy waters, bathing children sprinkled each other playfully and shrieked with delight.

Slowly and cautiously, Master's car entered the water, low, shimmering waves running on both of its sides.

Stopping at the edge of the pond, we all got out, looking to see what would happen to the Master.

In the middle of the shallow body of water, His car careened slightly to one side, probably getting into a side ditch, then came to a halt.

We gasped in horror, immediately rolled up our pants, rushed barefooted through the pond to render help and, pushing the car, in a few minutes had Master safe on the other shore.

Satguru stepped out, smiling, looking more bewitching than ever before. The radiation of His all-encompassing Love was utterly breath-taking, saturating us to the very depths of our Souls and having a wondrous effect as the veils of the mind stopped fluttering in the breeze of desires, and the mind stood still. From behind these veils came heavenly Bliss, incomparable to anything at all in this world. And the heart wished for nothing more than to stay forever in the Bliss of this heavenly Love.

Like bees filled with honey, brimming over with His Bliss, we waded and splashed our way back to our car only to find that the Ambassador was stuck to the bottom of the pond.

As we joyfully pulled, tugged and fumbled around the car, Master stood placidly on the distant other shore looking, watching and waiting.

Slowly, slowly, inch by inch, we pushed the auto towards that blessed shore where the Beloved was patiently waiting.

It took quite some time and quite some effort before we were on the road once again headed towards that dreaded leper colony.

"Yes," Bob said in a deep voice, "you see, the insignificant difficulties have now come true!" Werter grinned with relief.

On both sides of our road stretched endless fields and barren wastelands, nothing but limitless, airy emptiness--a deathscape indeed--when our cars suddenly stopped as our hearts quivered with apprehension.

Master, strong and stately with a brisk, firm walk, was already approaching a small, one-story high building some distance away with a solitary tree growing next to it. Under this tree, lepers were waiting.

In wet clothes spotted with mud, we stood on the road and with trepidation eyed this group of wretched people, who in turn eyed us while waiting, waiting under the solitary tree.

Gerald silently held Sushila on his arm, a dry faraway look on his face. Swen, his mouth slightly open, fixedly watched the lepers. Werter stared as if hypnotized, breath ceased, camera hanging loosely from his shoulder. Fear was heavily stamped upon my face, while Bob looked grim.

"We have nothing to fear," Mira Ji said confidently. "We are under Master's protection. We are the children of the King of Kings.   We should behave like that with humility, dignity and knowing no fear.

We have to acquire this precious habit of following the Master without hesitation no matter where He goes, as this habit will prove to be of paramount importance in the inner planes. Otherwise, the mind will have the upper hand and our progress will be retarded."

Mira Ji left us and with no hesitation whatsoever firmly walked behind the Master over some heavy, dark soil, while Elaine in her rumpled and wet Indian outfit followed her.

Rooted to the ground, we stood close together, shoulder-to-shoulder mustering courage, then feebly trailed behind Elaine until all of us stood face to face with the lepers.

The lepers gently raised their hands in traditional greeting, "God in me greets the God in you," and silently smiled.

Maybe the smile showed a missing tooth and the faces were deformed, maybe some missed feet, some fingers and palms of hands, but in these eyes there was so much humility, so much tenderness, modesty and kindness that the only words appropriate would be, "What beautiful people."

One of them, an exceptionally handsome young man, stood apart, his features perfect, his beard black as tar, his eyes like coals of fire, simmering with hate.

We never looked at him again, as with all his physical beauty, he was frighteningly ugly.

Master entered the small house, which happened to be a hospital, and the local doctor showed us around. Truly speaking, there was nothing much to show as there were only 2 or 3 rooms in this hospital all in all with no equipment whatsoever save one barrel containing some unknown liquid into which the lepers dipped their hands and that was supposed to help them.

We stood around this barrel while the lepers surrounded us on all sides, and once again we were caught in a ring of people, only this time they were gravely ill.

The lepers gazed at us with shining eyes as if they saw before them some kind of angelic vision.

The doctor led us through the colony. The lepers had built for themselves small mud huts that looked like burrows. One could crouch there but not stand up. No doors, no windows, and these were their houses.

It was no surprise that we hadn't noticed these hillocks from the road and had mistaken everything to be just an empty field. With their sick and weak hands, void of muscles, with these fingers that were barely covered with dry scraps of skin through which yellow bones were quite visible, they had cleaned and polished their little village and made it look spick and span. Their kitchen utensils, consisting of a spoon and a cup, were cleaner than the dishes at our medical colonel's house.

The visit was brief, and Master folded His hands in the Indian greeting, "God in me greets God in you," and walked to His car.

We followed the Satguru with heavy hearts and yet with sighs of relief.

The lepers shouted pitifully behind us.

"What is it? What do they say?"

"We are starving. We are starving," Mira Ji sadly translated this sorrowful cry.

Once again the lepers assembled under the solitary tree next to the hospital, a God-forsaken bunch of kind and very weak people. They watched as we were leaving the colony that they had swept and cleaned just for us, and observed how the ray of bright hope dimmed and perished as our cars faded away into the fog of the distance ahead.

We were returning to the world of healthy people, but in our hearts of hearts, we shall forever carry the painful memory of these poor forgotten lepers and of their mournful, heart-rending cry, "We are starving. We are starving!"

We sat silently, each one engrossed in his own thoughts.

Turning to us, Mira Ji said soothingly, "Their souls are just as clean and perfect as ours, and there is no difference between them and us. They, too, can see the Light of God within. Only outside, they are a little bit filthy.

Once Master Sawan Singh initiated a leper who saw the Light of God within, but the Master, taking upon Himself the leper's karma, ever after had a white spot on one of His legs."

"What a tragedy. How awful it is to be a leper," Werter said faintly and sighed in anguish. "This is simply awful. One of them was breathing heavily down my neck!"

"We are under Master's protection," Mira Ji repeated firmly. "We are the children of the King of Kings. We should behave like that with humility, dignity and knowing no fear!"

"Oh, Mira," Werter moaned his voice breaking, "I know all that. You did not understand what I meant. I'm not afraid of anything. Oh, what a nightmare it is to be a leper!" Werter shrank into himself, face pale and drawn, shoulders drooping.

Bob's blue eyes turned grey, or so it seemed to me, as he sat there slumped in his middle seat, a prey to dark misery. "Oh, what a tragedy! How awful it is to be a leper!" Once again Werter spoke almost inaudibly in a hollow voice and stared ahead with a vacant gaze.

Our hearts bled in anguish for the lepers, and for the "spiritual lepers" as Gerald put it, the whole of humanity as well. The "Weltschmertz"* swept through us like the invincible Roman armies and reigned mightily within our souls.

Back at the medical colonel's house breathless and in utter exhaustion, we fell on our beds incapable even of moving a finger.

A knock at the door dispelled our visions of a restful sleep, and our hopes wilted and perished as a voice asked us to come out for a cup of tea. With difficulty, we got up and

____

*Weltschmertz: pain for the whole world over.

meandered into the corridor, wishing for nothing but to somehow get back to our Procrustean beds, which seemed to be almost paradisiacal now, but were told that the Master expected us for darshan.

A pitiful-looking bunch, we settled down in front of the Satguru in the big hall that resembled a temple. There was a church-like night stillness around, hushed and reverent, as subdued and pale light of the chandelier fell from above.

As we gazed weakly into Master's silvery blue eyes, we realized immediately that He was reading us silently, each and every one, like an open book. On His face not a trace of fatigue or exhaustion; in His glance warm compassion and strength.

After a little while, just before the holy darshan was over, Master said with a barely noticeable smile, "Get prepared for Satsang."

As there was still a little time left before Satsang, we finally had our chance to rest. Bob, almost in a state of complete collapse, lay flat on his back drugged with fatigue, resting his blistered feet on the bed railing.

Both of us were immobilized, stiff and mute, like 2 corpses ready for the cremation flames. Through the open window high above, the Indian night, just as black as the young leper's beard, was brooding. Hot, strong and powerful like glowing coals, the stars somberly watched us.

Under Bob's bed lay Gerald's new slippers as Bob's own Indian sandals, purchased at Connaught Circle, had fallen apart a day earlier.

Alas! Gerald's slippers were the wrong size and indeed were the cause of the blisters, I thought wearily.

In the dark corridor I could see Mira Ji as she stood at a big lantern informing those interested about the next day's timetable.

Werter, looking emaciated, appeared from his room, the same German razor as before in his hand as he obstinately refused to give up hope of shaving in India.

Noticing Mira Ji, he quickly approached her and stammered nervously, "Mira, I told you before that a leper breathed heavily down my neck, and now my fingers are numb and it itches under the finger nails!"

Barely holding back her laughter, she answered, "It is your mind that is itching!"

Stunned, with eyes looking like two brown raisins swimming in a sea of surprise, Werter stared at her for a minute, then realizing that she was indeed right, laughed with relief, immediately perked up and plugged in the razor, but the socket refused to be coaxed and continued playing dead.

"Unglaublich!" he then exclaimed in his usual way, looking at that socket in disbelief; then turned around, his back illumined by the lantern, and, as his own flickering shadow led the way, vanished into his room while we fell into a death-like sleep.

A loud knock at the door woke us up.

"It is time now to leave for satsang," I muttered in a debilitated voice while Bob feebly moaned from his corner, "This routine is killing me! I can't take it any longer. This intensity of life is absolutely deadly!"

Weakly, we followed Mira Ji along a dark, narrow corridor to the place of Master's satsang, barely dragging our sandals along the cobblestones of the Ferozepur street.

After a long, long walk, we stopped for a moment at a rather odd-looking building resembling the ancient Roman catacombs. Far below, surrounded with stone walls on all 4 sides, a deep reservoir of water lay calm and silent. This unusual construction was reminiscent of an Egyptian pyramid turned upside down.

Leaving the pyramid behind, we continued our journey along a narrow, winding path passing by turrets, bastions, towers, boulders that fell from somewhere, and lonely arches, that like graceful swans' necks bent pensively over the ancient ruins. The columns like gigantic, black hands stretched to the sky pleading for mercy, stood rugged and somber.

All this fantastic landscape flickered and glittered in the lights of thousands of candles thoughtfully placed everywhere. Truly, an inspiring, unbelievable and quite an unearthly sight!

Turning to the right, we entered an enormous hall filled to capacity with Indians. In the first row, right under the podium, we somehow squeezed in and sat down, cross-legged, as there was no space to stretch out our legs anyhow.

It was a scene bubbling with turbulent life. Tape recorders and microphones were checked; movie cameras buzzed; flash lights flared up like lightning.

On the podium, the Master sat serenely, hands in His lap. Behind Him, knees resting on the plastic air bubbles, Gerald perched with his eyes closed engrossed in meditation. At his left sat Michael and Betty like 2 Bodhisattvas, eyes open, observing the happenings with interest.

Master began His talk in Punjabi.

After 15 minutes both my legs were numb and aching. From the unbearable heat, perspiration ran down soaking the shirt, while some insects were climbing up my back, their little paws moving up and up as cobblestones pierced my knees.

A woman, suddenly and heavily, placed her elbow on my shoulder and propped her head with the palm of her hand. And thus it remained for the duration of the two hour satsang.

At the end of the first hour, Bob turned white as a sheet of paper. Gerald's plastic balloons gave out, and he was forced to straighten his legs, his eyes wide open, face void of expression.

Michael's tall head of hair that looked like a caracul hat had flattened down considerably. Betty continued sitting in the lotus posture with a faded smile and a vacant, dull stare in her eyes, while next to her Swen, head bending low, eyes closed, resembled a silent martyr. Only the sportsman Werter, who sat next to Bob, still continued gazing at the Master with fascination in his almost unblinking eyes.

Satguru's peaceful voice, like the waves of a melodious song, rolled placidly over our heads. This song, strangely hypnotic and strangely familiar, called the Soul to that distant shore where the Beloved was patiently waiting at His radiant gate in the land of Sach Khand, that ineffable Place from whence there is no more returning.

Masterji sang like one intoxicated with Love:

"Sach Khand or the Realm of Truth
Is the seat of the Formless One.
Here He creates all creations,
Rejoicing in creating.
Here are many regions, heavenly
Systems and universes, to count
Which were to count the countless.
Here, out of the Formless,
The heavenly plateaux and all else
Came into form,
All destined to move according to
His Will.
He who is blessed with this vision,
Rejoices in its contemplation.
But, O Nanak, such is its beauty,
That to try to describe it is to
Attempt the impossible." (48)

At 11 p.m. the satsang was over. We walked home through the same ancient ruins feeling like mystical, early Christians returning from a secret meeting just held in these dark caverns and catacombs. "How magnificent it all was!" exclaimed Werter joyfully, eyes shining with delight. "I could not take my eyes from the Beloved Master's beautiful face! I've learned so much, so much today! Oh, how wonderful." He briskly walked ahead of us all, and it seemed that his whole figure glowed with inner light.

We moved through the night silently. Above us stood the black Indian sky; to the left, the ancient catacombs lit up with the thousands of lights; to the right, the mysterious inverted pyramid full of deep, soundless water.

Ahead, Bob limped with his velvet pillow under an armpit, tassels dangling on all sides; in the back, a stray dog followed quietly right behind.

"I am tired." With these words, Bob greeted the beginning of a new day that started with a morning satsang.

A long, winding staircase led to a flat roof resembling a small square where, on a tiny podium, our Master sat. The patdi, the singer Masterji, next to Him, was untying a few knots on the colorful bundle containing the Holy Scriptures of the Sikhs.

Bundle opened, text selected, Masterji began chanting sweetly a hymn from Holy Jap Ji, looking just like a song himself.

"Pilgrimages, austerities, mercy,
        charity and alms-giving, cease
        to be of any consequence, when
        one gets an ingress into the
        Til--the Inner Eye.*
Communion with and practice of the
        Holy Word, with heart full of
        devotion, procures admittance
        into the Inner Spiritual
        Realms, washing away the dirt
        of the sins at the Sacred
        Fount** within.

---

*Til: It literally means the mustard seed.
Here it is used for the ganglion between and
behind the two eyes. Hindus call it Shiv-Netra
or the Third Eye. In the Gospel it is termed as
Single Eye. The Sufis call it Nukta-i-Sweda.
It is the seat of the Soul in man. It is the
first stage, where the Soul collects itself and
is enabled to rise in the higher spiritual
planes.

**Sacred Fount: The Sacred Fount of Nectar in
the Amrit-Saar or Amritsar in man, situated in
Dasam Dwar. The Mohammedans call it Hauz-i-
Kausar and the Hindus term it as Prag Raj. It
is here that the Pilgrim Soul gets its baptism
and is washed clean of all impurities and
regains its pristine purity.

        All virtues are Thine, O Lord,
            I possess not one,
        There can be no worship without
            Practicing the Holy Word.
        From Thee has emanated the Bani or
            the Holy Word, which is the
            Path to salvation;
        Thou art Truth* enchantingly
            Sweet, and my mind yearns
            For Thee." (49)

Master commented, "Good actions, like acts of mercy and charity, although commendable in themselves, do not have an important bearing in the highest spiritual attainment. They cease to be of consequence once the soul begins its inner journey from the 'Til' or the Third Eye.

'If, therefore, thine eye be single, thy whole body shall be full of light.'** Borne along the current of the Word, the soul reaches 'Amrit-Saar' or the Fount of Nectar, the Amritsar in man. There, any impurities that may be still clinging to the soul are finally washed away.

---

*Truth or Sat Naam resides in Sach-Khand, which is the highest of the 5 spiritual planes, where the Formless One dwells.

**Matthew 6:22.

Thus, the soul is made fit for the onward journey to the highest spiritual plane of 'Sach Khand' which is of ineffable greatness and glory." (49a)

The translator vanished somewhere while the Master continued talking in Punjabi to a silent audience.

As we sat in the first row, we had a splendid view of the Master. Once in a while He would lift up His hand to adjust His turban or touch His silken beard with His palm.

"Take a look at Satguru's palm. Can you determine Master's fate?" Bob whispered almost inaudibly.

One indeed could see the lines on Master's palm, but not being a gypsy or a fortuneteller, the significance of the combination of these lines remained a deep mystery to me.

The voice of the translator sounded again behind our backs: "The soul beholds God when it enters into Sach Khand, the highest of the spiritual planes. How can it be otherwise? How can one behold what is pure spirit with these material eyes? One must transcend on the wings of the Word, and one can only do so through His Grace." (51)

In a short while the satsang was over. Masterji lovingly tied a few knots on his little bundle of Holy Books while sweetly singing to himself:

"Exalted is the Lord and exalted
His abode.
More exalted still His Holy Word.
He who reaches His height,
He alone may glimpse Him.
O Nanak, He alone knows His
Greatness; and it is only
His glance of Grace that can
Lift us to His height." (50)

Master left after satsang in the company
of the host.

As we went downstairs, we passed an open
door and beheld the Superior One sitting on a
flowery couch, people crouching all around Him
on the floor listening attentively to His words
of supreme wisdom.

Limping painfully, Bob barely made it to
the colonel's house, and for quite some time
groaned while lying on his thin mattress.

"Bob," I pleaded with concern, "the Master
is back and is expecting us for darshan."

"I can't make it," he almost cried. "I
can't. I have no energy left in me. No energy
left. I need rest! I desperately need rest!"

Nevertheless, though barely able to get
up, he hobbled to the big hall where Maharaji
was waiting in a low armchair. As we sat before
the Master, no questions were asked anymore.
The Westerners were clearly displaying symptoms
of exhaustion and fatigue.

Bob, by now akin to a pale spectre, gazed
at the Superior One, Who in turn observed us one
by one.

Turning to Bob, with a barely visible smile in His all-knowing eyes that twinkled with warm humor, Master asked, "Well, dear friend, did you determine my fate?"

Aghast, eyes bulging in disbelief, breath ceased, Bob flinched away, then froze, mouth open, stricken with dumb perplexity staring at the Master.

Master chuckled. "As you see," He continued, "Master has no rest whether in the ashram or on the tour!"

After these additional words, Bob's face grew as red as fire as he flushed from high emotion. Nervously shivering, he became quite a sight to observe.

Master laughed gently. "Know ye for certain that the essence of all knowledge and wisdom lies in Dhuni.* (51a)

God's bounty is supreme. Magnanimous as He is, He showers His gifts on all alike whether good or bad. All have their share. None is ignored. He knows us all, better than we do, and bestows on us what is the best for us." (52)

Leaning back in His chair, Master fell silent while the muted light filtered through the colored squares and rhombuses of the high stained windows and descended quietly into the chamber below. In the dark and hollow niches, somber statues lurked, secretly watching us with their marble eyes.

----

*Dhuni: Sound principle, Eternal Song, Naam or Word.

The Lieutenant Colonel, sitting humbly to the right of the Master, reverently asked a question in Punjabi to which the Superior One replied in English. "God is Love. The way back to Him is also Love.

It is only with the wings of Love and devotion that we can reach God, and not by intellectual wrestlings and flights of imagination. (51b) This creation is His manifestation. We should love all and everything that lives."

The thought drifted through my mind. "Oh, I can't love cobras. No, I can't."

Master chuckled as He looked at me. "Cobras, too," He said.

When the darshan was over, Bob limped slowly towards our room while I trailed behind him.

Still nervously shivering and frustrated, he dropped onto his bed and complained sadly, "How can one live this way? The Master knows our every thought whether we sit before Him, in our rooms or at a satsang where thousands are present! There is absolutely no privacy here. None! How can one keep a little secret?"

And like Sushila, Bob uttered exclamations, hands propped under his head, elbows sticking out from both sides of the flat pillow, then sighed again.

Listening to Bob's sad wailing, I could not get up to help him as my back gave out once again, while Master, without rest, without any trace of exhaustion, full of life, Love and compassion, with boundless energy continued doing God's work.

Toward evening, a bit rested, Bob arose. However, crying "I can't get up" I remained lying on 2 mattresses and 1 quilt while Bob doggedly hobbled out the door and left for satsang.

All the noises in the house died out as everyone left, and it became heavenly quiet. In the deep silence of the room only the ancient clock marked time with the sound of old age in its voice.

Suddenly, I fancied that between the ceiling and the wall in a huge cobweb an enormous vampire was lying in wait. He hung there, ominous, silent and motionless, looking fixedly with his almost human eyes straight at me.

I took a deep breath, returned its gaze and realized with horror that this monster was no fancy but an enormous spider hanging right above me, as big as a human fist. Hairy legs surrounded its bloated body covered with thick, rusty fur. Two long claws, or maybe fangs, protruded from its black, slimy mouth.

As we stared at each other, my voice vanished.

"None can die before the allotted time. Noone can live one second after the sands of time run out. The script of one's life is already written, and noone can change his fate, save the Master, and if this is the time, and this is my fate, then most certainly death is staring into my eyes at this moment."

As these words of the Master shot throu_ my mind, I thought, "Be brave!" but was petrified with overpowering fear.

"Fear not!" I sternly commanded myself once again and again but failed.

Fixedly, we continued looking at each other as Bob's comment to Werter came back to me: "We believe in a lot of things, but can we live up to them? That is the question."

Helplessly, the lights flickered in the colonel's house and went off in another blackout. Cold perspiration in large, moist drops oozed out on my forehead, while in the stillness--magnified by pitch darkness--the clock, indifferent and unconcerned, creaked on in her aged voice counting time.

Meanwhile, along the winding streets Mira Ji led the others in our party on the way to Master's satsang that was to take place in a Sikh Gurudwara. Werter followed her firmly and energetically. Bob hobbled weakly behind, Gerald's sandals on his blistered, painful feet, and Elaine walked at the back of the procession.

In the dense night, the structures, the houses with their stucco mouldings, the street itself illumined only by the pale rays of the moon, the lonely clapping of a loose window shade against the peeling walls--all that was like a weird setting in an old movie dealing with a nonexistent world.

Entering a large and beautiful Gurudwara, everyone settled down on the floor, turbans on the right, sarees on the left.

Master was surrounded by patriarchs, looking like Biblical holy men of yore: white turbans, white attire, dark, noble faces, dark, silent eyes.

Satguru talked on the absolute importance of having a Living Master, as to cross Sarm Khand, the mental world or the realm of ecstasy, is not so easy." He said,

"It is the most delusive world, where even the Mahatmas and the Rishis with all their learning and tapas, fail to hold on to their own ground. What is there in that vast universe which Brahman would not like to offer to those earnest souls who try to escape through his domains and reach the True Home of their Father! At every step, be it in the physical world, the astral or the mental, he tries to block the way of the aspiring souls.

The great Prophets and Messiahs and all others have given their experiences of the fierce encounters that they had with Satan, Mara, Ahriman; the evil spirits, Asuras, Demons and their agents in countless ways, fair or foul, whereby they try to obstruct the way, to win over the seekers after Truth by assurances of worldly kingdoms and principalities; and if they do not succumb to these temptations, then by threats of violence by fire, thunder, earthquakes, heaven-splittings, cloud-bursts, lightnings and what have you.

It is in predicaments like these that one can only stand these trials and tribulations when one has by his side his Guru or Murshid, for the Guru-Power then draws and absorbs the disciple's soul into Himself and takes him along the Path of Ringing Radiance.

For each soul, the Brahman stakes his all and does not yield, unless he is convinced that the seeker clings to the protection of the Master-Power (Akal or Timeless).

Do we not see even in the material world that the rulers and governments of one state seal their borders to prevent unauthorized emigration of their subjects, and devise laws to control such outflow?

Great indeed is the power of Time, and none can conquer it, and yet Time itself is in mortal dread of the Timeless Music lest he himself may get lost in the Divine Harmony." (53)

Back in the house of the lieutenant colonel, the lights suddenly flickered and came on.

I looked up with boundless horror, but to my immense relief, the spider was gone. Only the silky cobweb continued swaying lightly in the breeze of the rejuvenated fan.

The sounds of human voices suddenly filled the premises as everyone returned from satsang. Bob limped into the room tired, happy and pale. Throwing off Gerald's sandals he said, "It was beautiful. It was simply beautiful!" and immediately fell asleep.

In the morning cascades of rusty water flowed explosively from the bathroom faucet. We washed our faces in its bubbling coolness.

Bob decided to do some investigative work in the corridor and opened the door just as the Master was passing by. "I see you still have a little energy left," smiled the infallible Satguru, "and I am going strong!" Master left as He had to visit the murderer incarcerated in the Ferozepur jail.

Quickly closing the door, Bob stepped back completely forgetting the scouting attempt. Sitting on the edge of the bed, he sighed, "Did you hear that? Just yesterday I said in private that there was no energy left in me, and even that little Master knew!"

After a short pause, Bob stated, "There is positively no privacy here, and the only way to live around the Master is to repeat simran* all the time so no thoughts are left in one's head for the Master to read! And maybe that is exactly what Maharaji is teaching us in this particular way: 'Repeat simran, as simran brings one's attention from the circumference to the center of one's being, where, as we well know, the path begins.'"

After a long period of silence, Bob continued, "Just imagine! Mira Ji told me that Master sleeps only 1 or 2 hours a night. How can He work like that day and night, month after month, year after year with just 1 hour of sleep?

Incredible! Absolutely incredible! Can you understand anything? I certainly can't."

----

*Simran: Five charged words.

After missing the events of a whole day, we appeared at the evening darshan in the big hall of the lieutenant colonel's house and settled down in front of the Master. It was quite obvious that we Westerners were continuing to fall apart rapidly at the seams, like Bob's Indian sandals. Even Elaine had dark circles under her eyes, what to say about the rest of us.

But Master sat there strong and magnificent, glowing in His Divine Mystery completely beyond any mortal comprehension. His Godly aura of loving-kindness and mercy enveloped each and every one of us. Sitting on the rug at His holy feet, we gazed up at Him in awe.

"Sir, at the previous morning satsang you said that salvation can only be achieved through His Grace. What can I do to win Your Grace?" Bob asked in a subdued voice.

"Don't complain!" answered the Master. The holy darshan continued to the very end in total silence.

Back in our room sitting in the solitary, splendid chair next to the bathroom, Bob mused, "That Master knew of my complaints does not astound me in the least. A Godman, being One with Almighty God, is omniscient and omnipotent.

But when Master said, 'Don't complain,' it seems to me that He gave advice to everyone of us to take to the path of self-surrender to the Divine Will and become like the perfect disciple, Bhai Bhikari.

Whatever happens in one's life, be it hunger, misery, pain or pleasure, everything should be accepted as a gift from the Beloved, coming as a welcome remedy for our shortcomings.

Perfection is the goal of human life, as we know, and whatever is needed to achieve this goal will be given: pain or pleasure. So, as Master said, don't complain as God is chiseling out of the rough stone, which we are at present, something that is precious, pure, rare and sterling—a perfect man.

That was a rough leson," Bob finished, and neither complained, sighed nor groaned any more.

As the time of the night satsang approached, we left the colonel's house and settled in the car while repeating simran.

Leaving the city of Ferozepur behind, we drove out a distance on a cement road, then turned right to a bumpy dirt road. The frisky chauffeur lessened the speed.

Bouncing up and down on our back seats, we listened to Mira Ji: "The satsang will be held in an open field tonight," she filled us in, "closing Master's itinerary for Ferozepur. Tomorrow morning after initiation we all leave for Amritsar."

We were quite overjoyed and could hardly wait as once again we would drive along the peaceful roads of rural India and rest while passing lands and fields.

The Ambassador stopped a short distance away from a large field where again thousands upon thousands of people had assembled to listen to the words of the Saint.

We settled way back of the crowd on a flat
boulder, a barbed wire fence stretching on our
left, feet resting in the soft earth.

It was dark below, and it was dark above
and amidst this darkness Master's podium,
brilliantly lit up, stood out as a shining focal
point.

Maharaji sat in a lotus posture at the
front edge of the platform dressed in His usual
white outfit as lights streamed at Him from all
sides. The Superior One was the glowing center
of all this bright, fiery mandala.

Quietly His amplified voice rolled towards
us: "Communion with the Holy Naam—the Divine
Word—together with meditation on His Glory, is
the open sesame," said the Satguru, "to the
realization of the One Being.

Word is the substance and the power by
which all life is made. Holy communion with its
rapturous strains is a gift that can be attained
only through a Living Master.

In His company, a life of holy inspiration
and love of God is followed, and the Inner Eye
is opened to see the Presence of God in all
things. A True Master is not a mere human
being, but has become One with God, and as such
contains in Himself the powers of all the gods
and goddesses. He is veritably the Word made
flesh and blood.

The one lesson that such a Master teaches
His disciples is to meditate always upon the
Lord, the Creator of everything, and never to
forget Him." (53a)

Masterji chanted, "He is the
Supreme Master and does what
He Lists.
He is the King of Kings,
The Almighty Lord, and ours,
O Nanak, is only to abide by
His Will." (53d)

As the Master talked, the pale moon in her silvery armor and the hosts of her sparkling knights stood transfixed in the highest heavens caught by the sight of the King of all possible Kings.

When back in the colonel's house, we packed our suitcases preparing for tomorrow's trip while the clock on top of the spiderlegged table talked to us in its wise, ancient voice.

Early in the morning, we sat in a large courtyard under a canopy, surrounded by walls, repeating simran and waiting for the initiation to start.

As usual Master sat on the podium leaning forward and penetratingly looked at His future disciples, among whom we noticed our host, the lieutenant colonel.

Then the Satguru walked among the rows of silent people, head slightly bent as if listening to something. Once in a while, Master would stop and motion somebody to leave.

All that was not surprising. By now, we had started to understand at least a little something, although the working power behind all these events was still hidden from our eyes by a thick, impenetrable veil.

After the hour-long meditation was over, Maharaji said, "Leave off, please. Who saw the Radiant Form of the Master within? Please stand up."

More than one-third of the assembled people stood up, while the others reported that they were on the way to the second plane of creation. And that, too, was no surprise. Rather, like Werter, we would have been utterly perplexed if it had been any different.

Leaving the initiation grounds, we lingered on the square, watching Master's podium being taken apart and preparing to get into our Ambassador.

The crowd surrounding us suddenly gave way, and in the narrow opening, Master appeared. As He slowly approached us, we bowed, overjoyed.

Master looked at us, smiled, softly folded His hands and said, "God bless you all," then walked towards His car.

"AS THOU ORDAINETH, SO DO WE RECEIVE.

THOU ART IMMANENT IN ALL,

AND NOTHING IS WHERE THY WORD IS NOT.

WHAT POWER HAVE I TO CONCEIVE OF

THY WONDERFUL NATURE?

TOO POOR AM I TO MAKE AN OFFERING

OF MY LIFE TO THEE.

WHATEVER PLEASETH THEE IS GOOD.

THOU ART FOREVERMORE, O FORMLESS ONE!"

_____Jap Ji

CHAPTER SEVEN

AMRITSAR

Leaning back in our comfortable seats once again, we enjoyed undisturbed, unhurried life, a cool breeze, basked in sights of peaceful pastures and gazed at shepherds who looked like sages of times gone by.

We passed a flock of large, green parakeets, noisily perched on a big, branchy tree. Below, lilies and white lotuses grew among heart-shaped thick leaves in a wide ditch full of dark water. A monkey eagerly quenched its thirst crouching on the sandy edge. Two bare-footed, saffron-clad yogis, staffs in their hands, black hair falling to their shoulders, eyes glowing with inner power, quietly passed them by.

The chauffeur honked as an enormous elephant blocked our way. On its back sat a whole family under a colorful, silken palanquin. The elephant slowly gave way and stepped to the side as we drove cautiously by.

Returning to the middle of the road, the elephant, like a noble maharaja, continued plodding ahead unhurriedly, lifting its heavy feet one by one. Werter, spellbound, looked out the back window, a half-eaten banana in his hand, until the elephant completely vanished from sight.

"Werter, why do you always eat these bananas? You will turn into a monkey towards the end of this trip," I laughed.

"Because," was his thoughtful answer, "if one wants to stay healthy in India, one should eat bananas, as all the filth is peeled off with the skin, and the fruit inside is sanitary and spotlessly clean." And he bit into the sanitary product with all of his white teeth.

"When Elaine came to the ashram," Mira Ji began, smiling at us, "after a short time she got sick. The doctor discovered a large tumor in her abdomen."

"Oh," Elaine exclaimed with boredom, "you've told this story so many times already!"

"So what? It is a good story." Mira Ji laughed heartily and continued. "The doctor said an operation was a must if Elaine wanted to live. Yet Master advised her to wait until He returned from a tour.

In a week, the surgeon after another examination said that it looked so bad that Elaine had no time to wait. Yet Elaine continued waiting for the Master to return from His 2 weeks' trip.

When He did get back, the Satguru advised her to wait with the operation still longer until He returned from His next impending tour.

This time when He arrived at the ashram again the surgeon was called in immediately. He checked Elaine thoroughly and for quite some time, and to his utter surprise found no tumor!"

Both girls looked at us with the happiest possible expressions on their faces when abruptly we stopped at a railroad track. The guard rail was down.

Werter, getting out of the car, exercised with precision; then approaching a hawker, who stood next to the roadblock with his small tray on wheels, bought bananas for 1 rupee while Bob purchased oranges that looked dwarfed and green. Thus, our trip came to a pleasant halt, and we comfortably stretched our stiff legs on a green hillock just off the main road.

The chauffeur plucked a blade of grass, lay down on his back, hands behind his head, legs one on top of the other, chewed the blade and gazed into the wild, blue yonder where almost invisibly a silver plane was crossing the sky leaving behind a fluffy, cloudy trail.

All around us stretched fields and meadows from horizon to horizon, where the far-off, snow-capped mountains looked pale blue in the windless heat. On nature's plush, emerald carpet here and there, tall and slender cypresses stood like soldiers on guard. A few dark poplar trees were artistically scattered around.

Not a human soul was in sight, as far as we could see. Not even a cow! The summer day snoozed as if enchanted, while the fiery globe of the sun imperceptibly moved along its pre-destined path.

A red bird with an orange beak twittered, entranced, "Kabir, Kabir, Kabir" as if piping her praises of this great Indian Saint, while the diligent cricket orchestra provided a cease-less accompaniment for her song of faithful love.

In that precious, rare solitude, far from the noise of the world, its haunting passions, martyrdoms of vanities and greed, lost in the vastness of nature, pampered generously with the rays of the Eastern sun—in this undisturbed, primordial stillness, it seemed that some mysterious powers suddenly stirred within the depth of one's soul. And like the beautiful red bird in love with Kabir, the soul began singing in happy surrender:
> "Oh Master, Thou art a
> 'Type of the wise, who soar,
> But never roam;
> True to the kindred points of
> Heaven and Home.' (53b)
> 'Thou art the pilgrim's Path,
> The blind man's Eye,
> The dead man's Life.
> On Thee my hopes rely.
> If Thou remove, I err,
> I grope, I die.
> Disclose Thy sunbeams;
> Close Thy wings and stay.
> See, see how I am blind,
> And dead and stray,
> Oh, Thou, that art my Light,
> My Life, my Way.'"*

Time passed. The train was not in sight. Bananas and oranges were eaten.

---

*Francis Quarles.

"Well," said Mira Ji, and smiled with a rare mixture of humor and shyness, "Why not tell you one more story?

Once upon a time, there lived a Saint in India, who had a disciple. This disciple rose to Dasam Dwar, where he washed all his karmas away, and then believed that he had become a Saint himself!

Leaving his venerable teacher, he became an independent Guru. People flocked to him. He would take upon himself their karmas, rise to Dasam Dwar and wash them off.

Once a tuberculosis patient came to him. Again, he took the illness upon himself and went to the inner Amritsar. But his venerable teacher blocked the way and sent him back. This self-styled Guru died from T.B., as he could not wash the sickness off anymore."

"Why was he so severely punished?" Werter asked with regret.

"You see, Werter, only a Perfect Master who has reached the 8th plane of creation, like our Satguru, knows the Absolute Truth, the whole ray of Creation from the beginning to the end. Everyone else, who has not reached at least the 5th plane, Sach Khand, will still be subject to the different degrees of delusion.

Such people, believing--in their ignorance--that they are doing good, perform evil unintentionally. Not only do they harm themselves, but others, too. And that is why it is not wise to disobey a Perfect Master, you see.

I'll tell you another case to illustrate that point. It happened to our own Master.

A very young disciple of our Satguru could see the past and the future, like we see the present moment—just that clearly. His brother, who was spiritually dense and absolutely undeveloped, decided to use his relative's powers in the stock market and told his brother to get ready for a trip.

Satguru appeared to this young disciple 3 times from within, ordering him to stay away from the market. However, the boy disobeyed, and the brothers became well off financially. But the powers to see the future dimmed and vanished to the great chagrin of the boy.

So this youngster came to me, and begged with tears in his eyes to ask Master's forgiveness and restore his inner sight.

It took me quite a while to get Satguru's consent. As the boy fell at Master's feet, he was told, 'I have warned you 3 times from within, and you disobeyed. Now I will awaken your powers again, but you will defy the orders once more."

Wholeheartedly, the boy promised the Master to keep His commandments from there on, but fell at the first temptation. Master drew the curtain over his powers, and now he does not even see the Light!"

In the distance, a muffled whistle sounded. Instantly, we rose to our feet and strolled to the roadblock, listening with fascination to the almost inaudible rumbling of wheels and puffing of the train's engine, getting louder and louder as time ticked on.

First in sight was an ancient locomotive, followed by a long, noisy caravan of splattered freight cars.

Passing us by, it spouted glowing red and golden sparks from its funnel. Then a clear whistle rippled the sleepy air in a friendly 'hello.'

When the sounds of the spinning wheels and the vision itself dimmed and died in the distant mists, we continued looking trying to catch at least a faint trace of it.

The chauffeur yawned, got up from the grass and leisurely settled behind the steering wheel as all of us waited for the rail block to go up. We waited and waited, but the railblock remained down.

"So was! Unglaublich!" exclaimed Werter, staring in disbelief at the lifeless rail.

"Oh, dear Werter!" I thought, shaking from inner laughter.

"Oh, dear German Andre Stoltz,* when in the nineteenth century you visited the large Russian estate of 'Oblomowka' and faced its sluggish, lazy life, your practical, efficient German nature could absolutely not comprehend it. Yet it took you, Andre, to save 'Oblomowka' from inevitable bankruptcy.

---

*Andre Stoltz was a fictional character in the novel "Oblomowka" by I. Goncharov in the nineteenth century.

And today again in the twentieth century, you are facing the same type of life, and with the same result, only in another land, in another place and with another name--Werter Meinhardt."

I leaned forward and peeked at him from the corners of my eyes and heartily enjoyed Werter's perplexed face.

Eventually from nowhere, a sleepy, dishevelled figure appeared, pulled the rope, and the railguard groaned as it went up.

"Oh," I sighed with sincere regret, "why, oh, why, did all that wonder have to end so very quickly!" We were back on the road to Amritsar.

Suddenly, I felt feverish and shivered. My temperature climbed. The chauffeur refused to close the window. My head buzzed like a beehive, and we were still far, far away from Amritsar.

"In Amritsar, you will see the sacred Golden Temple of the Sikhs, standing in the midst of a pool of water," said Mira Ji, and her words proved to be prophetic as our Master sent us all to tour the temple a bit later.

The lively talking in the car seemed to go on endlessly. One hour dragged after another. Disinterestedly, I slumped in the back seat as my health declined.

Finally, our Ambassador turned in to the city of Amritsar and stopped at a wide gate leading into a large ashram courtyard. With difficulty, I got out of the car, leaning against its side as everything seemed to sway.

AMRITSAR

We stood some distance away from the Master Who was addressing a big crowd that filled the courtyard. Motioning everyone to continue sitting, Master got up and walked firmly towards the Westerners.

"Go and rest immediately as you are over-tired and sick," He ordered.

Hands folded, we bowed while the Satguru returned to the wicker chair and from there on satsang continued undisturbed as the Westerners were swiftly driven away. "At least we were present for His Holy Darshan," Bob sighed.

The Ambassador stopped just a few yards away from the ashram in front of a millionaire's mansion which occupied a lordly space. The facade was covered with a variety of intricate, ingenious architectural inventions suggestive of excessive wealth.

The lush garden, behind a tall, white wall, presented a lovely picture. Everything here was luxuriant, blossoming and aromatic, intended to please the most exquisite taste. The trees stood solemnly in carefully planned designs. Bushes were scattered around, a path twining amidst them like a golden thread, while different flowers arranged in esthetic bouquets enlivened the landscape, and one could enjoy this exotic orchard as one would enjoy a painting in the Louvre or at Versailles.

We entered the mansion where spacious halls were silent and cool, the decor pleasantly simple. There were numerous rooms and corridors here, staircases, balconies and bathrooms, too. It was a beautiful place to stay.

An excellent large room was assigned to us. Thick shutters closed the wide windows. An elegant fan worked noiselessly above. The sun was excluded from this chamber, and it felt inside like a perpetual, quiet evening.

A table surrounded by stylish chairs stood gracefully on a colorful Persian rug. Two beds with soft mattresses and fluffy pillows rested at opposite walls.

As I dropped onto the bed, I felt sure I had reached the end of my rope.

"Tile!" exclaimed Bob in surprise, as he peeked into the adjacent bathroom. "It is all sparkling clean here. There is a tub, a sink and a toilet, too!"

Sharing his joy with me, he continued, "Finally, oh, finally, I can take a bath and soak in a tub!" Grabbing a towel, he instantly disappeared behind the open door.

In a few minutes he reappeared, just as dirty as before, a disillusioned expression on his haggard face as he reported, "The tub is not connected to the plumbing. The toilet is clogged, and the pipe under the leaking sink is just one foot long. Wash your hands, and you will get a free bonus as your feet will be washed at the same time. The water floods the floor and disappears somewhere into an opening in the wall. We'll have to wait for a bath until we are back in America!"

Pensively, he stood there with an American cotton towel in his Yankee hands, clad in a long Indian shirt that looked as if for a whole century some elderly spinster had dusted her moldy closet with it. Then he said, "Maybe it is not that bad after all as many of these gadgets in the West made us weak and dependent turning us into slaves of comforts.

At the beginning of the trip, if you remember, Mira Ji told us that the Westerners are weak people and cannot cope with difficulties."

With determination Bob abruptly turned around, and once again vanished into the bathroom. The faucet clanked and snarled as hideous sounds shot from the rusty plumbing, coarse blasts and ghoulish screeching rang from behind the bathroom door and triumphantly echoed along the mansion halls as water gurgled and splashed. Bob was washing Indian-style.

My temperature continued to rise rapidly while slowly everything greyed and blurred. In spite of Bob's desire to stay with me, we decided that it would be wiser for him to attend satsang. Uneasy and worried, Bob left.

I thought, "Didn't Christ say, 'If you pray to God, He may give it to you or not give it to you. If you pray to God in my name, He may give it to you. But if you pray to me, you'll surely have it." (53c)

Eyes closed, I prayed to the Master, "Oh, Satguru, please grant me health just for one more day. Let me come to your last satsang and then have your darshan just one more time! One day, one day, one day." Over and over again I deliriously repeated the words.

"Master's orders!" a cheerful voice brought me back to consciousness as I opened my eyes.

"Master's orders!" repeated Mohan as he stood there in the middle of the room, a large tray in his hands.

"Master's orders!" he exclaimed once again, and put the tray with a tea kettle, a cup and biscuits onto the table top. "Master said, 'She is very, very sick. Take this tray to her. She has to drink up the tea and eat up the biscuits.' Parshad! Parshad!" Mohan rejoiced.

Bowing, hands folded and grinning happily, Mohan left the room.

I forced myself to get out of bed and settled in front of the tray of parshad. Sipping and eating, eating and sipping, my tears like raindrops mixed with the tea.

Where in the world would one find such compassion, such flawless warm love and such concern? How is it that the Beloved Master, having thousands upon thousands of disciples, knows who went and who did not go to satsang? How can He know who is sick and who is healthy?

Sobbing, I drank parshad tea, ate Master's crisp, round cookies while understanding remained beyond me.

The tea was finished, cookies eaten to the last one when suddenly I realized that the fever was gone and my legs once again felt quite normal.

The wave of health continued, surging up and up and up, till my whole body felt completely well. Just my head remained a little fuzzy. Then, in a flash, as if someone had pulled off a woolen cap, the sickness was gone, and gone without a trace!

Thunderstruck, in awe, I gasped, immediately got up, walked around on the Persian rug and stretched. There was no sign of illness remaining anywhere, no pain, not even a twitch!

Completely healed and well all over! My gratitude knew no bounds.

"A cause for a feast!" Thinking thus, I jubilantly entered the beautiful, tiled bathroom and celebrated by washing my dusty face in the clear, cool water. Bubbling out from the one-foot long pipe under the sink, the water poured onto my dirty feet, and I felt better than the Mogul Emperor Shah Jahan as he feasted while triumphantly surveying his fabulous riches.

Bob returned from the satsang quite worried, and opening the door stared in utter disbelief as he saw me sitting in the stylish chair in front of an empty tray, healthy, happy, clean and grinning as wide as Mohan.

After I told him what had happened, Bob exclaimed in utter wonder, "Who can comprehend such Power? Who can sing of such greatness!"

Graciously, Maharaji fulfilled the last part of the prayer as well. In the early morning hours, we were present at His Holy Satsang.

The rays of the emerging sun meekly trickled through the green foliage from the sapphire sky softly playing on the colorful turbans and sarees, glowing warmly on the rims of Gerald's spectacles, and gently sliding down

Werter's back. Bob in his newly washed, rumpled Indian shirt sat in the shade of the ashram wall on his velvet, tasseled pillow.

The Superior One spoke thus: "There is a hymn of Guru Nanak in which he presents a vivid picture of the world drifting into illusion and oblivion, and how the individual can be rescued from this drastic plight, if he so wishes. (54) So Guru Nanak describes it as a vast, dangerous ocean containing mighty breakers and treacherous whirlpools. And what is the cargo of the ships that sail in this ocean? Poison!--and every ship overladen with it. One can picture each physical form as a ship or a boat drifting aimlessly on the vast ocean of life laden with the poison of Maya (55) (delusion).

Birth upon birth, he tosses about in the storms of life. Sometimes the soul goes under; sometimes it rises to the surface; but it can see no end to this existence. One knows nothing of the past, or of what will happen in the future. One is just going wherever the current carries one. The ocean of mind contains limitless waves upon waves. Sometimes they are waves of enjoyment, sometimes of anger or lust or greed, attachment and ego. (56)

Man is pushed from pillar to post. We are drenched in whatever color that comes along-- dancing to the tune of the moment, saturated in forgetfulness. God is forgotten; self is forgotten. We just drift along aimlessly. This condition is terrifying. (57)

And who can see this true condition of affairs? Only he who stands on the edge, for he who is drifting is not conscious of what is happening, has no awareness of what is to come. Learned or illiterate, rich or poor, cultured or uncouth, yet all are in the same position. (58)

Masters come into the world. They see the souls in these dire straits. (59) They stand on the edge, you see.

On board a ship, two things are most necessary: a captain and some radar or equipment to guide the ship away from rocks and shoals. Without these, what hope is there of saving the ship? (60)

He (God), who has given salvation to millions, will bring us to the feet of the Guru, who places this tiny boat of ours on the mighty ship of Naam. On very large ships, many tons of wood, iron or stone can be carried without any danger of the ship sinking; so the Guru puts you on a spiritually unsinkable ship, and he himself is the captain. (60a)

So know that if you meet a True Guru, you have met the Lord. He is not only a Guru, but a messenger from God come to take you back to Him. Go wherever he leads you. If you obey him, you will become what he is. If not, if your mind steps in and interferes, you will not be able to get anywhere near him.

Those who have met a Perfect Master are greatly blessed. Those who have not should go and search until they find one, for this is not a theoretical subject but one of practice, to rise above the mind and senses. (61)

Only an experienced person can give an experience of higher knowledge. If one desires an experience of the Truth itself, it can only be experienced through one who is experienced in Truth. This law has ever been and ever will be." (62)

Master finished His talk, and the translater added cheerfully, "Sail on the Satguru's ship!"

Bob smiling at the translator said, "And with the breeze of His Love filling out the sails of our souls, on the frigate of Naam, we shall sail safely back to our Heavenly Home."

I pondered, "When Ivan Goncharov's around-the-world trip on the frigate Pallada came to an end and he returned back to St. Petersburg after 3 years of absence, so, too, will our incredible trip around the cosmos come to its inevitable end as we sail on the Satguru's ship back home to Sach Khand after eons and eons of exile."

"The prodigal son of God, the soul," Bob continued his thought, "thus will return home. What greater luck could one imagine?" And he warmly thanked the translator, who in turn nodded his head in full agreement.

Satsang over, everyone went where one desired, while a small crowd followed the Master as He crossed the courtyard. When passing us, the Satguru lifted His head and looking straight at me asked with an all-knowing smile, "How is your health today?"

"Oh, Sir!" I exclaimed with great emotion, "only with Your Grace am I completely well!   I don't know how to thank You." Master chuckled almost imperceptibly while I bowed deeply before Him.

Maharaji, the Superior One, motioned us to come with Him to His darshan inside the ashram on the second floor.

There again, we sat before the Master, basking in the Bliss of His Holy Presence.

Satguru spoke thus: "No Perfect Saint has ever failed His disciples. Realize fully, this one will not fail you. Think deeply upon this rare privilege. A Divine Dispensation has been granted to you. Master is not the body. He is the Power functioning through the body, and He is using His body to teach and guide man." (63)

"Satguru," Bob said, worried and almost inaudible, "spiritually we are quite undeveloped. Our inner progress is so very small, and we are never up to the mark. We are simply unworthy."

The Superior One smiled, "What are you worried about? You are safe!"

In a delighted mood, we left after the darshan was over. Mira Ji caught up with us in the courtyard. "Maharaji wishes that we should go and visit the Holy Temple of the Sikhs," she said.

Noone wanted to go there save Bob, who was quite willing and overjoyed; yet Mira Ji herself seemed reluctant and Werter looked bored. But Master's wishes are orders, and we all drove off, our sighs enlivening the drab atmosphere in the car.

Bob chuckled. "Back in Sawan Ashram," he recalled, "Mira Ji told us how the building of the Golden Temple of the Sikhs in Amritsar started, and when accomplished became a replica of the unearthly heavenly white and gold temple that Guru Ram Das beheld in Dasam Dwar as he stood there on the shores of the wondrous Lake of Nectar. I remember thinking then how thrilling it would be to see even this replica. And now, as you see, this wish was granted!" And Bob laughed with a few undefinable emotions in the tone of his voice.

Stopping in the middle of a square, we approached a tall, impressive arch. Standing under it, we beheld a deep blue lake as smooth as the sky above, sparkling amidst an array of buildings.

In the center of it towered a magnificent temple. On the white marble walls of the first floor rested the golden walls of the second floor, all covered with tracery, fretwork and mosaic. A narrow walk led around the temple with a delicate balustrade on one side, while its golden domes, large and small, shone and glittered in the rays of the sun reflecting in a watery mirror the white and pale blue marble sidewalk also seemingly afloat in these placid waters of the earthly Lake of Nectar, the Amritsar.

Leaving our shoes at the arch, we descended a long marble staircase to the blue and white marble sidewalk which surrounded the lake. The pavement was as hot as silver ready to melt.

'Its golden domes, large and small,
shone and glittered in the rays of the sun.'
Page 266

In the pool a few grown-ups and noisy children were taking a dip. Observing them attentively, Bob exclaimed, "My goodness, they really believe that one can wash off inner sins with outer water!"

"So was!" Werter said in unison, looking at the wet, happy faces.

After walking around the lake, we finally stood in front of a long, narrow bridge leading across the blue, shimmering waters to the temple itself. Another splendid, golden arch guarded the entrance to the bridge, the arch being a magnificent work of art. In its deep, golden niches were sayings from the Holy Scriptures carved out in salient, golden letters. In the shade of the arch, a few people were sitting, heads bowed in reverent supplication.

After Werter and Bob put handkerchiefs on top of their heads, in place of non-existent turbans, we were permitted to enter the temple itself where we were greeted with fantastic Eastern luxury. Walls, floors and ceilings were covered with exquisite carvings, bas-reliefs, mosaic tracery, and everything was done in the finest taste imaginable. Verily a divine sight!

A noble patriarch sat in an alcove, a large book--the Adi Granth Sahib--lay opened before him. In a voice soft and melodious, he chanted the sacred hymns of the Sikhs.

"In this Adi Granth," whispered Mira Ji, "the sayings of Saints of a number of religions are collected. The Truth, as you well know, is one and the same, and whosoever realizes it says one and the same thing.

'They really believe that one can wash off
inner sins with outer water!'
Page 267

'In the shade of the arch, a few people
were sitting.'
Page 267

How can there be any difference? In the Adi Granth are collected the utterings of the Mohammedans, Hindus and Sikh Saints. And each and every one of them sings the praises of the all-powerful Naam."

Going one flight up, we found another noble-looking Sikh sitting in front of a smaller-size Granth softly chanting the holy words of Truth. Bob went further up and later reported the temple had 5 floors in all and on each one of them was another patriarch singing from an ever smaller book.

Fascinated, I gazed through the windows at the paradisiacal sights in front. Probably, I thought, we have all landed in heaven if not even somewhere better than that.

Reverently Mira Ji whispered, "This chanting from all of the 5 Adi Granths never stops. Only the patdi, the singer, changes, yet the singing itself goes on and on 24 hours a day, day after day, month after month, year after year, ceaselessly, endlessly, and forever it will continue going like that."

Very happy with our visit to the Golden Sacred Shrine of the Sikhs, we disembarked at the gates of our host's mansion. Mira Ji left to see the Master, and when she returned, informed us that the orders were to go back to Sawan Ashram as no more houses of millionaires or lieutenant colonels were forthcoming on the last leg of Master's tour as Maharaji was about to visit simple villagers living in mud huts out in the fields somewhere.

Our little group, rather the worse for wear, once again stood in front of the cars on the street between the ashram wall and the mansion waiting and wondering whether the Satguru would come out to bid us goodbye.

Sushila on all fours crawled along the road in a wet diaper and shrieked loudly. Swen was blowing his nose, flaxen hair disheveled, deep blue eyes full of pain. Kim was shaking with fever. Michael was ravaged by bloody dysentery, being nauseous all the time. Bob looked haggard, his legs having developed more bruises and blisters from touring the Shrine of the Sikhs. All Westerners had physically collapsed, except the sportive conductor Werter and me with the Grace of the Satguru Himself.

In my soiled Indian shirt, I shifted from one foot to another wondering what the fantastic secret behind practical spirituality was, where lay the root of its solution.

In the distance, we saw Maharaji as He unhurriedly moved towards us, and once again, with a thrill in our hearts, we beheld His noble gait, His glowing countenance, His royal bearing. We gazed at Him; we watched Him; we observed Him and did not comprehend, as He remained to us a treasure safely hidden within a secret vault.

Quietly, the Superior One reviewed our battered group just as a kind and concerned father would; then turning to me whispered sweetly, "The secret lies in attention."

The brief darshan over, Master slowly walked towards the ashram building in the back of the yard while Bob said humbly, "True indeed are the words of the Persian Saint, 'He (the Master) is beyond comprehension, apprehension, conception and even conjecture. He outstrips the faculties of sight, hearing and understanding.' (63a) And, 'Those that claim to understand Him, They are surely the most foolish of men.'" (64)

The cars were loaded; the suitcases and bags tightly fixed on the roofs; medicine, pills, vitamins and the blue, plastic water-jug were all safe, packed and in place. Bob and I sat in our usual back seats and waited, while Werter, leaving the car, walked towards the mansion and vanished in the winding path of the blossoming garden.

In the back window of the station wagon, there was no more Kim and no more Swen to see as both lay motionless on the floor of the luggage compartment, Kim wrapped in a warm blanket, Swen stuffed with vitamin C concentrate. Bob gave Betty more aspirin for Michael and the whereabouts of Gerald we did not know.

Returning dreamily from his secret safari, pants splashed with mud from a passing car, feet sprinkled with dirt, Werter put his head in the open window of the Ambassador, a silent smile on his healthy face. Sniffing at a little bouquet of exotic flowers, looking like enormous forget-me-nots, that he had just picked in the blossoming garden, Werter tenderly handed his present to Mira Ji as a delicate fragrance reminiscent of lilacs in early spring suffused the inside of the car.

Since no order had come from the Master for our departure, Werter climbed into his seat and all of us continued waiting idly. By now the sun, strong and powerful in royal abundance, poured its undimmed rays on the earth beneath, sparkling in muddy puddles, interplaying in hot, bright designs of light and somber shadows everyplace we looked.

Suddenly, we noticed Mohan quickly approaching the Ambassador with a broad smile on his face. He informed everyone that Maharaji would like to see all of us once again. "How do you feel?" he asked me, eyes twinkling with joy.

"Excellent, Mohan, excellent, thank you!"

"I knew it," Mohan laughed. "I knew it from the very start."

We were told to stand and wait at the door of the ashram wall. Werter and I walked firmly behind Mira Ji while the rest of the Westerners, collecting their last bits of strength, limped and brought up the rear. In soiled, rumpled Indian outfits, splashed with mud, bedraggled, faces haggard, battered, exhausted and drawn, we stood there barefooted in deep silence and waited, waited at this shabby door, at this naked wall, presenting a truly dismal sight strikingly resembling Napoleon's defeated and retreating army from the land of the Russian Czar.

As in legends of old, the door was suddenly opened and on its threshold, immaculate and peerless outside and inside, glowing with ever undimmed light of Love, healthy and strong, the Perfect Man, the Godman, the greatest wonder of this world, like blinding sunlight appeared.

In utter wonderment, I thought, "Verily, verily, pale indeed were all my dreams when compared to this superb reality!" Transfixed, we gazed at Him, while my heart, like the patriarch in the Golden Temple of the Sikhs began ceaselessly and forever chanting within,

"The Master is the Song Eternal or
Word personified.
He is the Vedas, the scriptures.
He is saturated with the Divine.
The greatness of the Master,
Even if known, cannot be described
With mortal eloquence.
My Master has taught me one thing;
He is the Lord of everything;
Him I may never forget." (65)

The Superior One had just 2 minutes free as in front of the ashram a huge crowd was waiting and another in back of the wall.

"Goodbye, Master," Bob spoke with a sorrowful tremor in his voice, hands folded, heart downcast.

"I never say goodbye. I am always with you," the Satguru fondly replied with a tender expression in His silvery, blue eyes, and putting the palm of His hand on Bob's shoulder added affectionately, "I love you all."

For the very last time we looked at our Satguru, souls heavy with the pain of parting, when suddenly a golden ray of sun fell onto the Master's brow. In astonishment we watched as right in the middle of His forehead in God's own handwriting the Sanskrit letter "God" swelled up. This letter "Om" was so big, so noticeable, that it threw a shadow to its other side. Speechless and breathless, we gazed at this letter "Om," this Sanskrit letter "God."

The immutable God, the Word made flesh and His disciples in blessed, loving silence stood there on that holy Indian soil at that naked ashram wall. Silently, Master smiled, silently, turned around, and silently, left for satsang.

Our last 2 minutes with the Godman thus came to an end.

MASTER KIRPAL SINGH

EVEN KINGS AND EMPERORS WITH HEAPS OF WEALTH

AND VAST DOMINIONS, COMPARE NOT WITH AN ANT

FILLED WITH THE LOVE OF GOD.

_____Jap Ji

CHAPTER EIGHT

ON THE WAY BACK

The ignition key was turned; the motor started; and we were on the way back to Sawan Ashram. Elaine had a cold; Mira Ji was silent; Bob had no questions; all was grief. Second by second, minute by minute, hour by hour the time passed by.

Bob finally sighed loudly, "I feel like a blind man at the beach who just stepped into the cool, refreshing waters of the ocean up to the ankles, yet his blind eyes do not see the limitless vastness of it, and his mind cannot comprehend. It feels something like that with the Master."

"True," said Elaine, her deep voice betraying flu. "Our Master tells us 'we are aware of this outer ocean of consciousness only so far as it operates on the plane of senses, but the major part of it is hidden at the root or center of the soul in the eye focus within and of which we are totally ignorant.' (66) If we really want to know, we have to become one with this ocean, like our Master."

After another considerable period of silence, Elaine suggested that a cup of coffee and a little rest would not be such a bad idea. As everyone else left in search of a coffee house, I remained behind, hoping to rest in solitude and just to look around. Getting out of the car I stretched with pleasure.

A leper stood right in front of me, a metal begging bowl in the palm of his hand. Through the remaining scraps of his skin, yellow bones were clearly visible. One foot was there; the other was missing.

Gasping in horror, I instinctively recoiled, turned around and raced off with constantly accelerating speed as Werter's words, mournful and clear, reverberated in my ears, "What a tragedy! Oh, how awful it is to be a leper!" awaking conflicting feelings within. Meanwhile, the unfortunate leper ran after me, shouting and puffing.

How long can one run on only one foot? The miserable, sick man could not keep up the pace and got lost somewhere in the Indian crowd.

In distress I looked around hoping to glimpse Mira Ji and Bob, but in vain. Fancying lepers everyplace now, fearful to walk on the street, I quickly got back into the Ambassador, and with a sigh of relief ground down the window as the heat inside was stifling.

Noisy beggars rushed up from all directions and surrounded the car with a dense human wall. The sun was blotted out as all windows were covered with rowdy people. They yelled and pushed their hands and begging bowls through the open window which I quickly ground up.

Mira Ji's warning after our first memorable encounter with beggars back in Delhi, sounded in my mind, "Never give alms to the beggars, as some are just clever professionals living comfortably and well."

ON THE WAY BACK

The heat inside now became absolutely unbearable. "It will surely not be any hotter in the cremation vault with the fires burning," I thought, as one beggar sitting on the top of the car pounded ferociously with his fist over my head while the others continued screaming hysterically all around. This nightmare of menace seemingly had no end.

Leisurely strolling back from the tearoom, enjoying the views of the boulevard and the street side cafes, our valiant chauffeur suddenly noticed the threatening situation around his car. With lightning speed, he ran over, eyes flashing fire, yelling at the top of his voice and shaking both fists. The raggedy crowd hissed back like a bunch of hooded cobras but dispersed reluctantly and boiling mad.

Barely able to get out of the car, close to a swoon, I took a deep, invigorating breath as something rattled violently inside my head and bright, yellow lights like gigantic amoebas popped in front of my eyes.

"Oh, what a gallant hero this frisky chauffeur really is! Fighting his way all alone through the ranks of those beggars!" Filling with both admiration and gratitude, I sincerely thanked him for the timely rescue.

"On the other hand," I pondered, while feeling secure under the gallant hero's protection, "aren't we humans all just like these mendicants and beggars? Constantly, but constantly, we are begging for gifts at His door? How true are the beautiful words in Jap Ji,

'Many are the warriors, who are beggars at
His door, and many more, whose number is
Beyond reckoning. (67)
Many are those who misusing His gifts,
Wallow in sensuality;
Many, who receiving His gifts, deny Him;
Many the fools who only eat and enjoy,
But think not of the Donor.
And many lie afflicted by hunger, misery
And pain, which too are Thy gifts, O Lord.
He knows all and bestows accordingly. (68)
All, all receive their share,
As He ordains."

After prolonged and much needed rest, Bob
and Werter returned carrying a large pitcher
full of cool water, while Mira Ji and Elaine
trailed behind them.

"Mira, I lived up to your advice," I
exclaimed, "but do not ask what the price was!"

Out of the pitcher Werter poured clear
water on everyone's hands as we washed and
luxuriated in its cool freshness. "Oh, how
wonderful," he laughed joyfully, "oh, how
wonderful. What excellent, marvellous water!
And to make our joy complete, all we miss now is
ice cream!"

"Ice cream? What a splendid idea,"
grinned Bob, blue eyes sparkling with delight,
as he himself was quite a passionate lover of
ice cream.

Mira Ji's eyes twinkled mischievously.
"Let us feast," she cried out. "Let us find an
ice cream parlor and begin our sumptuous feast!"

Slowly driving past the rows of little stores, we carefully and intently looked for an ice cream parlor, but the Indian hieroglyphics did not make us any wiser. Finally, pointing at a little, dark entrance under a squalid canopy, Mira Ji ordered the driver to stop.

"Naughty, naughty," chuckled Elaine, promptly getting out of the car.

Forgetting our colds and blisters, like a happy flock of noisy sparrows, we entered a dark hole in the wall and looked around. Everything here seemed to be quite usual, and exactly the way it should be.

The counter and the furniture were chipped and rather bruised; a splattered stain with rays of dirt around it, like a heavenly star, adorned the wall; above it a lizard sat in traditional lizard's fashion.

The wonders of Indian culinary art were piled up on the counter in disarray. Flies gorged themselves on the food. Bananas, nuts and other eatables were strewed around, while dust, spots and dried-up blots covered everything visible and invisible.

We passed a refrigerator that for some unaccountable reason stood right in the middle of this small tearoom; a real old-timer, probably the first model ever manufactured.

This ice cream parlor had three areas, one above the other, connected with narrow steps, each possessing an individual, original squeak.

We climbed up to the top platform, and with complete delight settled around a bedraggled table right under a rusty fan. Werter, in

Gerald's large shirt, in pants splashed with the mud from the ashram puddle, stood before the owner and explained to him that we needed 5 portions of ice cream.

The owner stared at Werter trying to understand what his foreign customer wanted, eyes round as the beady eyes of the lizard sitting right above his head. Leaning over the counter, head stretched out, forehead rumpled with horizontal wrinkles from concentrated strain, mouth slightly open, yet try as he might, the owner could not understand a word, as English was Greek to him.

"Sahib?" he questioned.

Taking the owner to be hard-of-hearing, Werter lifted his hand up and, showing 5 fingers, said in a voice that could have raised the dead, "Ice cream!"

"Sahib?"

From her elevated position on the third platform, Mira Ji observed the goings-on below choking with laughter; then standing up full height, with a commanding voice she ordered in Punjabi, "Sahib wants to buy 5 portions of ice cream. Fill the plates and bring them over here!"

The owner's face brightened up with jubilation. "Acha! Acha!*" he exclaimed and ran to the old refrigerator.

____

*Acha: yes, O.K.

"Finally, oh finally, Mira," Bob cried out as if he had won a trophy, "the princess was talking in you!"

"Victory! Victory! We shall be served ice cream in a moment!" grinned Werter, running up the musical stairs.

Five magnificent portions of natural ice cream, aromatic and sweet, were brought up. We ordered coffee and Coca Cola in addition, and while waiting for them observed the spots and greasy fingerprints on our cups in place of artistic designs. As a waiter brought up 5 bottles of coke, carrying one under his armpit, Mira Ji pointed to the dirty cups.

"What is that?" she said firmly. "Take the cups back; wash them thoroughly; and only then bring them to us!"

The waiter looked puzzled while Mira Ji spoke to us in English. "I teach servants cleanliness, but it proves to be useless because most Indians are accustomed to live like that."

After grasping the idea, the waiter carefully put the bottles onto the rickety table and with an obliging smile on his innocent face, quickly wiped the cups with the edge of his grimy shirt and triumphantly placed them back one by one.

"What more is wanted?" Bob said as he attentively inspected his empty cup. "Either the cup is clean or my sanitary standards have changed. Take your choice!"

Mira Ji burst into spontaneous laughter. "They've changed! And you are turning native!"

"Ja, ja, es ist ganz klar. Everything is relative," remarked Werter.

Like bumblebees over sugar crystals, we voraciously consumed the delicious ice cream, thoroughly enjoying every spoonful of it.

Plate empty, Werter quickly wiped his sticky fingers with the edge of Gerald's shirt, then leaned back in his chair and said slowly and dreamily, "Why do we have to rush any place? Why do we have to go when it is so marvellous and wonderful here?

The people are kind and good. This little ice cream parlor is a veritable splendid heaven right in the middle of our planet Earth!" Suddenly getting up from his seat, he exclaimed enthusiastically, "Five more ice creams up here! More coffee, more Coca Cola!" And Werter signalled the owner with both his hands, as if conducting an orchestra.

Feasting on her second helping of ice cream with nuts, Mira Ji looked impishly at Werter. "This tearoom is not wonderful. These people are not kind and good. This owner is not marvellous. In any other tearoom you would say the same words.

The secret is that you love the Master so much that this limitless love of yours radiates to all and everything around and turns this world into a veritable Paradise. In the ashram even bugs and lizards will seem as precious diamonds and rubies to you. You yourself are the cause of all this splendor as love beautifies everything. So says our Master." And Mira Ji gazed at Werter with deep understanding.

Stirring sugar in her cup, the appealing coffee aroma rising heavily with the steam, Elaine quietly recited, "Verily, from earthly dust he raised us into Love Eternal!"

Continuing her thought, Bob said, "Forever swept off one's feet by the tidal wave of His powerful Love, irresistible and magnetic, enveloped by it, caught by it, drenched by it, we fell in love with that mighty Godly Love and our never-ending Game of Love began, deathless, radiant, eternal, till fully alchemized we'll stand as Love personified."

The time, we did not notice it. Over the ice cream and coffee, we continued talking about God and the Satguru, about Sach Khand and sailing home along the sonorous rainbow bridge that spans the creation from end to end—the never-ending song. But to our great chagrin we had to leave this heavenly spot on Earth, as we had to get back on the road.

Werter lingered around the counter, bought a large bag of shelled almonds and reluctantly climbed back into his seat, the very last one of all.

The endless fields of India once again stretched on both sides as we drove along eating Werter's nuts. Elaine sneezed loudly and blew her nose. Obviously, the ice cream had not helped her cold in the least.

"Bob," asked Werter, "is vitamin C a preventive remedy against colds?"

"Oh, yes, yes, it prevents colds if taken in time."   And immediately Bob gave him a vitamin C concentrate tablet from a little plastic bag.

"I got these C vitamins back in a drugstore in Delhi," Bob explained.   "Put it on your tongue and suck for as long as you can."   So, as we left the city and entered the cross-country road, Werter sucked the vitamin C vigorously and with precision, then suddenly looked at Bob, eyes popping out of their sockets and groaned with disgust, "This vitamin C has completely removed the skin from my tongue.   I can't feel anything any more!   What a nightmare! Unglaublich!   Absolutely unglaublich!"

While Werter fidgeted in his seat, Bob said with concern, "One tablet actually is not enough to insure prevention.   You should take four."   Horrified, Werter refused.

"It is time for dinner."   Mira Ji smiled, as we entered a small city.   "We'll have to find a suitable restaurant here."   Searchingly looking out of the window, she finally ordered the driver to stop at an exceptionally tall gate and went to investigate.

At the entrance a policeman sat on a boulder holding a club in his hand, now and then keeping his watchful eye on a goat with a skinny beard nipping yellow grass from between the stones.   Further up, a speckled hen cackled busily, digging up the dirt with her claws.

"Yes, we can have food here," Mira Ji said when emerging from the open gate. Taking our groceries along, we followed her into the courtyard.

Uniformed soldiers with rifles were milling around both outside and inside the premises. Some wore turbans, some, military hats.

They were loading trucks and jeeps with wooden boxes. Two soldiers, while shoving a heavy, bulky mess pot, argued impulsively. From above, like a suffocating feather bed, the familiar heat pressed down.

In the courtyard, a number of one-story high buildings had been erected, their windows covered with heavy iron bars "to protect the inhabitants from thieves," we thought, as we entered the restaurant.

A long, single table stood in the middle of a narrow, empty room on the cement floor surrounded by 4 bare walls, 2 rough-looking benches on either side. A back door led into a small cell-like enclosure where on a metal bed without a mattress, the waiter was snoring, obviously in no hurry to go any place. A lonely mug of water stood under his bed.

The cleanliness of this place struck us as quite unnatural. While Bob was putting the bag of groceries on the table, Werter, looking around, exclaimed delightedly, "What a splendid place! What could be better than this? We can take a prolonged rest here, while having a meal. Where are we?"

"In jail," answered Mira Ji.

"Donner Wetter! Das ist schon ganz unglaublich!"* and Werter stared at Mira Ji like a trapeze artist who had just lost his nerve, while Bob, flabbergasted, threw his hands up in the air.

"In jail?" Then catching up once again with his thinking abilities he queried cautiously, "And who is this guy doing the snoring?"

"A thief. He is the only prisoner in the whole jail," Mira Ji responded cheerfully. "The thief, the guard with the club at the gate, the military and we are the whole population of the jail at this time."

Shaken, I thought, "Indeed, truth is not what it seems to be. These bars prevent thieves from getting out, not in as we believed a moment ago. And so many other things in life are just like that, the other way around."

The jail attendant interrupted my thoughts as he entered the door carrying a tea kettle and a big metal pot with steaming rice in it. Mira Ji paid him a few rupees, while Bob unpacked our grocery bag.

Still a touch jittery, we settled down around the long convicts' table. Adding our own chapatis and puris to the delicious rice, we sipped the dark Indian tea from the convicts' mugs and ate our first dinner in jail with relish.

---

*Thunder and lightning. That is completely unbelievable!

ON THE WAY BACK

As time rolled on implacably and steadily, we began to feel quite at home in this penitentiary as everything suited our taste: the jail's clean and quiet messhall, the prisoners' food, the Indian tea in the convicts' mugs, the snoring thief on his metal bed and the heavy bars on the narrow windows that prevented the world from entering in. The longer we sat around the rustic table the more we loved this secluded place. "Our soul is trapped in a small jail of the body," said Mira Ji, finishing her meal, "and thus is also trapped in the vast jail of Brahmand. The magic key that throws open all kinds of prison gates, the Masters keep in their Godly hands.

So Master's work is of the highest order as He comes to liberate the souls from the vast prisonhouse of mind and matter in order to take the prodigal sons of God back to the mansions of their Heavenly Father.

A kindly soul may direct the prison warden to provide delicious food for the prisoners under his charge. Another may grant the boon of other delicacies to them. A third may order good clothing and lodging for them and so on. Each of them, no doubt, may be doing something to ameliorate the prisoners' lot for the time being.

But if someone were to throw open the prison gate and ask them to escape the squalor and misery of the jail, his work would naturally be counted as one far excelling the work of others.

This is exactly the nature of the work of a Master Soul. He reveals to us the Lost Kingdom and restores us to Paradise.

Man had an ignoble fall from the Garden of Eden, and none could restore him to the good graces of the Father and bring about reconciliation except the Son of Man. He takes upon Himself the vicarious responsibility for the sins of man, purifies him of all ignominy and by a transfusion of His own Life Impulse makes him arise into cosmic awareness and gain everlasting life." (69)

As Elaine began packing the remaining food in the grocery bag, we realized that our pleasant, unforgettable moments behind the bars of this jail had drawn to an end, and once again we were quite reluctant to leave. "Truly," I pondered, "Michail Zostchenko* was quite right when after a life-long observation of humans he came to the conclusion that 'a man is not a flea and can get accustomed to anything.' Even to his semi-conscious, dim life in the jail of his body, even to his miserable and pitiful existence in this vast cosmic prisonhouse called planet earth where, stumbling in pitch darkness, void of comprehension, deluded, confused, he gropes, and loves it! What to say of Brahmanda's bewitching jail yet to come! With perplexity, and like Werter, one was really prone to exclaim, 'Unglaublich! Absolutely unglaublich!'"

----

*M. Zostchenko: a Russian writer of the 20th century.

After leaving the crowded city, we once again relaxed in our seats, as it was only a 3 hour trip to Sawan Ashram.

We drove along a shady alley with very old trees towering on both sides. Their shaggy branches, as if holding hands, created a living arch above us. A flock of multi-colored birds, like hopping flowers, adorned the foliage while singing with glee.

Leaving the musical arch behind, we passed a small, charming village and proceeded amidst ravines. Hidden by poplar trees and blossoming bushes, an ancient river sleepily moved along. Its mysterious ends and beginnings were completely unknown to us. As the river turned to the left, continuing its silent flow, we proceeded ahead towards the far-off horizon amidst pastures and fields.

Spotting a small, wooden cart standing at the side of the road, Werter exclaimed not without delight, "We can have juice here!"

The owner crouched barelegged on the ground next to his improvised little shop in front of a wicker basket full of green limes while a blackened juicer solemnly rested on top of his cart.

Instantly, we decided to make use of this strange service and disembarked without delay. The owner jumped to his feet ready to serve while Bob asked with sincere wonderment, "How did he get here?" looking with awe at the empty vastness around us.

"I don't know. Probably fell straight down from heaven," laughed Mira Ji, relishing her own joke for some time.

My valiant hero, the brave chauffeur, was already lying on his back, hands under his head, legs one on top of the other, enjoying a deserved rest. We settled on the hillside next to the road, lost once again in the middle of glowing space.

In the far-off distance, the firmament, like a silken curtain embroidered with a few rain clouds, touched the remote ground, the space around reminiscent of the limitless Russian steppes, that stretch from horizon to horizon where they meet with the silent sky.

As we relaxed and sipped the astringent lime juice, we enjoyed the softness of a light breeze, the glowing warmth of the sun, the rich color of the rustic scene, the delicate, uniden- tifiable aroma that filled the air suggestive of jasmine mixed with heliotrope, and admired a faint silken arch of a rainbow, shimmering in the humid air, far, far away.

"Rainbow!" whispered Mira Ji, a dreamy gleam in her dark eyes as she looked at this heavenly bridge. "Do you know," she asked us, "who the True Master is? The Word or Naam is the True Teacher for all mankind. Like a sonorous rainbow it connects the soul on one end with God on the other. Naam is the one for all. It was the True Teacher in the past. It is the same Teacher now. It shall ever be the Teacher for all times to come. There is no second Teacher or Guru of mankind. (70)

In the physical body of the Saint, we worship the Word Personified in this person. And as such the two are inseparably respected. It is just like one's beloved sitting inside a house with the doors closed. We want to bow to him but how can we?

We know for certain that it is the beloved to whom we want to bow and not to the mud, lime and mortar of the house in which the beloved resides. We bow down to whom? Do we bow to the mud walls? No, but before the indweller of the house behind the walls, however to all appearances we may look as though facing the mud walls.

The man who has found Him (Word-Guru), who has become one with Him--the Word in Him--is related to us in the same way as the beloved. It is the self-luminous Radiant Figure within the physical body of the outer man who is our True Teacher, and who is one with the Lord. It is none other than the Lord Himself as He Himself appears in the Form of a Sadh."* (70)

Elaine, looking under the weather, sniffed a few times, then added unmindful of her cold, "Therefore, the great Saint Maulana Rumi tells us, 'Learn to worship the Satguru.'"

Eventually, we once again sank into our Ambassador seats, leaned back and pressed on towards Delhi.

"Mira, you mentioned the Luminous Form of the Master within just a little while ago. What

____

*Sadh: The Godman.

is the tie between God in that Form and the initiated soul?" Bob asked.

Mira Ji smiled in her own mysterious way while eyeing us sweetly. "This Luminous Form of the Master or the Lord Himself receives His initiates at the time of death when 'the soul-currents begin to withdraw from the body or a little earlier. The Satguru in His Radiant Form appears within to take charge of the departing spirit.' (70a)

He 'leads the spirit into higher regions and assigns each one an appropriate place to which he may be entitled according to his sadhna or the practice of the Holy Word during his lifetime, and imparts to him the necessary instructions for further and fuller development on the spiritual path. With the darveshes, there is no reckoning of deeds of their disciples. The Master is all in all, the sole judge and arbiter. He is ever with His disciple in weal or woe,' (70c) as 'the bonds of relationship between the Guru and the disciple are the strongest in the world for they are tied by the Divine and Omnipotent Will of God,' (71) you see."

"And what will happen to all others who did not have the great good fortune to be brought to the feet of a Living Master by the Omnipotent Will of God?" asked Bob with some concern in his voice.

"You really want to know? They remain under the law of justice or the law of 'an eye for an eye and a tooth for a tooth.' As a result of actions that one had performed while on earth, one is summoned to the court of the Great Judge, Dharam Raj. His messengers of death, called Yamdoots, make their appearance when the breath is departing and bring the soul to that court. The scroll is then opened and the entire account is laid bare. (72) The judgment day commences."

Thoughtfully, Bob mused, nodding his head, "That is so as many cases are known to medical history of people who died, were resuscitated and then told about the judgment day that took place in the presence of a great 'Being of Light'* as they call the judge Dharam Raj."**

"Ja, ja," Werter said, "es ist ganz klar, or so it seems to me."

After a considerable drive, we stopped on a bridge that stretched out far into the distance while below it, long and muddy, the Jumna river lazily rolled its greenish waters along empty, sandy banks towards its ultimate destination. The rays of the evening sun sparkled and shone on its silent ripples brought to life by the tender touch of the wandering Eastern breeze.

---

*Dr. Raymond Moody in 'Life After Life.'
See also Kenneth Ring's 'Heading Toward Omega.'

**Dharam Raj: Keeper of the Law, who dispenses justice to souls after they have left the body according to their actions. (72a)

One had to be a Shakespeare to be able to describe the traffic on this Jumna bridge. Everything thinkable and unthinkable was piled there in a long bottleneck, and this bottleneck was indeed what this bridge was all about. Military trucks, jeeps, camels, bicycles, pedestrians, donkeys, horses, chickens, wheel-carts—you name it, it was most certainly there clogging this bridge, honking, yelling, shouting, cackling, a fantastic mess.

"Trapped," laughed Mira Ji, "and the only thing left to do now is, like Lord Krishna, jump into the Jumna river and on one's own then reach the shore!

Do you know that story of Lord Krishna? No? Lord Krishna, after jumping into this Jumna river, controlled the hydra-headed serpent here with a sound of his flute. The accounts of Lord Krishna's life state that."

"Oh, Mira, was a serpent living in this Jumna river?" Werter questioned in surprise.

"No, no," answered Mira Ji, "this many-headed serpent is the mind, which has a thousand ways of inflicting its poison, and without that Sound from the Beyond, it cannot be controlled or overcome. (73) You see, only the oscillations of the mind stand between you and your Creator. Master says, as you know, 'Still the vibrations of the mind, and when it stands collected in the eye, you will pass on to the regions of light.'

Mind is no small thing. It is the power of negativity."

As we slowly inched our way along the Jumna bridge amidst the noise of cackling Babel and oblique rays of the sun that was approaching the horizon, Mira Ji continued, "During the time of Guru Gobind Singh, there was a story that a rishi left everything and went into the forest to do meditation.

Now there was also a certain King who had conquered many people and places, but whose greatest ambition was to conquer the rishi and make him obey his wishes. This strange ambition arose from the fact that the rishi was formerly a great King himself before he renounced everything for a spiritual life.

The King and his army marched into the deep forest. On approaching the rishi, he found the holy man was in meditation. Undaunted, the King woke the rishi and told him, 'Prepare yourself for a fight. I have come to do battle with you.'

The rishi calmly surveyed the King and his army and replied, 'Fight? I ran away from the worldly life for fear of my one great enemy, and I hid myself here in these woods. My soul yet shivers to hear the sound of his name. Even to think of his name, my heart is quivering.'

The King grew angry and shouted, 'Is he stronger than me, this enemy of yours?'

'What is the use?' said the rishi. 'You will not be able to conquer him.'

The King boldly replied, 'If I cannot conquer him, I will burn myself to death.' The rishi then told the King that the great enemy he spoke of was the mind.

From that very day, the King tried everything possible, using all manner of means to gain control over his mind, but found that he could not.

Finally, after admitting that he had failed, he burned himself alive at a place called Katasraj. A monument was erected there in memory of this King, and one can see this structure even now, if one so wishes."

Elaine added, "We have to become Masters in our own house of the body first before we get Self and God Realization. How can the soul cross the mind zone when she is the mind's slave, a princess of royal blood dragged around by the nose and legs in a most undignified manner by her own servant—the mind." Silence fell.

As the heroic chauffeur drove off the bridge, the sun was already touching the horizon. The sky shone in a fiery sunset. Crimson, orange and gold dressed the Jumna's living waters, the trees and bushes. The mysterious shadows deepened. Moist fog arose in streaks from the becalmed sleepy fields as pale stars prepared to light up in full strength.

We entered the ashram in the darkness of night. Switching on the lights and the fans in our room, we stood mute for a moment at the doorpost, then walked around.

"How beautiful everything is here, how clean and comfortable!" I exclaimed as my heart leaped with gladness.

On the shelf the bronze Bodhisattva still meditated in his prominent place. A lonely dry stocking hung on the rope over our beds. The old bathroom equipment worked. The clear water ran out of all faucets. The shower head was firmly affixed to the wall, and the toilets were spick and span.

In the middle of the fluffy Indian rug, a green frog hopped, enjoying her life. The old lizard on the wall looked at us, his head turned sidewise observing, while a mischievous twinkle gleamed in his eyes.

"Without this pink lizard," said Bob, "the room would indeed miss something important. He makes it all seem perfect and complete."

"We are home," I finished Bob's thought.

Ramji's familiar voice sounded behind the door. "The meal is served. Do please come to the dining room."

"Acha, acha," we answered. "Thank you so much."

The remnants of the defeated army from the West were already assembled at the dining table. Swen sat silently under the sign "Simran" weakly driving his fork through the food. Sapphire eyes wilted, flaxen hair unwashed for some time, face waxen—he was obviously quite ill, presenting a vivid image of a martyred stoic.

Kim was absent; Michael and Betty were not there, and we noticed the ashram homeopathic physician Dr. Moolraj quickly walking along the ashram lawn. From Gerald's room we could hear Sushila cry and a few faint sounds of diapers being washed.

Sun-tanned and healthy, Werter briskly entered the room and joined us at the dining table.

"I will not make fun about your bananas any more," I said as Werter speedily filled his plate with dessert. "You won the race."

"It works!" he answered simply.

Interrupting Swen's simran, I asked him with compassion, "Did you pray to the Master to relieve your sickness?"

"Why? Sickness and health are both gifts from the Beloved. Whatever He sends us is for our own good. We should be constantly grateful to Him and let His Will be done," Swen answered.

"The grandest way of life is surrender to His Will," Bob agreed.

Still filled with the convicts' dinner and the astringent lime juice, our appetites were non-existent, yet Bob ate 3 portions of dessert and Werter ate 5 anyhow.

In the morning since our rupees had to be exchanged back to dollars, we had to get a taxi to drive to the American exchange office. Not wanting to bother Mira Ji, we decided to walk. Through the rich foliage, shafts of golden sun rays fell upon the courtyard grounds. In the fog of the humid air, millions of little sparks scintillated.

The young secretary, swinging his hands along his body, walked across the ashram courtyard towards the Sat Sandesh office as the light suddenly blazed up brightly on his white shirt and blushed when he entered the shade of the trees.

'The young secretary, swinging his hands along
his body, walked across the ashram courtyard.'
Page 297

ON THE WAY BACK

We passed a few sevadars sitting under an awning, eating chapatis and leisurely drinking tea. Everything in the ashram was as it was before we left for the Punjab, only so much better. The heat and humidity seemed quite mild. The stench from the sewer canal was not at all as benumbing as we took it to be earlier. More than that, by now we could not at all imagine that our Sawan Ashram could have been built at any other possible place.

While the sleepy "Oblomoka" continued its unhurried way of life, we left its secluded, blessed grounds, crossed the bridge over the sewer canal and entered the familiar street.

"It really must be very nice," said Bob, "to sleep on top of these flat roofs. The night's breeze cools you a bit; one forgets the world below while the world above looks at you starry-eyed and shimmers and trembles with millions of lights."

Three young Sikhs passed us by, folded their hands in greeting and bowed, as we, in turn, bowed to them. Both heart and soul rejoiced as realization dawned that by now India had become an integral part of us, not just outwardly thanks to the tailor's skill, but inwardly, as her way of life was now our way of life, her culture was our culture, her Saint was our Satguru.

Smilingly, we put our heads into the little, black hole in the wall, the place that sold us honey just a few days ago and greeted the owner with a warm, "Namaste!"

He grinned back happily, his teeth sugar-white. "Namaste! You need more honey?"

How nice everything was in this little store, delightfully comfortable and cozy in its own sort of homemade way. It felt as if one had just entered some old grandmother's home where you were born, grew up, and where everything long ago had become a part of your very self.

As if realizing our feelings, the golden Radha, the pure human soul, and blue Krishna, the God of Love, greeted us from the wall with tender smiles.

As we returned from Delhi, rupees exchanged for dollars, we left the taxi a few blocks away from Sawan Ashram to have a nostalgic last walk.

For the last time, we passed the white cow with begilded horns and a lonely hump on her back, as a skinny dog, all her ribs quite visible, stood next to her wondering what to do. For the last time we looked at the peeling paint of the ancient Indian homes, for the last time we entered the narrow bridge that spanned the sewer canal.

With poorly disguised emotion, Bob said, "How shall we live, away from our Master, away from India—now our home—away from our Sawan Ashram and its quiet, idyllic life?

We are, you see, not the same people anymore; we have become Easterners, and the West is now as good as a wasteland to us as there is no common denominator left!

All these great pandits, missionaries, great this, great that, have collapsed in mid-air like soap bubbles. We have met a Godman and died to the childish doll's play of the world. We have met the Satguru, and the attachments and outer effects have been finished."

A motorcycle honked behind us. We made way as a beturbaned Sikh, saluting us with one hand, roared by, skirting with admirable skill a buffalo entering the bridge on its other end. As his motorcycle hit the dirt road, clouds of dust shot from under its wheels, and our beturbaned Sikh disappeared around the turn of the street.

"From this new angle of vision the condition of this world of ours seems to be akin to that of our overturned Ambassador car as it lay there off the road, wheels up, roof down," I said, as we passed the heavy, trotting buffalo and entered the dust cloud left behind by our friend.

"No matter what one thinks, just the opposite is true." I sighed, "One trusts that God is far above, yet He dwells right within. One takes himself to be the body, yet he is soul, eternal conscious entity. One thinks it is the end when someone dies, but death is a 'laughable impossibility,' as our Master puts it, and a birth into the wondrous worlds beyond.

One is convinced he has free will, yet he has none. One prides himself on being an individual, but in Truth we are all one.* Man thinks he sees and hears, yet he is blind and deaf! And all this is just the beginning of the list of opposites. How could such a mind-boggling, terrible accident happen to the world? Oh, mama mia," I exclaimed in frustration like the woman in the plane's backseat in Rome.

"Alas," Bob sighed, "only a Godman can penetrate the mysterious veils upon veils that constitute the phenomena of human life. Only He knows what this mighty play of God's lights and sounds called cosmos is all about."

"And to understand all these secrets and mysteries, one has to become a Godman," I echoed. "Maybe so far we have not understood much, maybe nothing at all. Yet one thing became absolutely clear: nothing in this world will ever deter us, not even death itself till our goal is reached, and we ourselves become a Godman with the secrets all revealed."

"Then forevermore we shall remain in the eternal company of the immortal Saints!" added Bob, as we entered the ashram grounds.

Suitcases packed, we approached the Ambassador, parked in front of the Western gates. At the other end of the courtyard, we noticed Gyaniji standing at the door of the

____

*Illusion of individuality stems from soul's (highest unalloyed aspect of Divinity) identification with the lower and lowest parts of Divinity (mind and matter).

empty Sat Sandesh office yawning and resting, a silver bangle on his wrist.

Unflappable Mira Ji busied herself at the Ambassador while the valiant chauffeur, beamed sitting behind the steering wheel.

As we began loading the suitcases into the car, I asked Bob, "You didn't lose the return tickets?"

"No, no, I don't think so," and Bob quickly checked the innumerable pockets of his American suit in search of the tickets.

Mira Ji bemusedly observed him. "These material tickets," she said "one can lose, but never can the return ticket for the train to Sach Khand be lost as this invaluable treasure is a permanent gift from the Master and is forever implanted within."

"It's time to leave," said Elaine with a deep flu voice as she prepared to get into the car.

"What would be the best way to contribute to Master's expenses?" Bob asked her, lifting the blue, plastic container from the ground.

"Master says, 'Spirituality is free as air and sunlight.' There are no fees, no charges in Master's ashram for anything at all, and, as you know, Master Himself lives on His government pension," she answered and got into her seat while Bob walked to the back of the Ambassador.

Gerald, pale and drawn, clad in his Indian outfit, pushing at his spectacles, passed Werter by who had just finished his exercises in the middle of the ashram lawn. Sushila, her brave, little face besmeared with yogurt, comfortably sat on his right arm.

Approaching Bob, who stood at the open trunk putting the blue plastic container into the suitcase already filled to capacity with our Indian outfits, American fluffy towels, Buddhas, bronze Bodhisattvas and copper incense burners, Gerald said with a happy, loving smile on his face, "Keep in touch!"

Leaving the Western lawn, and briskly walking towards us, back in his embroidered shirt, bare feet in Indian sandals, Werter, eyes moist with the love of the Master, stopped next to Gerald. Pulling out one of his visiting cards, Werter said with deep, warm feeling, "Bitte schreiben Sie mir.*

What a magnificent time we all have spent together mit unserem grossem Meister!"**

As I watched all three gentlemen standing in back of the Ambassador involved in a lively conversation about the Satguru, the thought crossed my mind, "Verily, verily, even kings and emperors with heaps of wealth and vast dominions compare not with an ant filled with the love of God as of such is the Kingdom of Heaven."

"Goodbye, goodbye, auf wiedersehen," we said as the motor came to life with the turn of the key. Through the back window of our car, we cast a last glance at the ashram. Master's

––––––––––––––

*Please write me.

**Together with our great Master.

house, like a white dove in a fluffy nest, sat among the emerald foliage. Flowers as colorful as the velvet butterflies fluttering over their opened cups, surrounded the Western lawn.

On that lawn, two white figures stood— Werter and Gerald waving their hands, getting smaller and smaller as the car approached the gate. The words 'Be good, do good, be one' moved back and vanished behind the wall. Faint chanting from Holy Jap Ji softly rippled the sleeping air, and a train passed, wheels clattering, whistling loudly in a last adieu.

In melancholy silence we drove along the streets of Delhi, Mira Ji, Elaine and my heroic chauffeur in front, we in the back. Only there was no Werter as a suitcase stood on the top of his seat.

"Mira," a disheartened Bob asked, "we are going back to the world now, and who knows what the future may hold. What if we never see our Master again?"

"Letting the world ride high and tall in one's saddle once again would be just like letting an elephant into a China shop. But be of good cheer," she answered, "you have met and you have seen the Godman.

To meet a Saint, to have His holy darshan and company is the greatest pilgrimage of all. To meet a Saint is worth more than travelling to all the 68 places of pilgrimage, and you have done just that.

Even if you never again meet the Master physically, and He wishes to bestow separation upon you, know it for sure that separation, too,

'Master's house, like a white dove in a fluffy
nest, sat among the emerald foliage.'
Page 304

is a priceless gift from the Satguru, as separation is the plant on which the blossoms of longing will grow, from which will develop the fruit of unwavering and undying love, moist with tears."

We passed the Red Fort. Like black sentinels condors perched on its sinister towers, still guarding from force of habit the long-vanished treasures of Shah Jahan.

Mira Ji looked at us with concern, then said, "Once upon a time there was a certain fakir who went to an Indian village. He had an abundance of compassion in his heart, and he warned the villagers, 'Tomorrow a breeze is coming, and whomever the breeze touches will go mad.'

A few of the villagers who had faith in the fakir took notice of his words and when the time came, they hid themselves in their houses, shutting the windows and doors fast. All those who ignored the warning were touched by the breeze and went mad.

When the lucky ones came out of hiding, they saw that everyone was mad, except themselves. But the mad people, being in the majority and seeing that the few were different, insisted, 'They are mad!' The world's condition is something like that, you see.

Keep this story in mind," Mira Ji advised. "It will help you some day."

Then, as we arrived at the airport, she sweetly uttered her parting words, "If you cannot find congenial society, it is better that you live all alone.   There is no better luck than solitude.

Live with the Master speaking through books, speaking on tapes.   Live on memories, memories, memories."

Oh, what a sad goodbye!

The luggage was checked; the Air India Boeing 707 was already waiting for us on the runway.

"Mira is a bundle of wisdom," I sighed.

"True," Bob quietly agreed as in low spirits we walked to the waiting room surrounded by the Western passengers.

Tall, blond and fair-skinned men in immaculate European suits with matching ties, women wearing knee-length dresses, modern and fashionable, bare feet in patent leather shoes, a touch of lipstick and a bit of makeup on their faces, self-esteem and cold content in their expressions, in their smiles condescension, in their walk assertiveness.

Bob noted with pain in his voice, "As Mira would say, 'These are not the disciples of our Master. These are the rich, proud and beautiful people. Their ego is big and does not let them see the Truth.'"

"All these people are like a strange and frightening nightmare.   Everything in them is quite foreign to me!"   Freezing in my tracks with fear, I thought, "Oh, God!   Outwardly Westerners, inwardly Easterners, dead to the worldly life, yet trapped in the world. What a predicament. How can we live?"

ON THE WAY BACK

My heart broke. Emotions overflowed in tears, as silently around us fell the iron curtain of invincible fate.

END

EPILOG

It should be noted that our mood of dejection on leaving India in 1969 was not permanent. We flew there three more times, each visit a different, wonderful experience.

In 1970 we recorded a number of interviews with the Master and watched Manav Kendra being constructed.

In 1971 we stayed both at Rajpur--the Master's home--and Manav Kendra. Who can ever forget sitting around the huge Mansarover pool with the Great Master Kirpal Singh in the evening, as the glowing Eastern sun was slowly setting.

And in 1973 we were with Him again, this time at Sawan Ashram and in the new dormitories at Manav Kendra.

As our final three weeks in India drew to a close, we humbly asked the Master, "Have we been with You in the past lives?"

"What do you think?" He responded.

"We think we were."

Satguru smiled lovingly, then translated our reply into Hindi for Tai Ji.

In closing, this reminiscence: In 1971 the leave-taking was particularly painful. As we ate a final meal at the home of Tai Ji's daughter, Maharaji phoned us. After a few heartwarming words and knowing we would be making a report on our visit when we returned to New York, Master said, "Tell them if they knew how much I loved them, they'd be dancing in the streets."

EPILOG

There were no further get-togethers.
Satguru left the earth scene for the last time
on August 21, 1974.
For us, the sun has set.

Robert Redeen

CHART OF CREATION

CHART OF CREATION

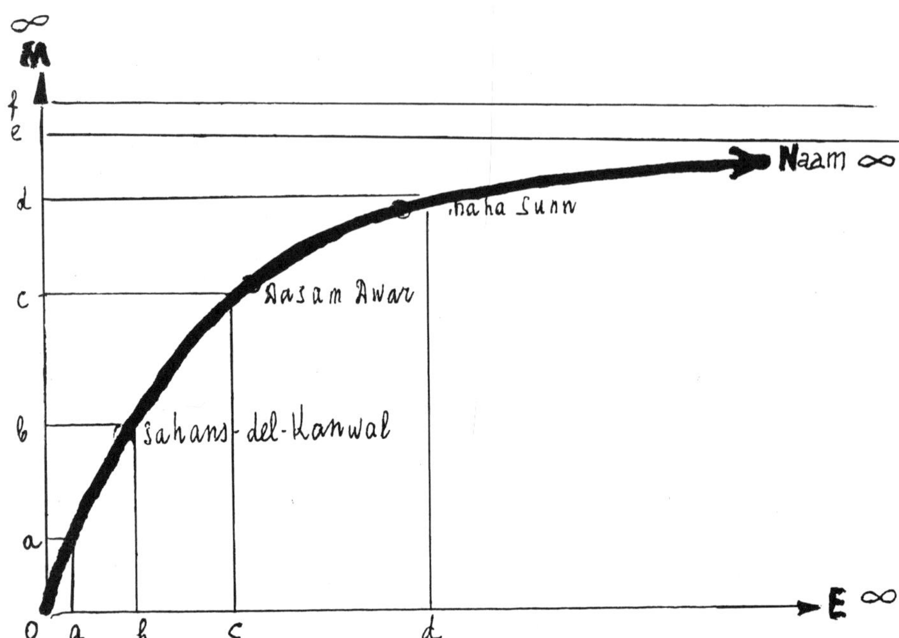

CHART OF CREATION

N.   The Creative Audible Life Stream, or Naam.
M.   The manifestation of Naam.
E.   The rate of vibration of Naam.
oaa. Material world, Dharm Khand or the realm
      of Action.   (Pinda)
obb. Astral world, Gian Khand or the realm of
      Knowledge.   (Anda)
occ. Mental world, Sarm Khand or the realm of
      Ecstasy.   (Brahmanda)
odd. Supramental world, Karm Khand or the realm
      of Grace.   (Par Brahm)
oe.   Spiritual world, Sach Khand or the realm
      of Truth.   (Sach Khand)
of.   Alak, Agam, Anami.

CHART OF CREATION
(A few explanations)

1.N. Naam, the essence of the Absolute God, the Nameless One (Anami) in vibratory action. This action produced Light and Sound, called Naam or Word, the only begotten son of God.

It is called variously Sound, Sruti (That which is heard), Shabd or Akash Bani (Voice from Heaven), Udgit, Sraosha (Music of the Beyond), Word or Harmony, Logos or the Holy Spirit, Kalma or Bang-i-Ilahi (Call from God), or Nida-i-Asmani (Heavenly Sound).

"Thou manifested Thyself as Naam and set up the Creation. Out of the Formless proceeded forms in varying degrees," said Guru Nanak. (73)

2.E. The rate of vibration of Naam.

3.M. Manifestation of Naam, as perceived by the soul.

The entire manifestation of the whole creation is "just of the Naam and there is nothing which is not of Him." (74)

The higher vibrations permeate the lower vibrations, but not in reverse.

The whole diapason of Naam is fully closed in Man, thus man alone has the possibility, the potential to know his Creator.

He is a microcosm, capable of realizing the macrocosm, as the Master tells us.

To rise along the sonorous arch of Naam, to merge into one's Source or God is the goal of human life, and is called God Realization or Salvation. Whosoever achieved that goal is called Param Sant, and such a personality is

CHART OF CREATION
(A few explanations)

rare indeed, and is nothing else but Word made flesh.

Everything that helps the soul, the spark of the very essence of the Absolute God, to return back to its Source or Home, is good; whatever drags her down the sonorous arch is sin.

The power that pulls the soul up is called positive, and in reverse, the power that pulls her down into creation is called negative, the difference being only in direction of the same power of Naam.

Thus, it becomes obvious that the terms "good" and "bad" or "sin" are relative, as the same event can have a different effect on different persons.

Let us close with the words of Guru Arjan:
"Listen ye to the Saints. Salvation lies
In the True World.
Service at the feet of the Master and
Devotion to His Word is the
True pilgrimage.
Such a one is accepted at His Court
And obtains a seat of honor.*
O Nanak! It is extreme good fortune
To cast aside pride and fall at the
Master's feet."**

---

*Gujri M4

**Jap Ji 30

REFERENCES

1. Letter to Raisa Scriabine Smith by K.S. Redeen, p.1.
2. Naam or Word by Kirpal Singh, p. 94.
3. Godman by Kirpal Singh, p. 15.
4. Naam or Word by Kirpal Singh, p. 286.
5. Naam or Word by Kirpal Singh, p. 288.
6. Naam or Word by Kirpal Singh, p. 288.
7. Spirituality by Kirpal Singh, p. 35.
9. Jap Ji by Kirpal Singh, p. 93.
10. Jap Ji by Kirpal Singh, p. 22.
11. The Holy Bible, St. John 1:1-3.
12. Discourses on Sant Mat by Sawan Singh (1939), p. 294.
13. Mystery of Death by Kirpal Singh, p. 29.
14. Mystery of Death by Kirpal Singh, p. 27.
15. The Holy Bible, Corinthians 15:51-55.
16. Mystery of Death by Kirpal Singh, p. 31.
17. Spiritual Gems by Sawan Singh, p. 231.
17a. Spiritual Gems by Sawan Singh, p. 232.
18. The Night Is a Jungle by Kirpal Singh, p. 277.
19. A Great Saint Baba Jaimal Singh by Kirpal Singh, p. 67.
19a. Heart to Heart Talks by Kirpal Singh, p. 172.
19b. The Pilgrimage of James by George Arnsby Jones, p. 92.
20. Godman by Kirpal Singh, p. 15.
21. Jap Ji, Stanza XXIV, by Kirpal Singh, p. 107.
22. Mystery of Death by Kirpal Singh, p. 10.
23. Mystery of Death by Kirpal Singh, p. 63.

REFERENCES

24. Heart to Heart Talks by Kirpal Singh, p. 1.
25. The Ocean of Grace Divine editor Bhadra Sena, p. 29.
27. Godman by Kirpal Singh, p. 174.
28. Godman by Kirpal Singh, p. 173.
28a. Godman by Kirpal Singh, p. 183.
29. Jap Ji, Stanza X, comment 2, by Kirpal Singh, p. 96.
30. Godman by Kirpal Singh, p. 175.
32. Jap Ji, Stanza XXXIII, by Kirpal Singh, p. 117.
33. Spiritual Gems by Sawan Singh, pp. 28-29.
34. Jap Ji, Stanza II, comments, by Kirpal Singh, p. 89.
35. Jap Ji, Stanza II, by Kirpal Singh, p. 89.
36. Jap Ji, Introduction, by Kirpal Singh, p. 67.
37. Wheel of Life (1965) by Kirpal Singh, p. 79.
38. Mystery of Death by Kirpal Singh, pp. 58-59.
39. Mystery of Death by Kirpal Singh, p. 51.
40. Mystery of Death by Kirpal Singh, p. 43.
40a. Ocean of Grace Divine, Ruhani Satsang, India.
41. Portrait of Perfection, p. 84.
42. Sat Sandesh, December 1971, p. 2.
43. Naam or Word by Kirpal Singh, p. 197.
44. Naam or Word by Kirpal Singh, p. 199.
44a. Naam or Word by Kirpal Singh, p. 192.
44b. Naam or Word by Kirpal Singh, p. 193.
44c. Naam or Word by Kirpal Singh, p. 193.
44d. Naam or Word by Kirpal Singh, p. 194.

REFERENCES

45. Jap Ji by Kirpal Singh, p. 94.
46. Sat Sandesh, April 1976, p. 10.
47. Sat Sandesh, October 1975, pp. 2-6.
48. Jap Ji, Stanza XXXVII, by Kirpal Singh, p. 121.
49. Jap Ji, Stanza XXI, by Kirpal Singh, pp. 104-105.
49a. Jap Ji, Stanza XXI, comments, by Kirpal Singh, p. 121.
50. Jap Ji, Stanza XXIV, by Kirpal Singh, p. 107.
51. Jap Ji, comments, by Kirpal Singh, p. 107.
51a. Godman by Kirpal Singh, p. 71.
51b. Spirituality by Kirpal Singh, p. 43.
52. Jap Ji, Stanza XXV, comments, by Kirpal Singh, p. 108.
53. Mystery of Death by Kirpal Singh, p. 117.
53a. Jap Ji, Stanza V, comments, by Kirpal Singh, p. 91.
53b. Godman by Kirpal Singh, p. 40.
53c. Sat Sandesh, December 1976, p. 41.
53d. Jap Ji, Stanza XXVII, p. 111.
54. Sat Sandesh, November 1971, p. 16.
55. Sat Sandesh, November 1971, p. 16.
56. Sat Sandesh, November 1971, p. 17.
57. Sat Sandesh, November 1971, p. 17.
58. Sat Sandesh, November 1971, p. 17.
59. Sat Sandesh, November 1971, p. 17.
60. Sat Sandesh, November 1971, p. 17.
60a. Sat Sandesh, November 1971, pp. 18-19.
61. Sat Sandesh, November 1971, p. 32.
62. Sat Sandesh, November 1971, p. 32.
63. Spiritual Elixir by Kirpal Singh, p. 234.
63a. Godman by Kirpal Singh, p. 5.

REFERENCES

64. Jap Ji, Stanza XXVI, by Kirpal Singh,
     p. 110.
65. Jap Ji, Stanza V, by Kirpal Singh, p. 92.
66. Spirituality by Kirpal Singh, p. 35.
67. Jap Ji, Stanza XXV, by Kirpal Singh,
     p. 108.
68. Jap Ji, Stanza XXV, by Kirpal Singh,
     pp. 108-109.
69. Godman by Kirpal Singh, p. 88.
70. Jap Ji by Kirpal Singh, p. 63.
70a. Mystery of Death by Kirpal Singh, p. 89.
70b. Mystery of Death by Kirpal Singh, p. 90.
71. Jap Ji by Kirpal Singh, p. 67.
72. Discourses on Sant Mat by Sawan Singh,
     p. 167.
72a. Jap Ji by Kirpal Singh, p. 111.
73. Naam or Word by Kirpal Singh, p. 21.
74. Naam or Word by Kirpal Singh, p. 21.

THE BOOKS OF KIRPAL SINGH

THE CROWN OF LIFE
A comparison of the various yogas and their scope, including Surat Shabd Yoga—the disciplined approach of Spirituality. Religious parallels and various modern movements cited. Paperback, 256 pages, index.

GODMAN
If there is always at least one authorized spiritual guide on earth at any time, what are the characteristics which will enable the honest seeker to distinguish him from those who are not competent? A complete study of the supreme mystics and their hallmarks. Paperback, 191 pages.

A GREAT SAINT: BABA JAIMAL SINGH
A unique biography tracing the development of one of the most outstanding Saints of modern times. Should be read by every seeker after God for the encouragement it offers. Paperback, 116 pages, glossary.

THE JAP JI: THE MESSAGE OF GURU NANAK
An extensive explanation of the basic principles taught by Guru Nanak (1469-1539 A.D.) with comparative scriptures cited. Stanzas of the hymns in English, as well as the original text in phonetic wording. Paperback, 182 pages, glossary.

THE BOOKS OF KIRPAL SINGH

MORNING TALKS
Consists of 40 discourses by Kirpal Singh
during 1967, 1968 and 1969 in India, which
relate to the ethical life of those under-
taking spiritual discipline. Paperback,
258 pages.

NAAM or WORD
"In the beginning was the WORD...and the
WORD was God." Quotations from Hindu,
Buddhist, Islamic and Christian sacred
writings confirm the universality of this
spiritual manifestation of God in reli-
gious tradition and mystical practices.
Paperback, 335 pages.

PRAYER: ITS NATURE AND TECHNIQUE
Discusses all forms and aspects of prayer
from the most elementary to the ultimate
state of "praying without ceasing." Also
contains collected prayers from all
religious traditions. Paperback, 153
pages, appendix, index of references.

SPIRITUALITY: WHAT IT IS
A straightforward explanation of man's
ultimate opportunity. Explores the
science of Spirituality. Paperback, 103
pages, plus Introductory.

THE BOOKS OF KIRPAL SINGH

SPIRITUAL ELIXIR
Collected questions addressed to Kirpal Singh in private correspondence, together with respective answers. Also contains various messages given on special occasions. Paperback, 382 pages, glossary.

THE TEACHINGS OF KIRPAL SINGH
Formerly in three separately-published parts now bound together in one volume.
Volume I: The Holy Path, 94 pages
Volume II: Self-Introspection/ Meditation, 188 pages
Volume III: The New Life, 192 pages
These are definitive statements from various talks and books by Kirpal Singh collected to illuminate the aspects of self-discipline necessary for Spirituality.

THE WHEEL OF LIFE & THE MYSTERY OF DEATH
Originally two separate books; now bound in one volume. The meaning of one's life on earth is carefully examined in the first text. In the second the reader is presented with the whys and wherefores of "the great final change called death." Paperback, 221 pages, plus index for the first text, and Introduction.

THE BOOKS OF KIRPAL SINGH

THE NIGHT IS A JUNGLE
    A compendium of 14 talks delivered
by Kirpal Singh prior to 1972, the
first four of which were given in
Philadelphia in 1955. The remaining
ten talks were presented in India.
All 14 were checked for accuracy by
Kirpal Singh prior to their com-
pilation in this book. Paperback,
358 pages with an Introduction.

____

Kirpal Singh's books may be obtained
from:

        Ruhani Satsang
        Divine Science of the Soul
        2618 Skywood Place
        Anaheim, California 92804

            or

        Sant Bani Ashram
        Franklin, New Hampshire 03235